To

....

From

....

Date

....

Compiled and edited by Brigitta Nortker.

Print ISBN 978-1-62416-642-6 (purple)
    ISBN 978-1-62416-643-3 (burgundy)

eBook Editions:
Adobe Digital Edition (.epub) 978-1-62836-291-6
Kindle and MobiPocket Edition (.prc) 978-1-62836-292-3

Published by Barbour Books, an imprint of Barbour Publishing, Inc., P.O. Box 719, Uhrichsville, Ohio 44683, www.barbourbooks.com

Our mission is to publish and distribute inspirational products offering exceptional value and biblical encouragement to the masses.

Member of the
Evangelical Christian
Publishers Association

Printed in China.

Daily Devotional

3-Minute Devotions for Women

BARBOUR BOOKS
An Imprint of Barbour Publishing, Inc.

Be Still and Learn

But his delight is in the law of the Lord,
And in His law he meditates day and night.
PSALM 1:2 AMP

Quiet time to learn of God's ways requires discipline. Yet our daily routine cries for our attention. We find ourselves with too much to do—and the ticking of the clock constantly in our ears.

Our loved ones cannot be ignored. Duty calls. There are meals to prepare, medicine to dispense, and clothes to arrange. When is there time for God?

It's easy to put our quiet time with God on the back burner. But the very thing we need most—hope—only the Lord can fill. He understands our exhaustion and frustration. He feels our pain and sadness. He's waiting to extend grace when we call upon Him.

Our quiet time—reading scripture and praying—is like water on a sponge. It fills us and expands our ability to keep going. It strengthens us for the day. It empowers us to fulfill what God requires.

Don't let the call of your duties drown out the need for quiet time. Discipline yourself to set aside a few minutes for the Lord. He is our hope, our salvation. We need His fellowship. To neglect that time is dangerous.

Father, help me to focus on You, to carve out minutes
from my day to spend in prayer and the Word.
My desire is to fellowship with You.

Who Helps the Helper?

*The Lord is my strength and my shield; my heart
trusted in him, and I am helped: therefore my heart
greatly rejoiceth; and with my song will I praise him.*
PSALM 28:7 KJV

Women tend to be helpers. They can't help it.

God made them that way. From the foundation of the earth, their primary job has been to help.

It is a woman's nature to assist, to nurture, to render care. Even in these days of more "equitable" roles, it is typically the woman who is found feeding the baby at 2 a.m., cheering the young soccer players, counseling the college student by long-distance phone calls, holding a shaky hand in a hospital room, and comforting the bereaved at a funeral.

Helping can be exhausting. The needs of young children, teens, grandchildren, and aging parents can stretch us—women and men both—until we're ready to snap. And then we find that we need help.

Who helps the helper?

The Lord does. When we are weak, He is strong. When we are vulnerable, He is our shield. When we can no longer trust in our own resources, we can trust in Him.

And we can trust Him before we snap. He is always there, ready to help.

Rejoice in Him, praise His name, and you will find the strength to go on.

*Father, I'm worn out. I can't care for all the people and needs
You bring into my life by myself. I need Your strength.
Thank You for being my helper and my shield.*

I'm Not Crazy after All

We have this hope as an anchor
for the soul, firm and secure.
HEBREWS 6:19 NIV

Am I going crazy? Am I the only person to feel this way? As we go through life, it seems like we occasionally lose our minds.

The challenge of balancing schedules, dealing with demanding personalities, and maintaining relationships and friendships can drive our entire life off course. Like a ship tossed in a storm, we can drift in a strange sea, overcome by uncontrollable waves.

But we do have an anchor—our hope in God. What does an anchor do? It prevents drifting by attaching firmly to the unmoving floor of the sea. God is that seabed, firm and secure, and Jesus is the anchor connecting us to the Father. Our anchor of hope is deep within the seabed of God.

The shape of an anchor reminds us of the cross. No wonder the first-century Christians used an anchor as a symbol of the cross. We are not adrift. We are securely fastened to God through Jesus.

No, you're not crazy when you feel lost and confused. We'll have stormy times—but we are held firm and secure by the anchor of hope.

Lord, I cling to You as my anchor. Although I may feel lost at times,
I know You are here with me, holding me secure, giving me hope.

Labor of Love

*Go to work in the morning and stick to it until evening
without watching the clock. You never know from moment
to moment how your work will turn out in the end.*
ECCLESIASTES 11:6 MSG

Have you ever had a job where the work was so routine that you were bored, watching the clock, willing the shift to end so you could get on with something you really enjoyed? Or maybe your job demanded so much of you physically, mentally, or emotionally that when you returned home, you wanted nothing more than to put out a large Do Not Disturb sign and "veg out" for the evening. Or perhaps you found yourself counting the days until retirement.

God says that any job, any ministry, is profitable. Don't look at the clock, wishing the time away. If you are too exhausted to reach out with God's love for others, then reevaluate what the Lord would have you do in service for Him. But don't hold out on serving Him because you are too "tired." He gave us His all because of His love. Respond in love for Him and give your all, showing His love to others.

*Father, may I find joy in serving You today—
because of Your love.*

Woe Is Me!

*And he said, I have been very jealous for the Lord
God of hosts: because the children of Israel have forsaken
thy covenant, thrown down thine altars, and slain thy
prophets with the sword; and I, even I only, am left;
and they seek my life, to take it away.*
1 KINGS 19:14 KJV

Poor Elijah.

The greatest day of his life had turned into the worst. From a miraculous victory on Mt. Carmel as the prophet of the one true God, he had become a sniveling fugitive. Weary of being chased, he sat under a juniper tree, wishing to die.

But God ministered to Elijah, and he went on forty more days to a cave in Mt. Horeb.

Still, the prophet pouted. "I've done all this for You, and I'm the only faithful one left. They're chasing me. This isn't fair!"

God met Elijah in his weariness, gave him a new assignment, and assured him that he was not alone. The Lord promised that the situation would be made right.

As God did for Elijah, He'll do for us. If you're feeling weary and overwhelmed as you carry your burden today, don't give up.

Rest in Him. He will nourish you and give you strength for the journey.

God cares for those who care for others.

*Father, if I could find a cave, I'd crawl into it. But I know
that's not where I should be. I know You have greater
things for me than what I see through my tired eyes.
Show me the next step and I'll take it.*

Sleepless Nights

I will lie down and sleep in peace, for you alone,
O Lord, make me dwell in safety.
PSALM 4:8 NIV

When we can't sleep, we squirm and adjust our pillows. Some try to count sheep. Others squint at the clock, calculating the number of hours left until morning—and the amount of sleep they're not getting.

For women, worry and fear are often the cause of insomnia. They plague us at night, because the busyness of life that keeps them at bay in the daytime dissipates in the quiet solitude of bed. Alone in the dark, it's easy to imagine the worst and feel hopeless about our situation.

But God longs to care for us and give us peace.

Lisa prays out loud when she can't sleep. She says her fight against worry is a spiritual battle and audible prayer is a key in winning the fight. Lisa finds rest from the burdens of life when she pictures herself handing her worries to God—and asking Him to hold them until morning.

God never sleeps. He cares for us all night long. We can rest in that care.

Father, help me to trust You in the dark of night. I feel alone and overwhelmed by my many responsibilities. Please give me the gift of peaceful sleep so I can face tomorrow refreshed.

Family Complications

And David said unto him, Fear not: for I will surely
shew thee kindness for Jonathan thy father's sake,
and will restore thee all the land of Saul thy father;
and thou shalt eat bread at my table continually.
2 SAMUEL 9:7 KJV

Like people today, Old Testament characters struggled in family relationships. David's wife Michal turned against him. Her father, King Saul, hunted David like an animal, though the younger man ultimately triumphed and was crowned king.

Most rulers executed their opponents—and their families. But King David, in a major risk-taking move, not only returned Saul's estate to his grandson Mephibosheth but also offered him financial support and a place at the king's table.

David's advisors probably thought him crazy. That is, unless they knew Mephibosheth's father, Jonathan. In the midst of family turmoil, he and David were fast friends. Jonathan even offered to step down as Saul's heir and support David's kingship. When his father threatened to kill David, Jonathan risked his own life by defending his friend. Later Jonathan died with Saul on the battlefield.

David's love for his late friend extended to Jonathan's children. When he summoned Mephibosheth, the terrified man probably thought David was planning to kill him. Instead, the king treated Mephibosheth like a son, welcoming him with open arms.

In our own difficult family situations, loyalty and kindness may also seem an unwise response. But God wants our actions to always reflect His readiness to bless amid heartache and hurt.

Father, when family forgiveness seems impossible,
help me act in accordance with Your unconditional love.

Spiritual Blessings

Praise be to the God and Father of our Lord Jesus Christ,
who has blessed us in the heavenly realms with
every spiritual blessing in Christ.
EPHESIANS 1:3 NIV

Discouraged? Dejected? Disillusioned? Sometimes life leaves us feeling downtrodden. Although the Lord has abundantly blessed us, at times it's easy to forget that truth. We may be struggling financially. We may be dealing with marital strife. We may be experiencing health issues. Is it possible to respond with praise when our earthly life appears to conflict with spiritual truth?

Regardless of our circumstances, God has blessed us with every spiritual blessing in Christ. We are not lacking anything in the heavenly realm. The problem is that many times our focus is on the earthly realm. Instead, we can purpose to turn our thoughts heavenward and count the spiritual blessings that are at our disposal. The Lord's indwelling presence guides our minds and comforts our hearts. His resurrection power enables us to persevere triumphantly. His sustaining peace imparts encouragement for today and hope for tomorrow. When we meditate on eternal blessings, our momentary struggles are put into the proper perspective. Earthly trials are temporary. Spiritual blessings are forever. Let's embrace the eternal gifts we have been given and praise Him for His abundant provision!

Dear Lord, regardless of my circumstances,
help me focus heavenward. Allow me to praise You
for the spiritual blessings I have been given. Amen.

Abide in Christ

"I am the vine, you are the branches; he who
abides in Me and I in him, he bears much fruit,
for apart from Me you can do nothing."
JOHN 15:5 NASB

Do we want the blessing of God on our lives? Of course we do. But how do we do it? By abiding in Christ. This means we are to remain, continue, and sink deeper into our relationship with Him. In doing so, we will bear much fruit.

In John 15:12, Jesus inspires us with the words, "Love one another, just as I have loved you." That means loving sacrificially, selflessly, totally, regardless of the other person's behavior or how we "feel" each day. When we apply that truth to our life, we will have an outgrowth of fruitful love we never dreamed possible.

We can be greatly encouraged by reading the entire text of John 15:1–17. Over and over Jesus tells us to remain or abide in Him. He assures us that apart from Him, we can't do anything. We can't be a good wife, mother, daughter, or sister unless we remain in Christ and seek His will for our lives.

Take time this evening to read through John 15:1–17, slowly and carefully. Think of ways you can implement all that Jesus is saying to you in these verses. Then pray for the blessing of God on your life as you sink deeper into Him.

Dear Jesus, I want Your blessing on my life.
Show me how to abide in You. In Jesus' name, amen.

Consolation amid Conflict

Our bodies had no rest, but we were troubled on
every side. Outside were conflicts, inside were fears.
Nevertheless God, who comforts the downcast,
comforted us by the coming of Titus.
2 CORINTHIANS 7:5–6 NKJV

Sometimes we feel so beaten down by life, battered by outside circumstances over which we have no control. During these unwelcome storms, fear begins to permeate our inner being. Seeing no way out, we may fall into depression and enter into self-preservation mode by withdrawing into ourselves. But in doing so, we cut ourselves off from those who would give us aid and comfort.

Fortunately, God has other plans. He knows what we need and lovingly provides it. He "comforts the downcast" by sending earthly "angels" to help us. These people of God, Tituses among us, give freely of God's love and fill us with the healing balm of His comfort.

In the midst of distress, we are not to withdraw from God's helping hand but immerse ourselves in His Word and reach out to others, allowing both to give us love and comfort in our time of need. And then, whole once more, we in turn can be a Titus for another.

Dear God, You know my frame, my circumstances,
my outlook, my troubles. Comfort me in this situation
through Your Word and the love of others. Give me
consolation in the midst of this conflict. Amen.

The Love Letter

*This is love: not that we loved God, but that he loved
us and sent his Son as an atoning sacrifice for our sins.*
1 JOHN 4:10 NIV

In the back of her closet, behind sweaters and boxes of seldom-worn shoes, was a carved wooden box. Every so often, she took out the box and slid off the lid. She sat on the carpeted floor in her bedroom and gently lifted out one sheet of paper after another. Each was wrinkled and stained, creased, and worn smooth with reading. Each was written in the same handwriting: her husband's.

Life was busier now; he didn't often tuck love letters under her pillow before he left for work in the morning or wedge a note between the milk and orange juice in the refrigerator. But his heart had not changed. Rereading his old letters helped her remember.

How would her husband have felt if he poured out his love to his wife in a letter and she was too busy or didn't care enough to read it? The same is true with God. And He hasn't just written us a few letters—He's written an entire book! If we want to show Him how much we love Him and desire to understand His heart, we need to read His words.

The Bible is our love letter from God, from the one true Lover of our souls. Read it; wear it out!

*Dear God, thank You for loving me so much.
Thank You for Your living, breathing, life-giving Word.
Help me to crave it as I crave food and drink. Amen.*

Self-Examination

Let us test and examine our ways,
and return to the LORD!
LAMENTATIONS 3:40 ESV

What if you could follow yourself around for the day, carefully examining all that you do? Look at your schedule—your choice of activities, the people you talk to, the things you listen to and watch, the habits being formed, the thoughts you think. Maybe your heart desires intimacy with God, but a real day in your life leaves no time for solitude. God often speaks to us in the stillness and silent spaces. How will we hear Him if we're never still?

Taking time to reflect, to think, and to examine oneself is a necessary step in moving toward intimacy with God. Before we can turn back to Him, we must repent of the things that moved us away from Him in the first place. As we set aside time for solitude and reflection, the Holy Spirit will gently show us these things if we ask. He will show us the sins we need to confess and give us the grace of repentance. Experiencing forgiveness, our fellowship with our heavenly Father is restored.

Lord, help me to still myself before You and be willing to examine my ways. Speak to me through Your Holy Spirit of what is wrong in my life. Give me the gift of repentance and allow me to enjoy the sweetness of Your forgiveness.

Precious Moments

. . .to whom God willed to make known what is
the riches of the glory of this mystery among the
Gentiles, which is Christ in you, the hope of glory.
COLOSSIANS 1:27 NASB

Do you ever lose sight of just how much you enjoy the presence of God? It's easy to become preoccupied with life's duties. When you finally find a moment to shut out the voices of the day, you quickly discover how little anything else matters but God. He is your light and your salvation. No one knows the path He's chosen for you quite like He does. He points to the truth and brings about the results He destined for you before the beginning of time.

Imagine—you were a thought, an idea with grand purpose, before He ever breathed life into the first man. Compare that to the things that penetrate your mind and cause you concern. In God's presence, there is little to worry about. The truth—freedom from everything—rests in time with Him. The more you lean into His higher purpose, the less you'll try to work it out on your own.

Why spend that precious time telling God all your worries—things He already knows? Instead give Him minutes of silence and moments of praise, and allow His wisdom to penetrate your heart and direct everything that concerns you.

Lord, help me to never lose sight of how much I enjoy spending time with You. Help me to take time each day to hear what You have to say. Amen.

God's Purposes

*Though I walk in the midst of trouble, you preserve
my life. . . . The Lord will fulfill his purpose for me.*
PSALM 138:7–8 NIV

It's hard to see that the Lord is fulfilling His purpose in our lives when
bad things happen, especially when it relates to our relationships.
These "bad things" usually happen when we place unreal
expectations on our family and friends—expectations of security,
peace, contentment, or fulfilled needs.

In Psalm 138 David praised God for guiding him through the rough
times in his life. As David looked back, he saw God's goodness to him
through the good times as well as the bad. And he realized that God
would continue to guide his life in the future as He had in the past.

What can we do when life derails our plans, desires, or
expectations? First, remember how God has led through difficult
circumstances in the past. Looking back helps us see how God has
fulfilled His purpose for saving us—molding us into the image of
Christ. Second, thank Him for His guidance and protection as He
brings us through hard times. Third, look forward, knowing that God
does not allow anything into our lives that isn't for our good. We can
trust Him to do what is best for us.

*Dear God, help me to not place expectations on my relationships
that only You can fulfill. Help me to remember that You
are working Your purpose in my life. Amen.*

Unexpected Treasures

Don't fall in love with money.
Be satisfied with what you have.
HEBREWS 13:5 CEV

When Dave asked Jen to marry him, he promised her love, faithfulness, and a lifetime of chocolate. He never said anything about money.

As years passed, Jen became increasingly frustrated with broken appliances, calls from bill collectors, and budgets strained to the ripping point. As her family struggled from paycheck to paycheck, she watched friends living comfortably. Discontent and envy stirred in her innards.

The Bible tells us not to fall in love with money, but it's incredibly hard to do—especially if we don't have enough. Money becomes a pseudo-savior, a way to rise above problems and enjoy the good things of life. We lose sight of the immeasurable wealth God *has* provided and become lost in the woods of discontent that border our blessings.

Jen recognized the brewing storm in her soul and stepped back to take inventory of the *needs* God had provided for her family, rather than focus on the *wants.* She knew the Lord was imbedding gratefulness in her heart the day she found herself dancing with the ailing washing machine as it mamboed across the floor.

Giver of all good things, quench my insatiable thirst for
the comfort money provides. Teach me that my security is in
You alone. When I fret about money, remind me that Your
beloved Son was born on a bale of hay in a barn. Amen.

Caring for the Temple

Honor God with your body.
1 CORINTHIANS 6:20 NLT

Our bodies are amazing gifts from God. Without any thought or effort on our parts, our hearts beat life-giving blood throughout our veins, providing us with the energy to accomplish the thousands of tasks we do each day. Our brains give the commands, our bodies obey. But these incredible structures aren't maintenance-free. Just as we are to be good stewards of our resources of time and money, we should also be good stewards of our bodies. God's Word calls them temples.

When we are busy meeting the needs of others, we often neglect to care for ourselves. But God wants us to treat our bodies with care and respect. This means exercising regularly, eating good food, getting enough rest. These are simple things but the dividends are high, for when we treat our bodies right they treat us right in return.

Father, thank You for the amazing body that You have given me, for all the things it does that happen without my knowledge. Help me to care for my body in a way that brings honor and glory to You. Amen.

Receiving God's Embrace

*How great is the love the Father has lavished on us, that we should
be called children of God! And that is what we are!*
1 JOHN 3:1 NIV

Some people are born "huggers." They greet family members or
complete strangers in the same way—with a hug. They just can't help
themselves. They must lavish love on those around them. They must
demonstrate affection. Most of us would agree that the closer the
relationship, the more meaningful the hug. Can you imagine receiving
an embrace from our heavenly Father, the God of the universe?

God lavished His love on us when He sent Jesus to earth. Jesus'
sacrificial death on our behalf paved the way for adoption into
God's family by faith. When we receive the gift of Jesus, we become
children of God. We are no longer strangers. We are no longer
alienated from a holy God. We have become family!

As you ponder God's great love for you, picture Jesus hanging
on the cross. With arms outstretched, He not only came to embrace
the world with God's love, He came to embrace you! Will you receive
God's hug? The unconditional love of our Creator is the greatest gift
we could ever receive. Will you allow His love to be lavished upon
you? Receive the embrace of your heavenly Father today!

*Dear Lord, I need Your embrace. May I receive
the abundant love You desire to lavish upon
me because I am Your child. Amen.*

More Than a Beauty Queen

*"If you persist in staying silent at a time like this, help and
deliverance will arrive for the Jews from someplace else;
but you and your family will be wiped out. Who knows?
Maybe you were made queen for just such a time as this."*
ESTHER 4:14 MSG

Queens usually begin their lives in royal palaces, living in the lap of
luxury all their lives.

If someone had told Hadassah, Mordecai's orphaned cousin, that
she would become Queen Esther of Persia, she would have laughed in
his face! But God had big plans for the lovely Jewish girl. She won an
empire-wide beauty contest and King Xerxes's love.

At this point, most fairy tales end with "they lived happily
ever after." But even a queen had no guarantee of protection from
powerful enemies. Mordecai discovered that Haman, the king's
closest advisor, had engineered the genocide of the Jews scattered
throughout the empire. While his heart yearned for Esther, whom he
regarded as his daughter, Mordecai realized that Esther might play a
role in saving her people—if she agreed to take the risk.

Few of us live the exotic, thrilling life of a queen, but all women
possess power within their spheres of influence—home, work, school,
community. God has brought us to this place in history for a purpose.
Will we take the risks?

*Father, I cannot imagine the plans You have for me.
But I know I can trust You with my hopes,
dreams—and life. Amen.*

He Is Here

And Jacob awaked out of his sleep, and he said,
Surely the LORD is in this place; and I knew it not.
GENESIS 28:16 KJV

No matter where we are, no matter what we are going through, God is with us. Whether we are on the run or rooted in the mud, in conflict with our husbands or reaching a compromise, deep in dreams or fully awake, He is here. He is in this place.

Jacob discovered this when he awoke from a dream of angels ascending and descending on a ladder. Having just stolen his brother's blessing, Jacob was on the run. But he could not outrun God. He was still with him, reassuring him: "Behold, I am with you and will keep you wherever you go. . . . I will not leave you" (Genesis 28:15 NKJV).

Jacob's God is our God. He has been, is, and always will be with His people. He is the Rock that never moves.

God holds us by the hand, telling us not to be afraid. Through thick and thin, amid dreams and waking hours, while at home and at work, amid laughter and tears, He leads, loves, speaks to, and cares for us. He is here.

Call to Him. He is listening. Love Him. He adores you. Pray and praise Him. He wants to hear your voice. Reach out and grab His hand. He wants to touch you. Never, ever let Him go.

Dear God, my heart overflows with joy and peace in Your
presence. You are here——hallelujah! Your spirit is with
me wherever I go, whatever I am going through.
Thank You, Lord, for never leaving me.

Deep Roots

> "And he said to the vinedresser, 'Look, for three years
> now I have come seeking fruit on this fig tree, and I find
> none. Cut it down. . . .' And [the vinedresser] answered
> him, 'Sir, let it alone this year also, until I dig around it
> and put on manure. Then if it should bear fruit next year,
> well and good; but if not, you can cut it down.' "
> LUKE 13:7–9 ESV

As we read this parable, we may ask ourselves, Why did God call us to Himself? After all, we often think we'll never win any awards for fruit-bearing. Our marriages often seem fairly ordinary, our testimonies less than exciting, our ministries faithful but limited.

Yet in the same way God did not chop down the barren tree, He has not cut us down. Looking to the future, He digs at our comfortable roots, challenging us to change. Then He fertilizes us with His Word, causing our roots to go deep into faith's soil.

Because God hasn't finished with us yet, let's put ourselves in the path of growth through study, prayer, and fellowship. One day, we'll see that long-awaited fruit and rejoice with God at what He's done through us.

Are we ready to grow? Let's put our roots deep into His Word today.

> Lord, thank You for Your gracious love that builds
> me up instead of cutting me off at the roots.
> Help my roots go deep in faith today.

A Request for Wisdom

"Now, O LORD my God, you have made me king instead
of my father, David, but I am like a little child
who doesn't know his way around."
1 KINGS 3:7 NLT

This prayer occurs one evening after Solomon has replaced David as the king of Israel. God appears to Solomon in a dream and offers to give him whatever he wants. Instead of asking for wealth or long life or triumph over his enemies, Solomon asks for wisdom. Solomon wants to rule wisely but, as he says, he feels like a little child. Therefore, Solomon asks for the ability to decide between right and wrong and to lead his people as a true follower of God.

Solomon's example stands out for us today. We need wisdom in our relationships, particularly as we strive to grow in godliness and love with our spouses.

At some point in your life, perhaps you have felt like a little child. A new situation arises—an argument you've never had before, a life-altering change, the death of a loved one. God is waiting for your prayer, and He desires to guide you in His unsurpassed wisdom. Like little children, we must ask God for help; He will help us find our way.

Dear Lord, You are wise beyond understanding. Grant me Your wisdom today in my relationships and in my current situations. Thank You for Your love and guidance. Amen.

But Seek First

But seek ye first the kingdom of God, and his righteousness;
and all these things shall be added unto you.
MATTHEW 6:33 KJV

Times were tough. Her husband's business was slowing down. Bills were beginning to mount. She was torn. Should she seek full-time employment or continue in volunteer ministry? Prayerfully, she and her husband sought the Lord's wisdom. They sensed the Lord asking them to trust Him financially while she served in ministry. By faith they followed the Lord's leading. Soon afterward, an unexpected check came in the mail to cover current expenses. Gradually, her husband's business began to prosper. God supplied their needs as they sought and followed His will.

Many times we are called to make difficult choices. We must glean God's wisdom for discernment. After seeking His wisdom, we must trust Him in obedience. That may require following our heads rather than our hearts or exercising faith rather than succumbing to fear. When we trust and obey, the Lord will take care of the rest. He will reward our faith. He will confirm that His way is indeed the best. He will meet our needs as we follow His will, despite the difficulties. Seek His kingdom and watch the Lord provide for you!

Dear Lord, may I seek You above all else and
trust that You will meet my needs. Amen.

Lifesaving 101

*Examine yourselves as to whether you are in
the faith. Test yourselves. Do you not know
yourselves, that Jesus Christ is in you?*
2 Corinthians 13:5 nkjv

How many times do we almost drown in the floodwaters of fear? How often are we overcome by waves of discontent or pulled by currents of doubt? How often do we forget that Jesus Christ, the Master of the Universe, is within us? He has already saved us from doubt, disappointment, dread, and death. In His strength, we can move mountains. We can change the world. We can be His representative of peace, strength, and love within our family, our neighborhood, and our workplace.

Jesus, the One with the power to rebuke the winds and calm the waters, is our lifesaver. The knowledge that He is within us boosts us up above the waves of fear and into the peace of His presence.

When caught up in the riptides of life, we are to examine ourselves to make sure we are acknowledging the *fact* that *Christ resides within us*. Buoyed by His presence, we can withstand the storm and rise up in the power of His strength.

*Jesus, You are the one who has saved my life, the one who resides
within me. Give me the wisdom to keep this in my mind
throughout my day, and give me the power to do Your will in
this world, knowing You have overcome it. Amen.*

Deadly Poison

*Thou shalt not go up and down as a talebearer
among thy people: neither shalt thou stand against
the blood of thy neighbour; I am the Lord.*
LEVITICUS 19:16 KJV

Gossip is the favorite pastime of far too many Christian women. Probably all of us have been guilty of it at one time or another. The truth is that God hates gossip, and it doesn't matter if a person is a casual talebearer or a chronic one. God is not fooled when we attempt to disguise gossip as prayerful concern, and most people probably aren't fooled either.

The really sad thing is that often when we gossip, we focus our discussion on those we love—our husbands, close friends, or other family members. It's possible that this is because we know more about these people and are more likely to pick up on their faults. Still, it is not right. Gossip is often as deadly as murder.

Another area we fail to acknowledge as gossip is "discussion" with our husbands. It's true that our communication with our spouses should be more open than it is with other people. There are times when talking things over with our husbands is necessary, even though the same conversation with someone else would be gossip. Just be careful not to "over-discuss" something. Otherwise it begins to fester and boils into talebearing.

Remember: You will not please God if you are prone to gossip.

*O Lord, I can bring all things before You.
I don't need to spread gossip like a virus.*

Looking Ahead to Where God Is

*But Jesus told him, "Anyone who puts a hand to the plow
and then looks back is not fit for the Kingdom of God."*
LUKE 9:62 NLT

We know that we shouldn't worry about tomorrow, but even worse is
to worry and feel regret about the past, which can only cripple us for
tomorrow. "I wish things could be the way they were." "I wish I were
younger." "I wish my husband treated me like he did when we first
met." "I wish I could fit into those jeans again. . . ." "I wish, I wish, I
wish."

Although the Lord doesn't want us looking back at what once was,
our enemy does. He wants us to feel discouraged and helpless over
what we face today and drown in self-pity about how it was in the past.
But God wants us to look ahead to the future. The future is where He
is. He promises to give us hope in our futures. Let's claim that promise
for ourselves, for our spouses, and for our marriages. Let's forget the
past—it's long gone already and cannot be changed. Let's move ahead
and press toward the new things that the Lord wants to do in our lives.

*Jesus, please help me to lay aside my past regrets and longings
for the things that have already faded away. Let me find
contentment in the present and hope for the future. Guide
me into the future in accordance with Your will. Amen.*

Change

*Jesus Christ is the same
yesterday and today and forever.*
HEBREWS 13:8 NIV

Are you experiencing a lot of change in your life right now? Maybe a career change, a big move, or a child going off to college? Or maybe you aren't facing a huge change but every day seems to hold quite a few variations and challenges.

Change can be very unsettling and downright scary sometimes. Even the small daily changes tend to eat away at us and have us wishing for something predictable! If we aren't grounded in Christ, change can send us tumbling over the edge. Isn't it wonderful that He gives us the assurance that He will never change? He is the same yesterday, today, and forever! Jesus Christ is with you always. He sees all of the unpredictable moments that creep—or slam—into your life. Remember that these moments have passed through His hands before He allows them to greet you.

Change can actually be a good thing! It might not seem like it at the time, but the Lord will work all things together for your good (Romans 8:28) if you love Him. You can trust that God has a plan for your life and He will be with you through all of the changes you will face.

*Dear Jesus, help me to trust in You through all of
the changes in my life. Thank You for never changing
and always being there for me. In Your name, amen.*

Giant Killers

"Go. . . . And may the LORD be with you!"
1 SAMUEL 17:37 NLT

Feeling bullied? Are others trying to fit you into their mold? Are giant-sized problems looming before you?

Welcome to David's world. When he boldly claimed that he would fight Goliath, his brother Eliab assaulted him with dispiriting remarks. But David simply defended his position and then walked away.

King Saul told David he was no match for Goliath. But David, remembering how God had helped him in the past, responded with "The Lord who rescued me from the claws of the lion and the bear will rescue me from this Philistine!" (1 Samuel 17:37 NLT).

The resigned Saul then tried to fit David into his battle gear—an uncomfortable fit for a shepherd boy. So David shed the armor, along with Saul's sword, and picked up his usual weapons—a sling and some stones.

When the Philistine giant saw David, he mocked and abused him. David said, "I come to you in the name of the Lord. . . .

Today the Lord will conquer you" (1 Samuel 17:45–46 NLT). Then he took out a stone and hurled it at Goliath. The stone sank into the giant's forehead, and the behemoth fell facedown.

Ladies, we, like David, can refuse to allow the words of discouragers, naysayers, molders, and giants to affect us. We, too, can walk forward in God's name and power. He will help us vanquish every negative word, thought, and deed—and lead us to triumph!

God, give me the strength and the power to walk forth in Your name, to turn away from the negative remarks of others, to be who You've called me to be, and to conquer the giants of this world.

Smart, Brave, and Beautiful

*And it was so, when the king saw Esther the queen
standing in the court, that she obtained favour in his sight:
and the king held out to Esther the golden sceptre.*
ESTHER 5:2 KJV

Queen Esther, a lovely Jewish girl who married King Xerxes of
Persia, found herself in desperate straits. Not knowing her ethnic
background, Haman, her husband's advisor, plotted the annihilation
of all Jews throughout the empire. Esther wanted to save her people,
but the king had not invited her to his side for thirty days. Had he
found a new trophy wife?

Nevertheless, Esther risked her life to connect with Xerxes. She
fasted for three days, but Esther did not use a "spiritual" approach
in dealing with her husband. Instead, she appeared in royal robes,
looking her best. She did not blurt out demands but piqued the king's
curiosity with dinner invitations that included Haman.

By the time Esther presented her request for mercy, Xerxes had
offered her half his kingdom. Upon hearing of Haman's treachery, he
dispatched him in no time flat.

Few of us win Miss America titles or compete with Martha
Stewart's entertainment skills, yet God has gifted us with wisdom,
beauty, and hospitality that impact our husbands and others. While
we may not rescue an entire nation, we can make a difference in—and
even help save—the lives of those around us.

*Lord, please help me recognize the gifts You have invested
in me and how I can best use them to help others. Amen.*

Well-Watered Gardens

The Lord will guide you always; he will satisfy
your needs in a sun-scorched land. . . .
You will be like a well-watered garden.
ISAIAH 58:11 NIV

Well-kept gardens are beautiful. The rows of plants are weed-free, the vegetables and flowers abundant, and everyone who sees such a garden admires it and wants the same.

When God is allowed to be our guide, our lives and marriages become like well-watered gardens. Even in the driest of times, God's beauty can shine through us. All we have to do is to allow Him the leadership in our home.

We do this by giving the reins to our husbands. This may sound easy, but often we want to take control. We want to be a subtle guide, ignoring God's blueprint and giving our husband's suggestions or bold statements as to how we should be living as a married couple.

This is not God's design and will lead to a garden full of weeds and haphazard rows. The fruit will be withered, the flowers stunted. If we want a garden that is a showcase, then we need to step back and let our husband lead. Even if he doesn't seem to be following God's path as we see it, we must trust God to bring His will to pass. He is a wonderful guide.

Thank You, Lord, for Your guidance in my life.
Help me to trust You in all things.
Help me to believe Your Word. Amen.

First Labors

She is energetic and strong, a hard worker.
PROVERBS 31:17 NLT

No matter what our occupation, whether that of homemaker or career woman, God's Word urges women to be hard workers, leading productive lives, not unlike the amazingly fruitful yet nameless wife of noble character described in Proverbs 31:10–31.

Several examples of industrious women can be found in the Bible. In the Old Testament, we can read about Deborah, who was a leader, judge, and prophetess. Then there was the widow Ruth, faithful to her mother-in-law, who worked in the fields, gathering wheat and barley. In the New Testament is Lydia, who was a dealer in purple cloth. There was also Dorcas, who made clothes. And there was Priscilla, who, along with her tentmaking husband, Aquila, worked in ministry with the apostle Paul. All these women seemed to have energy and appeared to be strong, hard workers.

But our work—whether inside or outside of the home—should not come before our relationship with God or our husbands. In all things, faith and family must come before the deadline we need to meet, the business trip we need to take, or the garage that needs to be cleaned out. Faith and family are even more important than whatever church project we've agreed to direct or community charity drive we've volunteered to participate in.

So let's be good stewards of the time we have here on earth. Give the first and best of your effort, energy, and strength to God and your husband. And the Lord will bless all your labors.

Father, remind me that my first labors are to
You and my husband. Help me to be a good
steward of my strength, time, and energy. Amen.

The Secret to Contentment

*I have learned the secret of being content in any
and every situation, whether well fed or hungry,
whether living in plenty or in want.*
PHILIPPIANS 4:12 NIV

We plan and dream. We imagine a life called *us*. And on the wings of our hopes we see "happily ever after" just over the horizon. The days come and go and dreams give birth to other dreams until our very happiness is put on a shelf, just out of reach. We wait for the day when our children are a little older or our husband's work schedule changes.

But waiting for the right circumstances to make us happy brings a tension all its own. Very often we mistake this tension as a sign that we are lacking something, but it is actually a tension born out of wanting what we do not have. Contentment, after all, is an inside job, and no amount of rearranging our lives will bring it to us. We must find it within ourselves.

The secret to contentment comes from understanding that where we are now is exactly where God wants us to be. He has a purpose for our lives, and He offers a peace that is separate from our circumstances. When we open our hearts to this, love comes rushing in the way the tide fills even the tiniest holes in the sand and blessings are scattered around like seashells.

*Lord, help me grow in the holy habit of contentment
by seeking Your presence and purpose for my life. Amen.*

Do the Next Thing

*"My food," said Jesus, "is to do the will of
him who sent me and to finish his work."*
JOHN 4:34 NIV

Busyness is the curse of modern life. There are lawns to mow,
meals to cook, gutters to clean, gardens to weed—enough chores to
last a lifetime of evenings and weekends. Even if you live in a tiny
apartment and eat only take-out food, there are still phone calls to
make, floors to scrub, letters to write, and errands to run.

But the Bible says that God has numbered our days as He
numbers the hairs on our heads. He knows how long we have to live,
and He knows best what we should do with the time He has given us.

Christian author and former missionary Elisabeth Elliot gives this
advice about how to decide what to do amid a myriad of necessary and
useful things: "Just do the next thing." These simple words are an
echo of Jesus', and in this He is our model. He did nothing that wasn't
God's perfect will, and He was perfectly content. When we feel harried
and stressed, it is often because we are trying to do more than God has
asked us to do.

God always gives us enough time to do His will.

*Dear Father, help me see all the things
I have to do and I want to do, and order
them according to Your will. Amen.*

In the Arms of a Friend

But we all, with unveiled face, beholding as in a mirror the
glory of the Lord, are being transformed into the same image
from glory to glory, just as by the Spirit of the Lord.
2 CORINTHIANS 3:18 NKJV

Shanna found the weeks following the birth of their second son emotional and a true test of faith. Finally, God had proven faithful and restored her newborn to health in spite of the doctor's words, "He only has a fifty-fifty chance of survival." Yet he completely recovered and was home.

The crisis over, Shanna's emotions were more than she could handle, and she found herself at the front door of her friend Barbie. As the door opened, Shanna fell into Barbie's arms.

Fighting to gain her composure, Barbie spoke the words Shanna needed to hear. "It's over. The baby's fine. Now get ahold of your emotions, girl! You're a woman of faith! With God at your side—you won!"

Tears turned to laughter. "I know," Shanna said, "but I needed to hear what you just said."

Have you ever found comfort from God through a friend? God brings His comfort to our hearts in many ways, but often He touches us most through the compassion of our brothers and sisters in Christ. Perhaps God wants to use you to touch someone today. Are you willing?

Thank You, Lord, for friendships. Give me compassion and a
willingness to be used as Your hand in someone's life. Amen.

The River

*Consider it pure joy. . .whenever
you face trials of many kinds.*
JAMES 1:2 NIV

Finding joy in the trials of life is like finding a precious stone embedded along a river's edge. As the water rages on, it is almost impossible to spot the stone's vibrant colors, but when the water is still, it is easy to see how it has been there all along. These are deep lessons that, when gathered together, strengthen our faith.

Turning away from trials is our natural response to life, but if we remember the river and the treasures that await us, they become easier to bear. Jesus tells us that throughout life we will have many troubles. At the same time, He offers us strength by reminding us that He has overcome them all (John 16:33). This is of great comfort to us when life becomes the raging river and we are struggling just to keep our heads above the water.

In time, as the water of our days ebbs and flows, eventually the turbulence passes. We gasp and cough and cling to shore to find that we survived not only the current that threatened to pull us under but our own doubt, as well. And blinking to us in the sunlight, caught along the riverbank, are pearls of wisdom and a jewel called hope.

*Father, I fear the trials when they come, but I
know that You are always with me. Help me cling to
You when troubles come, believing that through faith
there is a lesson waiting for me in the end. Amen.*

Treasures of Love

*He chose us in Him before the foundation of the world,
that we would be holy and blameless before Him. In love
He predestined us to adoption as sons through Jesus Christ
to Himself, according to the kind intention of His will.*
EPHESIANS 1:4–5 NASB

God sees us the way we seldom see ourselves—holy, pure, and blameless. It seems impossible. Did He forget the day we impatiently shifted back and forth in line, sending mental daggers to the person ahead who moved too slowly? Or all the times we complain and fret when our plans do not unfold in the way we hope?

We start our day with good intentions. But in our rush to achieve and be, we aim, fall short, and miss the mark, not seeing that who we are has already been named. We have already been claimed. And because of Christ's loving sacrifice, we are free to see ourselves as we really are—chosen and beloved.

Picked out of refuse of our failures, we are restored and covered in a blanket of His grace. Set apart for a glorious purpose, we are bestowed with the jewels of His love. It is not He who forgets, but rather we who need to remember. We are His living treasure here on earth.

Like the way light pours through a diamond, His light reflects best through the love we offer to others, especially to our husbands. We are not to be hidden away for safekeeping, for only in use do the jewels of compassion, kindness, gentleness, and patience (Colossians 3:12) sparkle brightly against a dark and colorless world.

*Father, help me to reflect Your love through my words and
deeds so that when others see me, they really see You. Amen.*

In God's Presence

Glory and honour are in his presence;
strength and gladness are in his place.
1 Chronicles 16:27 KJV

It is impossible for us with our imperfect minds to grasp the greatness of God. It is simply beyond our comprehension. However, God's Word gives us some really amazing insight into His character.

You know, in the Old Testament very few people were allowed into God's presence in the Holy of Holies because God is just that—holy. Now, because of Christ's blood, that veil separating the Holy Place from the Holy of Holies has been torn in two. Jesus is our High Priest, and because of that we have access to the Father. This doesn't make God less holy. It just means that because of Christ's blood those barriers have been removed.

In God's presence are glory, honor, strength, gladness, and a host of other wonderful characteristics. Our God is truly awesome. We can see that in creation, at Calvary, at the Garden tomb, and in our own lives.

Yes, God wants very much to be involved in our lives. He wants to be included in every aspect of our marriages, families, careers, and so forth. Great God that He is, He still cares for each of us individually. How about it? Will *you* let Him have the primary place in your home?

It's hard to understand why a great God like You
would want to invest so much in a sinner like me,
but I'm so thankful that You do, Lord.

Beauty Is Fleeting

Charm is deceptive, and beauty is fleeting;
but a woman who fears the LORD is to be praised.
PROVERBS 31:30 NIV

Let's face it. The aging process begins the moment we take our first breath. It's undeniable. We may color our gray or undergo plastic surgery, but we will never again look as we did in our twenties—something society tries to convince us is a problem. Accept the fact that beauty is fleeting. Years of gravitational pull eventually take its toll. Our physical bodies were not created to live forever. Someday we will return to the dust from which we were made.

Do not be distraught. Be encouraged! The Lord reminds us that the spiritual aspect of the aging process is far more important than our physical bodies. Our physical life is for a season. Our spiritual life is forever!

Choose to age gracefully by concentrating on the spiritual aspect of your being. Live in awe and respect for the Lord. Realize that your relationship with Him is the most important thing in this life. Then you will be able to laugh at your wrinkles while embracing your grandchildren. Your inner beauty will shine forth by the transforming power of the Holy Spirit. You will truly become more beautiful with each passing day!

Dear Lord, my physical beauty may not last forever, but my relationship with You will. So help me focus on that! Amen.

God's Wonder Woman

*Now Deborah, a prophetess,
the wife of Lapidoth, was judging Israel at that time.*
JUDGES 4:4 NKJV

Prophetess. Judge. Wife. Mother. All these describe Deborah, a
remarkable woman who answered God's leadership call and governed
Israel for sixty years. In an era when women did not learn to read,
let alone interpret the Law, Deborah held court every day under
a palm tree. Her countrymen arrived from near and far to entrust
their disputes to Deborah's godly insights. We don't know Lapidoth's
reaction, but during Old Testament times, a woman could not act
without her husband's consent. So by God's grace, Deborah managed
her home at the same time she managed the nation.

During the early years of Deborah's tenure, Israel struggled with
unstable spiritual and political conditions. Many worshipped idols;
as a result, God could not bless them. For twenty years, Jabin, the
cruel Canaanite king, and his general, Sisera, made constant raids on
their villages. Then God spoke through Deborah, summoning Barak
to lead an army against Sisera's forces. Barak refused to go to war
without Deborah, so she traveled far from home to experience the
same dangers he and his soldiers faced. God led them to victory and
disposed of Sisera through Jael, another woman. Deborah's praise
welled up in a warlike song of triumph that reminded the Israelites to
worship their powerful, wonderful God.

God has equipped each of us with the ability to perform the
duties to which He has called us. Are you letting Him work His way in
your life?

*Father, I often limit the possibilities You envision for me.
Help me to dream Your dreams. Amen.*

Burden-Bearing

*The heartfelt counsel of a friend is
as sweet as perfume and incense.*
Proverbs 27:9 nlt

Janet's friends and family often came to her for advice. She always seemed to have just the right words to say. Lately though, she was feeling overwhelmed because it seemed like everyone needed her at once. Besides, she had her own problems and responsibilities. What she really wanted was some time away—from her loved ones *and* their problems.

Caring for others, listening to them, and offering wise counsel is biblical. God created us to live in community, and we are instructed to bear one another's burdens. But there is often a fine line between bearing others' burdens and bearing *responsibility* for their burdens. It drains us and, more importantly, it can keep them from seeking answers directly from God.

It's essential to remember that our job is to point others *to* Christ, not become a substitute for Him. Allowing our friends unlimited access to our advice and counsel is one way this can happen. Sometimes the wisest words of advice we can offer are "Tell it to Jesus."

*Father, help me to wisely discern the difference between bearing
others' burdens and taking responsibility for their problems.
Help me to point others to You. Amen.*

Faith Booster

Therefore by Him let us continually offer the sacrifice of praise to God, that is, the fruit of our lips, giving thanks to His name.
HEBREWS 13:15 NKJV

Don't we just love it when people say "thank you" after we've done something for them? For some reason, it makes us more willing to perform some other duty, maybe an even greater task than the one we've already provided.

On the flip side, we consider it somewhat rude, even a bit disheartening, when we don't get that simple "thank you" for our efforts—whether that person is our spouse, our child, a neighbor, or a stranger on the street.

Imagine God not getting a thank you for all He's done for us. Imagine His disappointment when we neglect to say those two simple words.

Remember when Jesus healed the ten lepers and only one, a Samaritan, "returned, and with a loud voice glorified God, and fell down on his face at His feet, giving Him thanks" (Luke 17:15–16 NKJV)? What was Jesus' response? " 'But where are the nine? Were there not any found who returned to give glory to God except this foreigner?' " (Luke 17:17–18 NKJV).

Be like that good Samaritan: " 'Consider what great things [the Lord] has done for you' " (1 Samuel 12:24 NKJV) and give Him thanks. When you do, you will not only be pleasing God but also boosting your faith as you remember all the ways He has answered your prayers in the past. Such assurance of His hand in your life cannot help but fill you with peace.

So go ahead—make God's day. Thank Him, and then bask in that peace that surpasses all understanding (Philippians 4:6–7 NKJV).

Dear God, there are so many things You have done for me.
So here I am, falling down at Your feet to shout, THANK YOU!

Casting away Anxiety

Therefore humble yourselves under the mighty hand of God, that He may exalt you in due time, casting all your care upon Him, for He cares for you.
1 PETER 5:6–7 NKJV

A young bride stands at the window late at night, willing her husband's return from working late. He hasn't called to tell her where he is or what time to expect him home. Any moment now, she's sure the police will be at her door to tell her she's a widow.

Parents sit at the bedside of their child who is sick, unable to comprehend the illness that is sucking the life from her. Or a husband loses his job and is unable to find another quickly. The bills are piling up because there is no money to pay them.

These are extreme examples of circumstances that cause us to be anxious. Yet the little things cause just as much worry as the big things. The Amplified Bible expands on the word *care* in 1 Peter 5:7 by lumping together all our anxieties, all our worries, and all our concerns.

With every anxiety, God calls us to throw everything on Him, to let go of the burden of worry, large or small. The picture here is one of Him gathering them all together into one sack and carrying it on His shoulders. He wants to be our burden-bearer because He is able, because He cares for us affectionately and watchfully.

He knows the burden of anxiety we carry. Roll it off onto His mighty shoulders today.

Father, give me the strength to let go of this burden of anxiety I carry. You desire to bear my burden for me because of Your awesome love. Thank You for carrying my load. Amen.

Pleasing God or Pleasing Self

Obviously, I'm not trying to win the approval of people,
but of God. If pleasing people were my goal,
I would not be Christ's servant.
GALATIANS 1:10 NLT

A Christian camp director read the following statement, burning it into the minds of his listeners: "Only two choices on the shelf, pleasing God or pleasing self."

While this statement should sum up all our relationships, it especially applies in marriage. There is no room for selfishness in a marriage.

In Galatians 1:10, Paul states that his goal is to please God. And the proof he gives is that he wouldn't be serving Christ as he did if he were seeking to please others or himself. He could have done without the aggravations, the misunderstandings, and the persecutions he experienced. Yet he accepted them because he no longer mattered—only by choosing to please God instead of others or himself was he fulfilled and content.

Most of us wives fall into the trap of people-pleasing. But it seems that the harder we try to please others, the less we are fulfilled.

When we choose to put our focus on pleasing God, it doesn't matter what people say about us. Only in pleasing God, being obedient to His commands and guidelines for life, especially in our marriage relationships, do we truly feel fulfilled and content.

Father, I long to hear the words, "Well done, My good
and faithful servant." Help me choose to please You in
all things today, for only then am I satisfied. Amen.

The Bible in a Nutshell

The next day John saw Jesus coming toward him and said,
"Look, the Lamb of God, who takes away the sin of the world!"
JOHN 1:29 NIV

These words of John, spoken soon after Jesus' baptism in the Jordan River, contain the essence of the Bible in a nutshell. Though the Bible was written by different men from different countries, in different languages, over a span of thousands of years, it has a singular focus: Jesus. The books of history, law, and prophecy in the Old Testament point ahead to Jesus' coming; the Gospels and epistles of the New Testament point back to His ministry on earth and ahead to His heavenly reign. Essentially, the Bible is like a big neon arrow shining in the darkness, pointing to Jesus, saying as John did, "Look, the Lamb of God!"

The Bible may be our road map to heaven, but if we don't read it, we may lose the way. The world flashes many bright and enticing things before our eyes. Detours, shortcuts, potholes, and pitfalls in the form of missed opportunities, wrong choices, and sinful relationships all threaten to derail our spiritual journey.

The world will try to pull our eyes away from Jesus. Staying faithful to reading and meditating on God's Word will keep our eyes focused where they should be, on the Author and Perfecter of our faith (Hebrews 12:2).

Dear Father, Your Word is a lamp to my feet and
a light to my path. Help me read Your Word
daily and keep my eyes fixed on Jesus. Amen.

Flying off the Handle

*A gentle response defuses anger,
but a sharp tongue kindles a temper-fire.*
PROVERBS 15:1 MSG

The "love is patient, love is kind" passage in Paul's letter to the Corinthians (1 Corinthians 13:4) is one of the world's most well-known descriptions of love. After giving the positive attributes of love, Paul flips the coin to explain what love is *not*: It is not rude or easily angered.

The Greek word for "easily angered" is *paroxynō*. In different Bible versions, it is translated to mean greatly distressed, easily angered, irritable. Bottom line, Paul was saying that love means we don't fly off the handle to our husbands and children.

When we snap at those we love, what happens? Our actions create emotional and physical distance. People scatter! They escape to another room until we cool off. Or they might respond by getting even and snapping back. Irritability can quickly escalate into anger. Little things turn into big things, and big things turn into bad things.

We all have frustrating days that put us close to the edge. So what's a better way to handle irritability? Instead of expecting our family to excuse bad behavior after it happens, ask for some allowance. Be candid, before you snap. "I've had a horrible day and I'm not feeling very patient" is a much healthier response than flying off the handle.

Try it! There's nothing to lose and everything to gain: real love.

*Lord, put a bit in my mouth! Pull on
the reins so that I stop before I snap.*

Sheep and Shepherd

"I will be like a shepherd looking for his scattered flock.
I will find my sheep and rescue them from all the places
where they were scattered on that dark and cloudy day."
EZEKIEL 34:12 NLT

We've probably read passages about the shepherd and his flock
before now. Throughout the Bible, shepherd imagery is prevalent. In
many cases, the shepherd leads his flock and the sheep follow him
trustingly. In Ezekiel, God describes Himself as a shepherd looking
for his lost flock. The sheep to which God refers are not following
their Shepherd in a nice straight line, but rather, they are scattered.
Whether driven away by fear of the weather or if they have simply
wandered off through inattention, these sheep have ended up in
dangerous places from which the Shepherd must rescue them.

This image is a wonderful complement to the image of the
shepherd leading his flock. This image assures us that if we somehow
get distracted by carelessness or fear, God will come looking for us.
We are not completely lost and abandoned if we somehow wander
away. Even when we find ourselves in dangerous places, we can have
the confidence that our Shepherd will rescue us from all danger,
bringing us back to the fold, and eventually leading us to good
pastures and to rest.

Dear Lord, thank You for being my Shepherd. Thank You for
not only leading me in safe paths but for rescuing me when I
go astray. I'm so thankful You care so much about me. Amen.

Anxiety and God-Worship

*"If you decide for God, living a life of God-worship, it follows
that you don't fuss about what's on the table at mealtimes
or whether the clothes in your closet are in fashion."*
MATTHEW 6:25 MSG

Jesus knows how to get to the heart of any problem. In the Sermon
on the Mount He touched on a number of topics, but He especially
focused on things that cause anxiety. He says that the cure for anxiety
is deciding to live a life of God-worship. When our thoughts are totally
focused on God, we won't fuss about what we're going to eat or
whether we're dressed in the latest fashions.

As women, we tend to worry about the everyday necessities
of life. And it's easy to blame our husbands when these needs are
jeopardized. Food and clothing are basic needs, but at times it seems
that women are more concerned with these issues than men, probably
because of our nurturing natures. We need to be careful that we don't
put more emphasis on the necessities than God does.

If we decide for God, we must trust that He will provide exactly
what we need. While it may not be gourmet food or haute couture,
we can be content, knowing that many times He gives us our wants,
as well. Trust God to provide; rest in His love. And thank Him for
every provision. God loves to receive our worship for what we take for
granted.

*Father, thank You for providing all that we need,
many times even more than we ask for. You are good. Amen.*

Light for a Dark Journey

And I will bring the blind by a way that they knew not;
I will lead them in paths that they have not known: I will
make darkness light before them, and crooked things straight.
These things will I do unto them, and not forsake them.
ISAIAH 42:16 KJV

A blind person depends on unchanging organization in her home to help her navigate through life. No one can shift a piece of furniture. Every pan or dish must find its given place in a cabinet after washing. Matching clothes must be grouped together, or the blind person may walk out the door wearing a color combination never conceived in the civilized world!

Given such dependence on everyday consistency, why would God take a blind person down unfamiliar paths where she might fall? And while most of us possess physical sight, we may often find ourselves in dark circumstances where we feel ignorant, confused, even helpless. Does God enjoy our struggles? Does He laugh when we stumble?

No. Isaiah tells us that God promises to do the impossible for His blind, stressed people: He will give light to those who don't even know what it is. He will straighten our paths in ways we could never envision. Just as a faithful friend guides a blind person through a dangerous intersection in a strange city, God will help us deal with the unknown. He never leaves us alone.

Lord Jesus, my humanity blinds me to Your possibilities.
Please hold my hand and lead me along Your way. Amen.

Light

You are my lamp, O LORD;
the LORD turns my darkness into light.
2 SAMUEL 22:29 NIV

The Bible begins with light. Genesis 1:3 tells us, "And God said, 'Let there be light,' and there was light" (NIV). It also ends with light. Revelation 22:5 says, "There will be no more night. They will not need the light of a lamp or the light of the sun, for the Lord God will give them light" (NIV). Unfortunately, there's a lot of darkness in between. War. Murder. Pain. Loss. Scripture certainly doesn't candy-coat the difficulties of life; however, even in the midst of the darkness there are glorious glimpses of His marvelous light. David's sin is forgiven and he becomes a man after God's own heart. Paul is transformed from a murderer of Christians to a passionate evangelist. Peter denied Christ, but that wasn't his destiny—instead he defends Christ to the death. God has the amazing ability to turn even our darkest situations into personal and spiritual victories.

Perhaps you are facing a dark situation right now. Maybe you've suffered loss, a moral failure, or missed a chance to defend your faith. If so, you're not alone—you have a lot of company. When it seems that you're surrounded by darkness, remember that light is both your foundation and your future. Release the situation to God's marvelous light and know that He is able to transform it into something more than you could ever dream.

God, you are Light. In you there is no darkness
at all. Thank You for the truth that Your
light illumines even my blackest night.

The Power of Prayer

For the eyes of the Lord are on the righteous and
his ears are attentive to their prayer, but the face
of the Lord is against those who do evil.
1 PETER 3:12, NIV

The Bible tells us that when two or more are gathered together in Jesus' name, He is right there with us (Matthew 18:20)! God's Word also tells us that the prayers of the righteous are "powerful and effective" (James 5:16). Are you praying with others on a regular basis? If you are living a godly life, your prayers have power, and when two of you are praying together. . .there is even more power!

Most of us lead very busy lives, and we're lucky if we can squeeze in our own private prayer time, let alone finding the time to pray with others. But we need to do whatever we can to *make* time to pray with others—whether in person, over the phone, by texting, or via the Internet.

Prayer ushers us into the presence of God. Prayer allows us to hear and echo the needs of others. Prayer changes things. Prayer is crucial to a growing marriage, a burgeoning family, and your very life!

Father, I come here now, in Your name, to praise You, to know You
more, and to lift my concerns up to You. Help me make prayer a
priority in my marriage, my family, my life. Amen.

God's Picket Fence

The name of the Lord is a strong tower;
the righteous runs to it and is safe.
Proverbs 18:10 nasb

It's a dangerous world out there. Drunk drivers, heart attacks, rabid dogs, cancer, unemployment, terrorism, E. coli. . . The list goes on. It is easy to use a lot of energy thinking about all the bad things that could happen, as if our mental vigilance will somehow ward them off. But the Bible is very clear in commanding us not to worry. Jesus says it in unmistakably direct language: " 'Do not worry' " (Matthew 6:31). We should be very wary about disobeying a direct command from Jesus!

At its root, worry shows our lack of trust in both God's love and His power. The Bible is as clear about God's promises of protection for those who love Him as it is about the injunction not to worry. In fact, one necessarily follows the other: We shouldn't worry *because* God is taking care of us. The Bible says that we can rejoice; we can spend our days singing praise to God, knowing that His protection is all around us.

We don't always have fences around our houses, and even if we did, they couldn't protect our families from everything. But what we do have is a promise from God that He stands eternal sentry over those who love Him.

Dear Lord, I praise You for Your immense power,
Your love, and Your faithfulness. Forgive me for
worrying and help me trust in Your promises. Amen.

Receiving the Undeserved

"But the Lord our God is merciful and forgiving,
even though we have rebelled against him."
DANIEL 9:9 NLT

Rebellion is a word one comes across in many different contexts. One reads of historical rebellion, of literary rebellion, even of rebellious teenagers. Regardless of the context, rebellion—the flagrant defiance of the authority in charge—is often seriously punished. Rarely does one come across a case where outright rebellion is treated with mercy and forgiveness.

In his prayer to God, Daniel admits that he and his people have rebelled against God and His word. Punishment is the obvious recompense for such behavior. But Daniel doesn't talk about punishment; he speaks instead about the incredible mercy and forgiveness of God.

As Christians today, we remain a people of unclean hearts, rebellious and disobedient toward God. And yet, despite our rebellion, we serve a God who loves and cares for us, a God who desires reconciliation above all else, a God who sent His Son to die on the cross so that our sins could be washed away once and for all. Instead of punishment, we are graced with God's mercy and forgiveness. Praise God for His infinite love!

Dear Lord, although I sometimes rebel against You,
You continually show me forgiveness and mercy.
Thank You for loving me so. Teach me to obey Your Word
today and every day. Help me live to please You. Amen

The First and Last Word

O God, You are my God; early will I seek You. . . .
When I remember You on my bed, I meditate on You
in the night watches. Because You have been my help,
therefore in the shadow of Your wings I will rejoice. My
soul follows close behind You; Your right hand upholds me.
PSALM 63:1, 6–8 NKJV

Nothing starts a day out better than spending some moments in God's Word. Our perspective shifts, becoming His, not ours. We notice the wonder of His creation, seeing His hand in each leaf of the tree, each feather on the bird, each hair on our husband's head, and, in so doing, we are moved to praise Him for His glorious works.

As the day progresses, we turn to feel Him beside us, surrounding us, supporting us. We occasionally send up desperate prayers and are then strengthened as we feel His reassuring hand upon our shoulder. At times, we hear Him whisper and stop what we're doing to listen. And then, in God's power, we step out of our comfort zone to heed His direction.

When the day is done and we are about to close our eyes, we open His book to hear the last word of the day. As we focus on the Light, the world fades away, losing its strength, its hold over us, and we are renewed in His wisdom, falling asleep in the quiet comfort of His ever-loving, everlasting arms.

Lord, be my help, my guide, my strength as
I seek the light of Your Word—day and night.

A Master Builder

Every wise woman buildeth her house.
PROVERBS 14:1 KJV

What does your dream home look like? Is it a log cabin in the woods? A mansion in the country? A beachfront condo? Whatever it is, it takes skill to build. And while you may hire a contractor and construction crew to erect the physical structure, you are the actual builder of your home.

The most important part of any building is the foundation, and there is no surer foundation than Christ. He must be at the center of your family life. It is His wisdom that makes a home strong, His love that holds the bricks and mortar together. Once He is established as the groundwork for your structure, you can successfully add the walls, roof, and all of the interior details.

Your home should be a refuge from the world. A place that reflects who you are. It should feel warm and welcoming, tranquil and content. If it doesn't, then perhaps it's time to take a second look at your building materials. Don't settle for less than the best.

Remember that the home you are erecting now will become a heritage for generations to come. Dream big, dream bright, and with the right tools and a sure foundation, that dream will become a reality.

Dear Father, help me to be a wise builder. To make my
home a peaceful habitation that will stand the tests
of time and remain long after I am gone. Amen.

Raised Scars

And as we have borne the image of the man of dust,
we shall also bear the image of the heavenly Man.
1 CORINTHIANS 15:49 NKJV

As wives, daughters, mothers, and friends, we all bear scars from painful experiences. Some scars are visible, like the ones from childhood spills or the marks from an appendectomy, cesarean section, or some other surgery. Then there are the scars that are less visible. The wounds on our hearts when our husband speaks a cross word, a loved one has died, or a cherished relationship has been severed.

Yes, we all bear scars. But with Jesus in our hearts, we, although wounded, still have the victory. We have been born anew, into the life of Christ. Nothing in this world can ever truly harm us, for the Great Healer lives within. Amid the wounds and suffering of this world, we can access His peace, His life, His power.

Yes, like Jesus after the Resurrection on that long-ago Easter morn, we still bear the scars of this world, in our hands, our feet, our sides. They are proof of the pain we have endured. But because our Champion rose again—with His wounds disfiguring but not disabling—we are more than enabled to live mighty lives in Christ.

Don't let the scars you bear disable you. Instead, experience the peace, strength, healing, and victory you have in Christ. Then rise anew in His power!

Dear God, You know my scars inside and out.
Although the wounds have healed, the scars remain.
But Your Son has given me power, victory, and strength
over the pain of this world. In Him I have peace.
Thank You for giving us Your Son and raising Him again!

Who Do You Run To?

Immediately, when the entire crowd saw Him,
they were amazed and began running up to greet Him.
MARK 9:15 NASB

After Jesus' transfiguration, He came down the mountain. As soon as the people saw Him, they ran to greet Him. When Jesus asked what was happening, a man spoke up, telling Jesus how His disciples were having trouble healing his son, a boy who was seized by a mute spirit.

After giving Jesus an update on his boy's condition, the father said, "If You can do anything, take pity on us and help us!" (Mark 9:22 NASB).

Jesus responded with, " 'If You can?' All things are possible to him who believes" (Mark 9:23 NASB).

The boy's father cried out, "I do believe; help my unbelief" (Mark 9:24 NASB).

When the crowd began to gather around, Jesus rebuked the boy's unclean spirit and he was healed.

What do you do when you're having trouble at home? Who do *you* run to? Are you running to Jesus, pleading for Him to help you? Do you know that if you only believe, *anything* is possible? Are you confirming that belief to Jesus and asking Him for more?

Run to Jesus. Tell Him all. Cry out for more faith. And watch the miracles commence!

Jesus, I run to You today, amazement in my eyes,
my heart in my hand, my troubles on my shoulders.
Help me, Lord! Take pity upon me! I do believe in You!
Help my unbelief! Show me a miracle!

Picture Window

But the path of the righteous is like the light of dawn,
which shines brighter and brighter until full day.
PROVERBS 4:18 ESV

Have you ever looked at a classic stained-glass window at night? You don't see much. Though the leading around each form may give an outline of the subject, you can't see the bright colors that make such windows so appealing in the daylight.

When the sun rises colors begin to appear, and as bright sunlight shines through the panes of glass, a beautiful picture appears, portraying biblical characters, parables—most often Jesus.

Our lives are like those windows. Before we know Jesus, our window is dark. But when we come to know Him, His light shines in us and a spiritual picture appears—faintly, perhaps, at first, but with much potential for brightness. As we grow in Him, His light brightens, and our testimonies shine forth with increasing beauty.

Can those around us testify to the light shining through our lives? Do the robes of Jesus shine whitely, or has sin muddied the picture, blocking His light from our witness? As Jesus influences our marriages, our paths shine first in the power of dawn sunshine then ever increasing, till a more-than-noonday brightness enlivens all the colors of our picture window.

Lord, help me to live in Your brightness and reflect
that light in my life. May my husband and others
clearly see my testimony of faith.

Offensive Ways

*Search me, O God, and know my heart; test me and
know my anxious thoughts. See if there is any offensive
way in me, and lead me in the way everlasting.*
PSALM 139:23–24 NIV

Worry. Anxiety. Fear. It is easy to become consumed with anxious
thoughts, the "what-ifs" in life. What if my breast lump turns out
to be malignant? What if my husband gets laid off? What if my
friend doesn't forgive me? Our mind dwells on scenarios that may
or may not come to pass. Mental and emotional energy is expended
needlessly because worrying changes nothing. Instead, we are the
ones adversely affected. The stress generated by worry can cause
physical, mental, and emotional illnesses.

Worry, anxiety, and fear are also spiritual roadblocks. Did you
know that anxious thoughts are offensive to God? Anxiety is a red flag
signaling that we are not trusting God. Fear and faith cannot coexist.
We are either worrying or trusting, anxious or peaceful.

Come before the Lord. Invite Him to search your heart. Allow
His light to expose any anxious thoughts lurking in the shadows.
Acknowledge and confess your fears. Then trust Him with those
concerns. Ask that His will be done, knowing and believing that His
will is best. Then receive His peace by faith. Let's desire to live by
faith, trusting all your cares to God.

*Dear Lord, search my heart. Forgive my anxious thoughts.
May I trust You instead. Amen.*

Grace—It's Still Amazing

Create in me a clean heart, O God;
and renew a right spirit within me.
PSALM 51:10 KJV

Do you hold grudges? Sometimes it's really hard to let go of the grief and anger when someone has caused you hurt and pain. And it's often the ones who know you best that can hurt you the most.

You trusted them, perhaps opened up and became transparent, leaving yourself vulnerable. Maybe you've resolved never to do that again. Holding on to offenses, remembering the incident, and experiencing those feelings over and over again can't hurt the person who hurt you—it only hurts *you*.

The greatest gift you can give yourself is to forgive the offender. It's hard to let go, but think of it as not letting go but giving it up—giving it to God. Make a trade-off. Give Him your shame, anger, guilt, and memories of the assault or insult. Then when you're empty, really empty, let Him fill you with His grace! Try it, and you'll find that grace is still amazing every single time you experience it.

Lord, help me to let go of the injuries I've experienced
at the hands of others, from the smallest little hurt to
the deepest wounds of my heart. Show me how to really
let it go and live in Your grace every day! Amen.

Queenly Listening

He who answers before listening—
that is his folly and his shame.
PROVERBS 18:13 NIV

Nebuchadnezzar's wife, the queen, had been widowed for some time when her grandson, Belshazzar, decided to throw a big banquet. The queen wasn't planning on attending the party, but then she heard voices, upset and frightened. She was told that a hand had mysteriously appeared and wrote words on the banquet wall.

No one could interpret the meaning of the writing, but the queen knew someone who could. She hurried into the banquet hall to find King Belshazzar. "This man Daniel, whom the king [Nebuchadnezzar] called Belteshazzar, was found to have a keen mind and knowledge and understanding, and also the ability to interpret dreams, explain riddles and solve difficult problems. Call for Daniel, and he will tell you what the writing means" (Daniel 5:12 NIV).

This queen had apparently listened to her husband throughout their marriage really, really listened. She was raised in a pagan culture and was probably very young when she married King Nebuchadnezzar, yet she had the wisdom to pay attention to her husband's dramatic problems. On this fateful day, the knowledge she had gleaned was used to accomplish God's purposes.

Listening, really listening, is a rare trait. We all need to listen more attentively to our husbands, our children, our friends. We might learn something!

Father, sometimes I talk too much! Teach me to be
a good listener to others. Stop me as I start to interrupt
someone so that I can hold back and just listen.

No Place Like Home

*She looketh well to the ways of her household,
and eateth not the bread of idleness.*
PROVERBS 31:27 KJV

Taking care of a home is a lot of work, and no one can manage yours better than you!

You know where everything is. You know how much food to prepare to feed your family. You know when to start dinner to make sure it's served at the appropriate time. You're the queen of clean, a whiz at obliterating stubborn stains. You're a bargain hunter, getting the most for your money. When something needs doing, you roll up your sleeves and get to work. Your home is your pride and joy, and it shows!

If you have a lovely home, you know that it didn't get that way by chance. It took a lot of effort, and a great deal of that effort came from you. Give yourself a pat on the back. You have created a place of comfort and beauty that blesses your entire family. With your labor and skill, there truly is no place like home!

*Dear heavenly Father, thank You for my home and family.
Help me to always cherish it and to care for it
as You would have me to. Amen.*

Spiritual Health Tips

*But ye, beloved, building up yourselves on your most holy faith,
praying in the Holy Ghost, keep yourselves in the love of God,
looking for the mercy of our Lord Jesus Christ unto eternal life.*
JUDE 1:20–21 KJV

Wives spend untold time and energy nurturing other people—a
lifelong commitment to Jesus' command to love our neighbors as
ourselves. Sometimes, however, we're so busy working, planning,
celebrating, comforting, listening, and chauffeuring that we forget to
invest in our own spiritual health.

Jude calls on Christians to exercise their faith so they will not
only survive but also thrive in a culture that does not worship God. Of
course, exercise is never easy! We may spend days in endless activity,
yet our spiritual muscles grow flabby because we never stretch them
beyond the status quo. When we dare to dream God's dreams and
follow His direction, we gain the power to accomplish His will.

Jude urges believers to connect with the Holy Spirit in fervent
lifestyle prayer and remain close to God, not wandering off to
embrace destructive values and habits.

Finally, he encourages his friends to remain upbeat on a major
scale: "Expect God's mercy through Jesus Christ to bless you forever!"

When we follow God's regimen for good spiritual health, we can
anticipate great things in our own lives and in those we serve.

*Lord Jesus, I don't like change—yet if I'm to grow
and help others develop, I need to welcome it!
Transform me, God. Amen.*

Lift Up God's Name

*O Lord, thou art my God; I will exalt thee,
I will praise thy name; for thou hast done wonderful
things; thy counsels of old are faithfulness and truth.*
ISAIAH 25:1 KJV

Kendra sat at the kitchen table savoring the last of her coffee and enjoying her morning fellowship with her Savior. The brightness of the sun streaming through the window caught her attention, and she automatically looked toward the east, where the bright orb was just coming over the horizon. She gasped at the scene before her. Bold oranges coupled with rich pink hues and soft blues bathed the country landscape in a flood of cheerful color that only God could have captured.

She wondered for perhaps the millionth time how anyone could doubt the existence of this great Creator. Not only did God paint beautiful pictures in His creation, He also was the Master Potter who was in the process of molding her into a vessel fit for His use.

How thankful Kendra was to have God in her life. He who made her knew her best. He would give her the strength and wisdom to do her best in everything—her marriage, her career, her service to Him. He is truly a faithful and awesome God!

*How amazing You are, O God. Your hand in creation
and on my life are continual reminders of Your greatness.*

Pour Out Your Soul

But Hannah replied, "No, my lord, I am a woman oppressed
in spirit. . . . I have poured out my soul before the LORD."
1 SAMUEL 1:15 NASB

Hannah of the Bible had major problems. She was having trouble
conceiving and, because of that, was antagonized by her husband's
other wife, the child-bearing Peninnah.

So what did she do? She poured out her soul to God. Then, after
leaving all her cares at her Father's feet, she "went her way and ate,
and her face was no longer sad" (1 Samuel 1:18). The next day, she
and her family rose up early and worshipped the Lord (1 Samuel
1:19). Soon after, she conceived. The Lord had answered her prayer.

Are we as smart as Hannah? Do we go to the Lord when we are
distressed and pour out our hearts before Him? Or do we sit and sim-
mer in the juices of discontentment, sucking up our hurts and sorrows,
becoming so weighed down by our woes that we have trouble even
rising to our feet?

Got trouble? Get talking. Pour out your heart before the Lord.
He is ready and waiting to listen. Give Him the desires of your heart.
Leave your troubles at His feet. And then, knowing all is in His hands,
worship Him, letting your newly unburdened heart rejoice!

That's the order: Pour, petition, praise! Then watch the Lord
shower miracles into your life!

Lord, I pour out my heart to You, my Father, my God,
my Rock, and my Fortress! Give me hope, strength, and the
desires of my heart. I thank and praise You in Jesus' name!

The Time Is Near

Blessed is the one who reads the words of this prophecy,
and blessed are those who hear it and take to heart
what is written in it, because the time is near.
REVELATION 1:3 NIV

It's so easy to get caught up in the here and now. There are bills to pay, work to do, kids to raise, vacations to take. . .any kind of distraction you can think of. Satan tries to keep us so busy that we don't even realize we've gotten our focus off the Lord.

The Bible tells us that we are blessed if we read God's Word and take it to heart because "the time is near"! Are you living each day with that in mind?

There are several essential principles in this verse that we shouldn't miss. First, we need to be reading God's Word each day. Strapped for time? Go to an online Bible site and have scripture e-mailed to you every day! Second, take to heart what you've read. Meditate on a few verses of scripture each day, and ask God to teach you something from them. Ask Him to help you apply His Word to your life. Third, remember that "the time is near!" Live your everyday life like Jesus might be coming back today!

Jesus, help me to keep my focus on You. Give me the time and desire
to be in Your Word each day. In Your name, amen.

Intensely Emotional

Jesus wept.
JOHN 11:35 NIV

She was an emotional woman. Many times her passion for life was expressed with tears. She cried at her mother's death and her child's hospitalization. But she also shed tears at her granddaughter's birth and son's graduation. In celebration or sorrow, she wore her emotions on her sleeve. She embraced life by intensely feeling every hill and valley. Embarrassed by her tears as a teen, she finally learned to view her gift of passion as a blessing from the Lord.

Perhaps you, too, are an emotional woman. Take heart. Jesus wept. Although this is the shortest verse in the Bible, it speaks volumes. Jesus had emotions and was not embarrassed to express them. He cried when His good friend Lazarus died. In the Garden of Gethsemane, His soul was overwhelmed with sorrow. We read that His anger was unleashed when He drove the money changers out of the temple. Jesus cared. He felt intensely. He was passionate about life because, as the Creator, He knew that life was not happenstance. Jesus was sent to Earth for the divine purpose of redeeming fallen man. How could He not care? How could things not matter? How could He not weep?

We were created in His image. We were created to feel, to have emotions. Embrace them. Emotions are an expression of the heart. Don't be afraid to reveal your heart to others. Follow Jesus' example.

Dear Lord, thank You for creating me with emotions.
May I express them appropriately. Amen.

God's Grip

*"For I hold you by your right hand—I, the LORD your God.
And I say to you, 'Don't be afraid. I am here to help you.' "*
ISAIAH 41:13 NLT

Trouble comes into every life: We all lose jobs, have loved ones fall ill, and face spiritual crises. In our marriages, we experience sometimes-heated disagreements, confusion about what life direction we should take, and seemingly unsolvable dilemmas. As long as we are earthbound, unexpected and unwelcome problems remain our lot.

Often, we feel tempted to ask, "Where was God when this happened?"

The answer? He was gripping our right hands, ready to help us through it all.

It's not as if God didn't see ahead to our life-distorting events. No difficulty we face comes as a surprise to Him. The Omniscient One is aware of all that lies in our futures; but charitably, He does not give us warning. He knows we'd only fuss and worry or try to work things out for ourselves and land ourselves in even bigger trouble. Instead He walks hand in hand with even the most challenged believer who reaches out for His comforting grip.

Facing trouble today? Cling to this verse, believe it, and turn your concerns over to the Lord. Don't waste time in fear and worry. Your Lord knows just where the three of you are headed.

*Lord, help me cling to Your hand
and feel Your tight and loving grip.*

What's Your Fragrance?

But thank God! He has made us his captives and continues to lead us along in Christ's triumphal procession. Now he uses us to spread the knowledge of Christ everywhere, like a sweet perfume. Our lives are a Christ-like fragrance rising up to God.
2 CORINTHIANS 2:14–15 NLT

It has been said that the average human being can detect up to ten thousand different odors. Smells can evoke powerful images—the smell of mothballs can take us right back to when we were eight years old and playing in Grandma's attic. The scent of pine can transport us to the ski vacation we took in college with friends.

As followers of Christ we have been given a very unique fragrance. And whether we intend it to or not, our very presence in the lives of others always leaves a lingering scent. When we are kind to someone who doesn't deserve it, it smells wonderful. When we help a person in need, the fragrance lingers long after we've gone. Paul says that regardless of what we do, our fragrance should *always* remind people of Christ.

As you go about your business today, what kind of fragrance will you take with you? Pause for a moment to ask God to help you be a sweet representative of Christ, leaving His delightful aroma lingering in the air behind you.

*Father, help me to touch, in some small way,
each person I meet today. Help me to leave behind
a fragrance that reminds them of You.*

Different

Fear not; I will do to thee all that thou requirest: for all the city of my people doth know that thou art a virtuous woman.
RUTH 3:11 KJV

Ruth was not a nice Jewish girl. She hailed from Moab, Israel's enemy. Ruth had been exposed to idol worship, some of which may have included human sacrifice and fertility rites. When she arrived in Bethlehem with Naomi, her late husband's mother, the townspeople probably shook their heads at the way she dressed.

Yet Boaz, a prominent citizen, did not hesitate to marry Ruth. Why? Because she cared deeply for Naomi, a penniless old woman, and worked hard to provide for her. Ruth not only left her own family and culture behind but also vowed to follow Naomi's God. Boaz—and his entire hometown—soon recognized Ruth's kindness and determination to change.

Though Ruth lived more than three thousand years ago, her example of love and faithfulness is worth imitating. And when we ask for God's help in blessing those we don't understand and who don't understand us, we can be sure He will come to our aid, just as He helped Ruth.

Lord God, it's not easy to adjust to others' needs.
Let the loving fragrance of my life draw them to You. Amen.

Floating in Grace

"Be still, and know that I am God."
PSALM 46:10 NIV

Sometimes we want the answers while we are still thrashing in the waves of our own doubt, but the truth is, we seldom find wisdom until we are still. When tossed about, the horizon may, for the moment, leave our sight. And we are lost. These are the times when we are called to stillness. For many of us, doing *something* seems better than doing *nothing*, but it is easier to see clear to the bottom of our problems after all the ripples have faded.

Silence and stillness are the doorways that welcome our weary hearts in prayer. Prayer can be full of lamenting and asking, but when we realize that deep prayer is more a quieting of the soul, the power of who God is floods into our hearts. He is order amid the chaos, the foundation of all reason, and pure goodness in an unjust world. Through this kind of prayer, loves rushes in and renews us.

God is endless and unaltered love. The God that parted the Red Sea and calmed the storms is the same God that works His grace into our everyday lives. Eternity is on the horizon. All we need to do is look to Him, and we will float in depths where our feet can't touch and walk over anything that threatens to overcome us.

Father, You calm the storms and heal my doubt. Help me begin every day in prayer with a calm heart and stillness of mind, that I may have a better understanding of You. Amen.

Mrs. Potiphar

*"Keep watching and praying that you
may not enter into temptation."*
MATTHEW 26:41 NASB

Potiphar's wife had set her cap on her husband's servant. Scripture tells us that Joseph was a looker, "well-built and handsome, and after a while his master's wife took notice of Joseph and said, 'Come to bed with me!' " (Genesis 39:6–7 NIV).

But Mrs. Potiphar had underestimated Joseph's integrity. He explained that he could never betray her husband's trust. Even more indicative of Joseph's sterling nature, he said, "How then could I do such a wicked thing and sin against God?" (Genesis 39:9 NIV). Joseph's relationship with God was so well-established that he knew a sin—any sin—would be an offense against God.

Mrs. Potiphar wouldn't give up. "And though she spoke to Joseph day after day, he refused to go to bed with her or even be with her" (Genesis 39:10 NIV).

Her pride wounded, Mrs. Potiphar decided to punish Joseph. She waited until the house was empty of servants so there would be no witnesses, and then she accused Joseph of rape. Her husband threw Joseph into prison.

Why prison? Potiphar had every right to have Joseph executed. Did he suspect his wife's duplicity? We never learn anything more about Mrs. Potiphar, which might be scripture's way of telling us that we know enough. She was an immoral, scheming woman who sought to harm a man of God. And yet God used her treachery for good in Joseph's life. God can use anyone or anything to accomplish His purposes.

*Lord, guard me against any off-limits relationship.
Let me be like Joseph, who stayed clear of temptation.*

Your Talents

God has given each of you a gift from his great variety
of spiritual gifts. Use them well to serve one another.
1 PETER 4:10 NLT

Author Leo Buscaglia said, "Your talent is God's gift to you. What you do with it is your gift back to God."

What's your talent? Is it balancing numbers, writing stories, being a homemaker, caring for others, making people laugh, baking sweets, preaching, teaching?

Not sure what your gift is? Well, what are you good at? What do you enjoy doing? What talent do you feel a burning need to share? What do you feel God leading you to do? Whatever your answer is to these questions, that's your gift.

It may be that your gift or talent is not something you can use on the job. Perhaps it's not even something from which you can make money. That's okay. Use it anyway.

If you have a way with words, write an article for your church newsletter. If you have a drive to instruct, teach a Sunday school class. If you love to cook, begin by trying out some gourmet dishes on your husband.

Use the gifts God has given you. In doing so, you will find your life blessed and, at the same time, be a blessing to others. And, as an added bonus, you'll be giving your gift back to God. Is there anything better than that?

Lord, I owe You so much, and although I can never
truly repay You, I can use the gifts You have given
me to help others. Show me my gifts, Lord. And help
me find ways to use them. All to Your glory!

Sarah's Daughters

Through faith also Sara herself received strength to conceive seed, and was delivered of a child when she was past age, because she judged him faithful who had promised.
HEBREWS 11:11 KJV

Although the popular Narnia series by C. S. Lewis draws attention to the "daughters of Eve," this is not a biblical idea.

While we are daughters of Eve because she was the mother of all living, we are not to pattern ourselves after her. We are never told to be daughters of Eve. Rather, we are encouraged to be daughters of Sarah.

Eve was deceived and fell into a transgression. But Sarah was faithful.

Sarah obeyed Abraham, even in dangerous situations.

Sarah reverenced Abraham, calling him "lord."

Even though Sarah, when told that she would have a son in her old age, had laughed at the idea and then denied doing so, she still had the faith to conceive Isaac. However little her faith was, it earned her a place in the Hall of Faith in Hebrews 11.

How can we be daughters of Sarah?

Peter tells us that we should be in subjection to our own husbands, showing them reverence. We need to display chaste behavior, focus on our inward growth rather than our outward appearance, and have a meek and quiet spirit.

These qualities are lightly esteemed in our modern world but of priceless value to our heavenly Father.

If you would honor Him, be Sarah's daughter.

Father, it sometimes goes against my flesh to be quiet, meek, and reverent to my husband. I yield myself to Your Spirit now, Father. Amen.

Earth's Dark Glasses

For now we see through a glass, darkly;
but then face to face: now I know in part;
but then shall I know even as also I am known.
1 CORINTHIANS 13:12 KJV

She had been married for only a year. Her skin was smooth, her hair thick, her body slim and graceful. She knew her husband loved her, but sometimes she wondered if his love would be as strong when her hair was white and thin and her cheeks were sagged and spotted with age. Looking for reassurance, she studied the other couples in church on Sundays, especially one older couple who sat nearby. This husband and wife had been married for more than five decades, and the years hung heavily on them.

Week after week she watched them, and then it dawned on her. It seemed as if they did not see each other as the rest of the world did. When the wife took her husband's thin arm, she was holding the muscular arm of her young husband. When the husband smiled into his wife's face, he wasn't seeing the wrinkles and liver spots. He was seeing the young woman he married fifty years before.

Soon and very soon these bodies will be discarded and God will give us new ones. Until then, let us try to see each other—and trust that we are seen—as God sees us: spotless and without blemish, covered in the precious blood of the Lamb.

Dear Lord, help me be content with the body You have
given me. Thank You for the hope of the resurrection
and a new, glorified body in the future. Amen.

Asking for Trouble

"Therefore do not worry about tomorrow, for tomorrow will worry about itself. Each day has enough trouble of its own."
MATTHEW 6:34 NIV

God's Word is very clear about worrying. God says: Don't do it! Did you know that it is actually a sin to worry? When we worry, we are telling God that we don't trust Him enough with our future.

How often do we worry? Almost hourly, right? We have a lot of confessing to do then, don't we? We worry about how we're going to pay all the bills, if this person we're committed to will truly be committed to us for the rest of our lives, if we will get a life-threatening illness, and on and on it goes. We worry about so much, and God says don't do it! How do we stop?

We have to commit our life, our plans, and our thoughts to the Lord *each day*! Make this the first thing you do every morning. The Bible tells us to give all of our worries over to the Lord because He cares for us (1 Peter 5:7). It also tells us that worrying won't add one single hour to our lives (Luke 12:25). So why do it? When we worry, we're just asking for trouble!

*Father, please forgive me for worrying. Help me
to trust You at all times. In Jesus' name, amen.*

Honor God with Healthy Habits

When you eat or drink or do anything else,
always do it to honor God.
1 CORINTHIANS 10:31 CEV

The statistics are grim. Sixty percent of Americans are overweight or obese. Only about a third of us get the minimum recommended amount of exercise each day. Health problems that were once reserved for elderly people, like diabetes and high blood pressure, are now affecting us at younger and younger ages. In spite of living in a society obsessed with diet and exercise, many of us are becoming increasingly unhealthier. Yet the Bible says that whatever we do we are to honor God, and that includes with our bodies (1 Corinthians 6:20). We often think of this in relation to sexual purity. And it certainly applies. However, we also have an opportunity to honor God with our bodies by taking good care of them—by getting enough rest and enough exercise.

Take a look in the mirror. You probably need at least eight hours of sleep each night so that your body can function optimally. Do you make it a priority to get enough rest, or do you stretch yourself to the limit all week and then try to make up for it on the weekends? The surgeon general recommends that adults get thirty to sixty minutes of physical activity most days of the week. Is there time in your day for fresh air and exercise? Particularly as you age, healthy habits are an investment that will pay enormous dividends down the road. It sounds like a cliché, but you only get one body—make it a priority to honor God with it.

Father, thank You for blessing me with a body that
does so much for me. Please help me to make it a
priority to care for it in a way that honors You. Amen.

Becoming a Follower

I will instruct you and teach you in the way
you should go; I will guide you with My eye.
PSALM 32:8 NKJV

Sometimes life can seem to be careening out of control, so much so that you feel like a fireman running from here to there, extinguishing the fires breaking out in your life or the lives of those around you. Distractions, crises, and interruptions try their best to rob you of your peace, energy, and strength.

But when you accepted Jesus as your Lord and Savior, you were turned inside out. You have the ability to live from your spirit instead of your emotions. The Spirit of God within you wants to guide you and give you something that can't come from your emotions alone—daily peace.

Relax and let the real you—your heart—lead and guide you in all truth. Instead of reacting to your circumstances, stop and respond to the voice of God. Then perhaps you'll still put out fires, but you'll arrive on the scene when the blaze is more manageable, with a clear sense of direction of what needs to be done to bring about the best outcome for your life and the lives of those around you.

Heavenly Father, I want to respond to life, not react to it.
Help me to hear Your voice and follow Your lead. Amen.

Word or Deed

And whatever you do, whether in word or deed,
do it all in the name of the Lord Jesus, giving
thanks to God the Father through him.
COLOSSIANS 3:17 NIV

There is no such thing as a Sunday Christian. Bearing the name of Christ is a twenty-four hour, seven-day-a-week proposition. Whether at work, shopping at the grocery store, or playing golf, our lives reflect the One we profess. Once we are united with Christ, our secular and spiritual lives are also united. We should not live one way during the week and then act differently at church on Sunday. People are watching. Inconsistency is quickly recognized. Hypocrisy is offensive.

Although Christians are far from perfect, we are called to be Christ's ambassadors, His representatives. In a world filled with darkness, we have the privilege of being light to those that are lost. By reflecting His glory, we proclaim His truth: Jesus Christ is the way, the truth, and the life (John 14:6).

So whatever you do or say, represent Jesus well. May He be your focus so that others will be drawn to Him. Allow Jesus access to every part of your life, every day of your life. Don't hide your light under a bushel. Let it shine brightly to a world that is lost

May the light of Christ in you be clearly seen by others. Christ in you is indeed the hope of glory!

Dear Lord, may I represent You as I should.
May my words and actions be pleasing to You. Amen.

Daily Bread

"Give us today our daily bread."
MATTHEW 6:11 NIV

In our mega-warehouse culture, buying in bulk has become a trend that carries over into the rest of our lives. Who can argue that storing up on dish soap and paper towels doesn't bring some sense of security to our anxious hearts? So with our pantries full, we look toward the unknown with hope for similar assurances. In our spiritual lives, this is an entirely different matter indeed—our hands and hearts need to be emptied before they can be filled. God gives us just enough for one day.

The truth is that no matter what false securities we create, it is God who takes us into tomorrow. In our empty sleep, God refreshes and renews us so that each morning we have what we need to face the new day's demands. His grace is not something we can stockpile but rather something we give away.

Whenever we feel our heart tighten over outcomes we want, we simply need to loosen our grip and take rest in Him. Because we live in a world of independence and self-sufficiency, this faith feels awkward at first until we experience a joy unmatched by anything we can conjure up on our own. It is in these divine moments that we can throw open the cupboard doors of our hearts and give away everything that's there, knowing that tomorrow we will be full again.

Father, thank You for giving us our manna each and every day. Thank You for providing for all our needs as we continually reap the joy of knowing You as the trustworthy sustainer of our lives. Amen.

Personalized Prayer

I have hidden your word in my heart.
Psalm 119:11 nlt

Lots of Bible verses contain the words *he*, *him*, and *his*. One reason for that is that most of the Bible stories are about men and the deeds they performed, the prayers they prayed, the psalms they wrote and sang. Another reason is that the scriptures—Old and New—were written from the perspective of a male-dominated society. As a result, sometimes it's hard for us women to get close to a verse, to take it to heart when the references are made to a male and we are definitely female. So what's a girl to do?

Make it personal. If there is a verse that's really speaking to your heart, one that you'd like to commit to memory so that you can pull it from the recesses of your mind when needed, write it down using *she*, *her*, or *hers* (or, for that matter, *I*, *you*, and *we*) where appropriate.

For example, a great verse to store away for those less-than-peaceful moments is Isaiah 26:3. In the New King James, the original verse reads, "You will keep him in perfect peace, whose mind is stayed on You, because he trusts in You." Make this personal by changing it to "You will keep *her* in perfect peace, whose mind is stayed on You, because *she* trusts in You." Or better yet, "You will keep *me* in perfect peace, whose mind is stayed on You, because *I* trust in You."

It's God's Word meant for you. So truly take it to heart by making it your very own. Make it personal. Because if God is nothing else, He's personal.

Lord, I want to make Your Word truly mine.
Help me to understand, to make Your Word personal.
Let's talk. . .heart to heart.

Making Bread

*Be humble under God's powerful hand so he
will lift you up when the right time comes.*
1 PETER 5:6 NCV

When we reach the end of everything we know, that is when God rolls up His sleeves and does His best work in our lives. He waits until we are finished rolling our problems around like dough, pounding away until there is nothing left to be done. When we hand our mess over to Him with humble and sticky fingers, He takes it all and transforms it into a kind of bread that nourishes us.

There is a story about orphaned children during WWII who were left homeless and starving. Once rescued, they had trouble sleeping at night out of fear that they would wake in the morning and be hungry again. After all attempts were made to ease their fears, someone came up with the idea of giving each child a piece of bread to hold during the night. It worked. The children slept peacefully, holding their bread. We can take a lesson from those children and hold our bread as a symbol that God was with us today and He will be with us again tomorrow.

The art of spiritual bread making requires a deep patience that allows obstacles to rest, quietly covered in His grace so that they can rise into opportunities that give us strength. He works in miracles—turning even our most difficult ordeals into blessings that can heal us.

*Father, You are the Bread of Life. Give us the faith and the patience
we need to allow You to work in our lives. Amen.*

Busier Than the Prime Minister of Babylon?

Three times a day [Daniel] got down on his knees and prayed,
giving thanks to his God, just as he had done before.
DANIEL 6:10 NIV

Like clockwork, Daniel had a custom of praying three times a day.
He left his office, went home, and knelt by an open window that
faced Jerusalem. Taken from Judah as a young teenager and forced
into "friendly captivity" by King Nebuchadnezzar of Babylon, Daniel
excelled in his responsibilities. In return, he was treated well and rose
through the ranks of Babylon bureaucracy. Eventually he became one
of three "prime ministers" of Babylon! And still he knew who he was,
and he knew who his God was. He never forgot.

Are we praying faithfully for the people God has placed in our
lives? Most likely, our record of praying for them is spotty at best. But
are we any busier than a prime minister of Babylon? Daniel made a
habit of regular, effective prayer. It was just as important to him, if
not more so, than food.

We need to develop effective praying habits for our friends and
family. Prayer doesn't have to be locked to a time or a place or a
particular posture. We need to kneel in our hearts, whenever we
sense the Lord's inner promptings to pray.

Lord, forgive me for growing complacent in prayer.
Poke me! Wake me! Remind me to pray regularly for my
family, for their hearts to belong to You for all eternity.

Inside Out

*In like manner also, that women adorn themselves in modest
apparel, with shamefacedness and sobriety; not with broided hair,
or gold, or pearls, or costly array; but (which becometh
women professing godliness) with good works.*
1 Timothy 2:9–10 KJV

Is it wrong to have a desire to look nice? No! Are women required
to walk around looking at the ground? Absolutely not. The point of
this verse is not that women should do their best to look frumpy and
unattractive. It *is*, however, to point out that being well-dressed and
expensively adorned are completely pointless if inner beauty is absent.

It is possible to be neatly, even stylishly, attired and still be
modest. Your makeup and jewelry can be applied neatly and with
good taste, but it should not be done in a way that draws unnecessary
attention to yourself.

Your purpose is to be godly—to draw people to Jesus. You do this
by walking so closely with Him that His beauty is reflected in You. All
your designer clothes and expensive accessories are worthless—an
artificial beauty—if Christ's love is not radiating through your entire
being.

Get your priorities straight. Be sure your heart is beautiful, and
external attractiveness is sure to follow.

*Lord Jesus, let Your love shine through me.
May my heart be beautiful in Thy sight.*

Freely Give

"Freely you have received, freely give."
MATTHEW 10:8 NIV

As women, it is normal when we devote ourselves to do—and be—as many things as others need. Giving, for us, is as natural as breathing. That is, until we find that we are dancing delicately on a tightrope in a precarious balancing act between what we need and what others want. Despite all our efforts, gravity usually wins as the truth comes crashing down. We simply can't give what we don't have.

It was never God's plan that we spin through life with nothing but a bag of tricks to get us by. Talent and caffeinated energy only work for so long, until the moment comes when we reach into our empty pockets and conclude that we have nothing else to give.

Generous giving begins when we dig into the soil of God's sustenance and find what He has planted for us. We are nourished by this precious truth of who we are in Christ. He fills us with unlimited resources of love, patience, wisdom, and truth. From this place, we are free to give without fear of falling or becoming empty.

Every day the questions laid out before us are these: How can we enter into our day without being connected to the Source who offers His love like a spring? How can we attend to the myriad of demands placed on us without freely accepting the power that God offers first?

Father, help me to begin each day in Your Word so
that I can be filled with the Holy Spirit and give
from Your strength rather than my own. Amen

Female Issues

He said to her, "Daughter, be of good cheer;
your faith has made you well. Go in peace."
LUKE 8:48 NKJV

When it comes time for prayer requests, nothing can clear a room faster than a woman revealing she has "female problems." Even our husbands are sometimes embarrassed when we want to discuss womanly issues that they can't even begin to fathom. Yet Jesus didn't waver when "a woman having an issue of blood twelve years" (Luke 8:43 KJV) came to Him for help. Talk about issues!

This was one brave woman, considering that Leviticus 15:19 made it clear that any female with an issue of blood was to be set apart from everyone else for seven days. She was deemed "unclean," and anything she'd even *touch* would turn unclean.

Yet this particular physically weak woman, who was full of faith, boldly approached the Great Physician, knowing that if she just touched Him, she would be healed!

When she felt Jesus' garment, the power left Him and immediately healed her! When He realized what had happened, He wasn't embarrassed or repulsed. In fact, Jesus responded with wonderful words: "Daughter, be of good cheer; your faith has made you well. Go in peace." Ah, words to live by. Words that heal.

If you have an "issue" that you are reluctant to share with others, take your faith and bring it to Jesus. He's waiting for you to receive His power, to be healed, to find peace.

Lord, thank You for allowing me, Your daughter, to share
everything with You. I come to You with my issues and
am ready to receive Your power, blessing, and peace.

Transparency

Do not conform any longer to the pattern of this world,
but be transformed by the renewing of your mind.
Then you will be able to test and approve what God's
will is—his good, pleasing and perfect will.
ROMANS 12:2 NIV

Lack of communication skills is one of the greatest hindrances to healthy relationships. Most of the time, when we pray, we are seeking change. We cannot change others, but we *can* submit to God's design for our life through the transformation of the Holy Spirit.

Your words are powerful! They shape the atmosphere of your home and the hearts of all who enter. Your very words build up or tear down relationships. Take a breath and realize that your husband and children have a right to express themselves. Make room for their ideas and opinions even when they are different than yours.

Allow yourself to become transparent to God. Ask God to reveal the real *you* to you. When we allow Him to expose the truth of who we are, He brings everything to the light. When we are reproved by His love, then our weaknesses are made visible and He is able to heal the past wounds and hurts that have controlled our behavior and speech.

Focus your words on building up, and when you do need to speak a difficult word, ask the Lord to help you say it with His love.

Lord, teach me to guard my heart with all diligence, and show me
how to speak the truth in love in my home, in my church, with my
friends, and in all my relationships. Amen.

Good Things

*And the people spake against God, and against Moses,
Wherefore have ye brought us up out of Egypt to die in
the wilderness? for there is no bread, neither is there
any water; and our soul loatheth this light bread.*
NUMBERS 21:5 KJV

At this time in their journey of deliverance, the Israelites had seen many miracles. They had followed a cloud and a pillar of fire and had been fed with manna. They had seen the Red Sea part (or had heard about it). More recently they had seen the earth open to swallow up their rebellious brothers.

Yet when the going got tough and they were without real bread and fresh water, they complained against God. In fact, they said they *hated* what God had supplied!

We look back at them and are amazed. How could they be so dense, so faithless? God was obviously with them. How could they possibly doubt His love and care for them?

But are we any better?

Believers have the indwelling Holy Spirit. God is *in* us; He is always with us. He has promised to never forsake us.

Yet when the going gets tough—when our finances and relationships are strained and when we don't have what we think we need—we complain just as the Israelites did.

Let us learn the lessons they did not. Let us trust in our Father, knowing that He cares and is always working for our good.

*How often I complain about the little irritations and
miss seeing all the good things You give me, Father.
Have mercy on my fickle heart. Amen.*

First Things First

*In the morning, O LORD, you hear my voice; in the morning
I lay my requests before you and wait in expectation.*
PSALM 5:3 NIV

No team takes the field without first meeting in the locker room for
a pregame talk. No actor takes the stage without first getting into
character. It would be foolish to build a house without consulting
with an architect and drawing up plans. For any successful endeavor,
preparation is key.

Throughout His earthly ministry, Jesus modeled this principle.
He was an incredibly busy Man. There were disciples to train, people
to heal, and children to bless. No matter what He did or where He
traveled, something or someone always seemed to need attention.
However, in spite of the many demands placed upon Him, scripture
tells us that Jesus got up early in the morning, while it was still dark,
and took time to meet His Father in prayer (Mark 1:35). Jesus was
perfect, and yet even He knew this discipline was essential to ensure
the effectiveness of His ministry.

What is the first thing you do each morning? Many of us hit the
ground running, armed with to-do lists a mile long. Unfortunately,
this means we try to take off in a hundred different directions, lacking
focus, and then falling into our beds each night with a sense that we
haven't accomplished anything at all.

While it doesn't ensure perfection, setting aside a short time each
morning to focus on the Father and the day ahead can help prepare us
to live more intentionally. In these moments we, like Jesus, gain clarity
so that we can invest our lives in the things that will truly matter.

*Father, help me to take time, each morning, to focus on
You and the day ahead. Align my priorities so that the
things I do will be the things You want me to do.*

Serving the Lord

*Whatever you do, work at it with all your heart,
as working for the Lord, not for men, since you know
that you will receive an inheritance from the Lord as
a reward. It is the Lord Christ you are serving.*
COLOSSIANS 3:23–24 NIV

God has given all of us some work to accomplish. Whether it's
a daily job, raising a family, taking care of a home and a business. . .
some of our tasks tend to be tiresome jobs that we wish we could hire
someone else to do.

As Christians in today's society, we really need to change our
thinking about the little jobs. We need to keep Colossians 3:23–24 in
mind anytime we are working so that Christ will be glorified. If we
take these verses to heart, our attitudes will change and we will be a
strong witness to others.

Try getting up five minutes earlier this week and spending that
time memorizing these verses. Write them down and ask the Lord
to change your heart and attitude about any grunt work you don't
usually enjoy doing. You will see a change in your life and marriage
as you take these verses to heart. Your attitude at home will be much
better as you mop the floor and clean the toilets because you are
doing these tasks as an act of worship to the Lord!

*Dear Lord, I want to worship You in everything I do.
Change my attitude about the little things so that I
may be a good witness to You always. Amen.*

Sacred Ground

*"Until now you have not asked for anything in my name.
Ask and you will receive, and your joy will be complete."*
JOHN 16:24 NIV

Every day, Jesus invites us to enter into a holy place with Him by praying in His name. So often we ask for things in our daily rush from here to there: "Lord, please give me a parking space close to the door." Or things that do require some miracle making: "Please change my husband." Certainly these prayers, if answered, would make our lives easier, but Jesus isn't talking about prayers that simply make us happier. He is talking about prayers that bring us complete and utter joy.

When we step out of ourselves and into a life with Jesus, we begin to see how this mystery of joy unfolds. Over time, His words take root and weave into our own, until we find ourselves unsure where His thoughts end and ours begin.

And one rainy day, in a crowded parking lot, we see a woman we've never met but suddenly know she needs help getting to her car. Or we gain new insight into the pressure our husband is under and we feel tenderness toward him we haven't felt before. In those moments of clarity when our words and prayers become one with Jesus', the sacred ground on which we walk is the ten steps it takes to offer an umbrella and an extra hand or a loving embrace.

*Father, teach me how to enter into a relationship
with You so deeply that I can hear Your voice and
feel Your joy as I pray Your words as my own. Amen.*

Timing Is Everything

*"Go and gather together all the Jews of Susa and fast
for me. Do not eat or drink for three days, night or day.
My maids and I will do the same. And then, though it
is against the law, I will go in to see the king."*
ESTHER 4:16 NLT

Esther was an orphan in a foreign land. Suddenly she found herself on
center stage as King Xerxes of Persia's new bride. Barely accustomed
to her new duties as queen, Esther faced a crisis of enormous
proportions. She learned that the king had unwittingly placed all Jews
living in Persia, including herself, in jeopardy. Prior to risking her life
for her people, she humbled herself by fasting and asking for prayer
support from others.

How did God direct her? To wait patiently for the right time to
speak. In ancient times, the queen risked her life by appearing in
front of the king's throne unless she was summoned. Esther had
something she needed to say to King Xerxes, but she paused and
prayed and proceeded cautiously and carefully. Xerxes saw her
standing in the hall. Pleased, he was in a mood eager to give Esther
anything she wanted. Timing was everything.

This is a wise reminder for us to choose our words carefully and
to deliver those words at the right time. We want our message to be
well received. Is our husband hungry? Tired? Irritable? Distracted?
Those aren't the moments for heart-to-heart conversation. What we
say matters, but so does how and when.

*Lord, give me Esther's restraint. Make me sensitive to
Your guidance. May I learn to practice instant obedience.*

Humility Brings Glory

"For everyone who exalts himself will be humbled,
and he who humbles himself will be exalted."
Luke 14:11 niv

The tree was bare. Every leaf had been shed. Winter had arrived. Yet beyond the barren tree, the sun peeked its head above the treetops. Dawn was breaking. As the sun ascended higher, its rays were visible through the bare branches. Before long, the entire tree was glowing as the sun's radiance shone through it.

Many times our lives seem barren, as if we've been stripped of everything. We find ourselves humbled, humiliated, forsaken, or rejected—standing alone, like a barren tree. But our story does not end there. God's glory will burst forth. Wait. At just the right time, like the sunrise, He makes His appearance. When He does, His light will shine through because our branches are bare. The world will see. Our humility allows others to see the Lord clearly through us because the focus is no longer on us but on Him. When we decrease, the Lord will increase.

Do not view humility with distain. His glory can only be revealed when we are humble. Humble yourself before the Lord and He will lift you up. He will shine through you. You will reflect and make known His glory. May it be so!

Dear Lord, may humility characterize my
life so that You may be glorified. Amen.

Michal's Choice

As the ark of the LORD was entering the City of David,
Michal daughter of Saul watched from a window.
And when she saw King David leaping and dancing
before the LORD, she despised him in her heart.
2 SAMUEL 6:16 NIV

Nine years earlier, Michal was hopelessly in love with David. She even betrayed her father, King Saul, to save David's life. But today, that love was dead. His abandoned joy only embarrassed her.

Michal couldn't identify with David's joy because she didn't share it. She had no appreciation for the significance of the return of the ark of the Lord to Jerusalem. But to David, it meant basking in the presence of the Lord.

When David returned home, Michal met him at the door, eyes blazing. She blasted him with hot hatred! And he responded by distancing himself from her.

Like most couples, Michal and David once loved each other passionately, but nine stressful years later, that passion had died. Instead of replacing her emptiness with God, Michal let her heart remain. . .empty.

We think passion will be enough to sustain a marriage, but it isn't. Only God can satisfy our heart's deepest desires.

It could have been so different for Michal! She was David's first love. She could have been his last one.

Make God your first choice. Allow Him to fill your heart. He'll keep your love alive!

Lord, may I have a heart like David. He seemed to
intuitively understand that You belonged first in his life.

The Dawn of Mourning

"Blessed are those who mourn,
for they will be comforted."
MATTHEW 5:4 NIV

When dreams become shadows and sadness tramples our heart, mourning becomes the way we learn to breathe again. It is sanity, really, which prompts us to cry out and break the silence that simply absorbs our loss. Giving voice to our grief joins us in song to all those who have suffered before. It releases our sadness and keeps it from settling into and numbing our hearts.

We mourn many things throughout our life. . .loss of loved ones, our health, our ideas, or our expectations. But bemoaning our earthly losses is not the type of mourning Jesus is talking about in the Beatitudes. He is referring to what happens when we are hit with the overwhelming realization that we are spiritually lost beings in need of a Savior. Simply put, we are the walking dead, living a useless life over a fixed amount of time. And the clock is running.

Jesus says that those who grieve over their enlightened spiritual condition are blessed. Yes, blessed because He has great news! He offers us everlasting life with Him through His Son, Jesus. He gives the dead new life. Every time we stumble in sin and fall on our pain, He promises to comfort us and restore us to Him. His love and complete forgiveness turns our mourning into a new day.

Father, thank you for the comfort You give me when I can't help but see myself as I really am. Thank You for Your forgiveness and promise of everlasting life. Amen.

Run Home

But now, God's Message, the God who made you in the first place,
Jacob, the One who got you started, Israel: "Don't be afraid,
I've redeemed you. I've called your name. You're mine."
ISAIAH 43:1 MSG

Remember when you were a child and you ran outside to play? When it came time for dinner, your mom called you in. She called you by name. And you stopped whatever you were doing and ran. You ran home. Because at home, your parents (the ones whose love created you) protected you and provided for you. They fed, clothed, and nourished you. They answered all your questions. They gave you direction.

Now you're all grown up. And there is still one who protects you, provides for you, and nourishes you. It's God, the One who got you started. He calls you by your name. You are His! He longs for you to run home to Him!

Listen! Be still. Quiet your thoughts. Do you hear Him? He's calling your name!

Drop whatever you're doing and run! Run into His arms. Allow Him to fill you with His Spirit and peace. Allow Him to love you with an everlasting love. Allow Him to feed you on His Word. Allow Him to hold you tight. He will never let you fall, never let you go. You need not be afraid. You're home!

Lord, I hear You calling my name!
Here I am, Lord! Hear I am! I'm coming home!

The Master Multiplier

And they said to Him, "We have here
only five loaves and two fish."
MATTHEW 14:17 NKJV

One day five thousand people were sitting on a hillside, listening
to Jesus. But as the day drew to a close, stomachs began to growl.
Knowing that they were faced with an inordinate amount of hungry
mouths, the disciples panicked, telling Jesus to send the crowd away
to buy bread from the surrounding villages.

But Jesus said to them, "You give them something to eat" (Mark
6:37 NKJV).

This, to the disciples, seemed like an impossibility! Focusing on
what they lacked, the disciples knew there was no way five loaves and
two fish would satisfy this hungry mob. Yet Jesus commanded them
to bring their meager stores to Him.

Then Jesus "took the five loaves and the two fish, and looking up
to heaven, He blessed and broke and gave the loaves to the disciples;
and the disciples gave to the multitudes" (Matthew 14:19 NKJV). And
here's the amazing thing: "They all ate and were filled" (Matthew
14:20 NKJV)! Not only that, but they ended up with twelve baskets
filled with leftovers!

With Jesus in our lives, we dare not look at what we lack—in our
marriage, our family, our job, or our church. Instead, He wants us to
take what we have and give it to Him. By doing so, He will bless our
meager store and multiply it. And in the end, we will find we have
more than enough!

Jesus, help me focus not on what I lack but on what I have.
I know that You can do the impossible. So please take my
meager store, bless it, and multiply it, to Your glory!

What God Doesn't See

*He hath not beheld iniquity in Jacob, neither hath
he seen perverseness in Israel: the LORD his God is
with him, and the shout of a king is among them.*
NUMBERS 23:21 KJV

Try has he might, Balaam could not curse the children of Israel.
Instead, he blessed them.

While God had control of Balaam's wicked mouth, he made an
unbelievable statement: God had not beheld iniquity in Jacob or seen
perverseness in Israel.

Really? Just a few chapters earlier, Korah, Dathan, and Abiram
had rebelled and the earth had swallowed them up. Then the
Israelites despised the gift of manna again, and God judged them with
serpents.

There was obvious rebellion and wickedness among the people,
but God said He had not beheld iniquity or perverseness in His
people! How is this possible? The next statement explains: "The LORD
his God is with him."

God is with His chosen people. He sets His love upon them. He
imputes His righteousness to them. Because God was in the midst
of Israel, when He looked on them, He didn't see their sin—He saw
Himself.

Likewise, when God looks upon His chosen now, He doesn't see
our sin. He sees Himself. He sees Christ's righteousness, imputed to us
through the death and resurrection of Jesus. "Blessed. . .[are] the people
whom he hath chosen for his own inheritance" (Psalm 33:12 KJV).

*Father, You have chosen me, saved me, sealed me, and declared
me righteous. I want to yield my whole self to You, as a servant of
righteousness. Show me where I should serve You today. Amen.*

Where Are You?

They heard the sound of the LORD God walking in the garden in the cool of the day, and the man and his wife hid themselves from the presence of the LORD God. . . . Then the LORD God called to the man, and said to him, "Where are you?"
GENESIS 3:8–9 NASB

Imagine having a meeting place with God every day at the same time. He waits for each of us, in our favorite place—in the shade under a tree or in the coziest chair by the fireplace. For Adam and Eve, it was in the garden in the cool of the day, after the sun made its steady decline.

One day, they were gone. The tragedy of sin filled them with shame and fear so great that they hid. He called out to them, for He knows that disease grows in the dark and hidden places of our heart. "Where are you?" was not a question of their whereabouts, but rather the cry of a Father longing for His children to come out of hiding and back into the healing light.

Now He calls to us. "Where are you?" Busy days have turned into weeks of silence. *It's been too long,* we think. *I've drifted too far.* But with God, no distance is too great. He has already gone to the ends of the earth to reach us and died on a cross to save us.

Father, it is hard to believe that You, the Creator of the Universe, longs to spend time with me every day. Help me hear Your call to come out of my busyness or despair and spend time in Your Word. Amen.

Divine Love

*"So now I am giving you a new commandment: Love each other.
Just as I have loved you, you should love each other."*
JOHN 13:34 NLT

It sounds simple, but rarely is it easy. Loving the people in our life is
often our toughest assignment. Isn't that why a part of us is always
searching for other people to love who seem less burdensome and
more deserving? Many times the behavior of those we live with
stirs up confusion and sadness in us. For we each carry a lifetime of
experience inside that tells us the painful truth about people. Whether
it happens today or years from now, eventually they will let us down.

It is hard to avoid the clarity of Jesus' message to love people to
the extent that He loves. Since God is the creator of love, He is the
standard by which we are measured. He loves sacrificially, completely,
and passionately, without keeping a record of past failures. Can we
really love others the way God loves us? Can we love our husbands
like that? Try it for just one day; it is easy to see why we need a Savior
in the first place.

We may think, *Well, it would be easier if he didn't leave his towel
on the floor or slam the kitchen cupboards and doors at every turn.*
It's true. Our husbands can make loving them a challenge. But Jesus
isn't saying that we should love our husbands as they deserve we
should love them in the way *He* deserves to be loved.

*Father, help me to love my husband the way You do.
Please show me how. Amen.*

The Devil's Triangle

For all that is in the world, the lust of the flesh,
and the lust of the eyes, and the pride of life,
is not of the Father, but is of the world.
1 JOHN 2:16 KJV

For all the complaining we do about the things we don't have, we sure miss out on a lot of the blessings of the things we do have. Our prayers are more focused on complaining to God than they are on praising Him. Why is this? Often it's because we're trapped in the devil's triangle. Our hearts are filled more with lust for things we don't possess and on sinful pride rather than on love for God and others and joy in the blessings He has bestowed on us.

The lust of the flesh doesn't have to trap you, though. Be aware that it is present, and arm your heart against it. As humans we *are* susceptible, but as Christians we *can* overcome. We must engross ourselves in the Word of God and let the Holy Spirit do a work in us. We need to daily crucify the old nature within us and let Jesus form us into new creatures. Once our hearts are habitually filled with true praise to our Creator, it will be easier to live in His love rather than in the lust of the devil.

Father, I praise You for Your greatness,
for You alone are worthy.

Heaven's Exchange

Because by one sacrifice he has made perfect
forever those who are being made holy.
HEBREWS 10:14 NIV

It sounds like a riddle, but it's true. We are a living work in progress all the while the final work in us has already been finished. We are forgiven and spiritually perfect at the same time we are living through the process. When this becomes too much to comprehend, just remember that we live inside Earth's time bubble, separate from eternity.

Jesus has completed the work needed to guarantee our future in heaven by dying on the cross for our sins. He has made us complete in Him by beating death and rising from the tomb. He stands in our place with a sinless record and trades our life's work with His. Because of that heavenly exchange, we are free to become who we were created to be here on Earth.

Too often we are fooled into not trusting this promise, believing that what Jesus has done is not enough and we must take matters into our own hands. We have been trained to find ways to secure our future and earn our own way, but Jesus tells us that in life's greatest ambition, we have already won the ultimate prize.

So before you face the day ahead with all its troubles, reflect on the power of this verse. Our strength lies in accepting its truth and living as we really are in Christ.

Father, thank you for taking my place on the cross
and securing for me eternal life. Help me believe
that You have completed a good work in me. Amen.

A Holy Longing

*As the deer pants for streams of water, so my soul
pants for you, O God. My soul thirsts for God, for the
living God. When can I go and meet with God?*
PSALM 42:1–2 NIV

When you think of the word *longing*, what images come to mind? We
long for so many things, don't we? We long for someone to love us, to
tell us how special we are. We long for financial peace. We long for a
great job, the perfect place to live, and even the ideal friends.

God's greatest desire is that we long for Him. Today's scripture
presents a pretty clear image. We should be hungering and thirsting
after God. When we've been away from Him, even for a short time,
our souls should pant for Him.

If we were completely honest with ourselves, we'd have to admit
that our earthly longings usually supersede our longing for God. Sure,
we enjoy our worship time, but we don't really come into it with the
depth of longing referred to in this scripture. Ask God to give you His
perspective on longing. He knows what it means to long for someone,
after all. His longing for you was so great that He gave His only Son
on a cross to be near you.

*Father, my earthly longings usually get in the way
of my spiritual ones. Draw me into Your presence,
God. Reignite my longing for You.*

Living This Day

"Therefore do not worry about tomorrow,
for tomorrow will worry about itself."
MATTHEW 6:34 NIV

So many things race through our minds, what will the next day or week or month hold? How will the test results turn out? How am I going to meet the needs of the rest of my family? When can I find some time for myself so I can regroup? Before long, our attention has shifted from the real needs of the present to the unrealized fears of another day.

God doesn't want us borrowing trouble from the future. He wants us to see how He's meeting our needs on this particular day. When we're busy projecting our worries on the days ahead, we miss what He's doing in our lives right now.

Think back to a day when you wondered how you'd have strength to get from sunrise to sunset. But you did it—because God gave you His power, not for tomorrow or next month, but right when you needed it.

God knows each day has its issues. But He told us not to worry, because when the next day comes He'll be right there again, ready to equip us for whatever we need to do.

God is *our* caregiver. Let Him minister to you *this* day.

> *God, I'm glad that You only ask me to think upon*
> *this day. I needn't worry because You know my*
> *needs and will meet them according to Your will.*

The Ultimate Caregiver

Casting all your care upon him; for he careth for you.
1 PETER 5:7 KJV

God is in the caregiving business. From the moment we each entered the world, He's taken care of us by meeting our needs, working tirelessly on our behalf, and shaping us into the men and women He longed for us to be. And He still cares for us—truly, passionately, intently. His great love, even when we don't deserve it, shows how much He cares.

Without question, the Lord is the ultimate caregiver. He's the best in the business. And that should motivate us as we set out to care for others. If we imitate God—not just in actions and deeds, but with our motives and intents—we can't go wrong. And when we feel overwhelmed, He has encouraged us to cast our cares on Him. Why? Because He cares so very much for us!

So run to the Lord with your struggles. Trust your heavenly Father to brush away every tear, wash away every pain, and then set you on your feet again—to care for others.

Dear Lord, as I seek to become the best I can be at what I do, help me to keep my eyes on You. Remind me that You were—and are—the ultimate caregiver.

Impossible Days

Out of my distress I called on the LORD;
the LORD answered me and set me free.
PSALM 118:5 ESV

Life is physically, emotionally, and spiritually draining. As we put forth all our effort, we may each wonder, *Will I have enough strength to complete this task?*

When our bodies and spirits weaken, our prayers—even the most desperate ones—often become more powerful. In our emptiness, as we ask, "Lord, how much more can I bear?" He comes immediately to our aid.

God knows every need of His overburdened people. And though we may not be able to spend much time in Bible study, church attendance, and prayer, He still watches over us, listening carefully for our most helpless communications. Then He answers powerfully, in ways He may never have responded in less-demanding times.

We don't need to pray perfectly or read six chapters of scripture a day before caring for our loved ones. Nor do we need to give up all our sparse personal time. God knows the service we provide and He blesses us for it—perhaps well beyond what we feel we deserve.

The One whose " 'steadfast love endures forever' " (Psalm 118:4 ESV) never deserts those He loves. He sets us free—even in the midst of our many chores, responsibilities, and impossible days. We can call on Him and feel His freedom no matter what our days include.

Thank You, Lord, for listening and
responding to all my troubles.

Crying Out

*I am worn out from groaning; all night long I flood
my bed with weeping and drench my couch with tears.*
PSALM 6:6 NIV

Crying is an important emotional release, but how often do we
suppress our tears? Maybe we think crying indicates we're giving up
hope. Or perhaps we're afraid others may think we're weak. Then
there's the false notion that crying means we're not trusting God to
handle our situation.

Like a cut that must be cleaned in order to heal properly, our
wounded hearts need a cleansing, too. Releasing our tears to God is
a way we can purify our hearts from the emotional debris collecting
inside.

Our Lord set an example for us to follow. Jesus, the creator of
tears, cried. He wept in front of others. He cried out to His Father.
Neither fear nor pride stopped Him from expressing these painful
emotions. Jesus knew that His Father would hear His cries and come
to His aid.

God will do the same for us, wiping away our tears and healing
the wounds of our heart. Crying may make us feel vulnerable—but
God's comfort reminds us we're loved.

*Dear Father, I pray I am never too scared or too proud
to bring my tears to You. How comforting it is
to know You're going to dry them for me.*

Alone?

*And he took the mantle of Elijah that fell from him,
and smote the waters, and said, Where is the LORD God
of Elijah? and when he also had smitten the waters,
they parted hither and thither: and Elisha went over.*
2 KINGS 2:14 KJV

For years, Elisha devoted time and energy to Elijah the prophet. He dreaded the end of his master's ministry. When the "sons of the prophets," Elijah's disciples, predicted his exit, Elisha refused to listen. When Elijah himself tried to take leave of his aide, Elisha said, "No way."

He watched miracles he did not want to see. First, Elijah parted the Jordan River with a slap of his mantle. Then a chariot of fire carried Elijah to heaven. Elisha could only cry, "My father! My father!" (2 Kings 2:12 KJV) and tear his clothes in grief. His future loomed empty and sad without his mentor and friend.

But Elisha had asked for a double inheritance from his spiritual father, a twofold portion of God's Spirit. So when Elisha slapped the Jordan with his mentor's mantle and yelled, "Where is the LORD God of Elijah?" (2 Kings 2:14 KJV), the Lord parted the river again.

When we have devoted our lives to loved ones—especially those who nurtured us spiritually—we may find it difficult to go on without them. But God is still there, ready to empower us with His love so we can accomplish His purposes.

*Lord, although I'll miss the dear one I've served, You'll send me
others to love. Help me see them with Your vision.*

Wonders of Music

*But I will sing of your strength, in the morning I will sing of
your love; for you are my fortress, my refuge in times of
trouble. . . . I sing praise to you. . .my loving God.*
PSALM 59:16–17 NIV

Talk about trouble—David had more than his fair share of it. Day
in and day out, year after year, David was a wanted man pursued
by a jealous king. Homeless, on the run, accompanied by a bunch of
lowlifes, David lays out an interesting pattern in the psalms.

First, he cries out to God in sorrow, complaint, even occasional
whining. But invariably, he then shifts to joyful praise.

We can be that real with God, too. We can tell Him our heart's
burdens and vent our hurts, disappointments, and struggles to Him.
He can handle it.

David didn't try to sound "spiritual." He was genuine with God.
Once he had cleared the air, his heart turned to thanksgiving and
praise. He'd bring out the instruments, write a song or two, and
regain his strength.

Music can be a source of strength to a weary soul. Whistling,
humming, or singing a song of praise can help refocus a grumbling
heart and restore hope when it's been waning.

Today, fill your world with songs of praise and worship.

*Mighty Father, I thank You for the wonder of music.
Help me to sing Your praises—of Your strength
and love daily, for You are my refuge.*

Good Works Are All Around

Well reported of for good works; if [a widow] have brought up children, if she have lodged strangers, if she have washed the saints' feet, if she have relieved the afflicted, if she have diligently followed every good work.

1 TIMOTHY 5:10 KJV

Often when we read the Bible, we miss its practicality. In Ephesians 2:10, for example, Paul tells us that we are created for "good works, which God hath before ordained that we should walk in them" (KJV).

How many times do we read this and wonder, "What good works am I supposed to do for God?" We may spend hours in prayer, laboring to find God's will and discover the works we are to do.

But the Bible shows us not many pages later—and from the same pen as Ephesians—the good works of a woman and services that believers of either sex can provide. In 1 Timothy 5, we see that our good works include being faithful spouses, bringing up children, showing hospitality to strangers and fellow believers, and helping those in distress.

Good work is not a mystery that we have to meditate to find.

We just need to see the needs around us and meet them as God gives us the strength and resources to do so.

That's practical—and pure—Christianity.

Father, how often I have wondered about Your will for my life, thinking it was something grand and glorious. But Your Word says it's all around me. Help me to see and follow the good works that are within my reach.

His Perfect Strength

"My grace is sufficient for you, for my power is made perfect in weakness." Therefore I will boast all the more gladly about my weaknesses, so that Christ's power may rest on me.
2 CORINTHIANS 12:9 NIV

How do you define stress? Perhaps you feel it when the car doesn't start or the toilet backs up or the line is too long at the grocery store. Or maybe your source of stress is a terrible diagnosis, a late-night phone call, a demanding boss, or a broken relationship. It's probably a combination of all of these things. You might be able to cope with one of them, but when several are bearing down at once, stress is the inevitable result.

It has been said that stress results when our perceived demands exceed our perceived resources. When the hours required to meet a deadline at work (demand) exceed the number of hours we have available (resources), we get stressed. The most important word in this definition is *perceived*. When it comes to stress, people have a tendency to do two things. One, they magnify the demand ("I will *never* be able to get this done") and two, they fail to consider all of their resources. For the child of God, this includes His mighty strength, which remains long after ours is gone.

In an uncertain world, it is difficult to say few things for sure. But no matter what life throws our way, we can be confident of this: Our demands will *never* exceed God's vast resources.

Strong and mighty heavenly Father, thank You that in my weakness I can always rely on Your perfect strength. Amen.

Why Me?

*I am Alpha and Omega, the beginning and the
ending, saith the Lord, which is, and which was,
and which is to come, the Almighty.*
REVELATION 1:8 KJV

When we find ourselves in difficult situations, what do we do?

Many people look at those circumstances selfishly and cry: "Oh,
God, why me? Why do these things happen to *me*?"

But we mortals have a too-narrow view of our existence. In our
minds, this world at this time is all there is. Sure, God is eternal—
but maybe that just means He was around before us and had some
supervision that we would come into being someday.

If that's our concept of God, we need to read His Word more
closely.

Jesus said He is the "Alpha and Omega." He's the beginning and
the end. Jesus, like the Father, *is.* He is the ever-present One who is
apart from time.

When God spoke our world into existence, He called into being a
certain reality, knowing then everything that ever was to happen—
and everyone who ever was to be.

That you exist now is cause for rejoicing! God made *you* to
fellowship with Him! If that fellowship demands trials for a season,
rejoice that God thinks you worthy to share in the sufferings of
Christ—and, eventually, in His glory.

Why do these things happen to you?

Because God in His infinite wisdom, love, and grace determined
them to be. Praise His holy name!

*Father, I thank You for giving me this difficult time in my life.
Shine through all my trials today. I want You to get the glory.*

Peace, Be Still

GOD makes his people strong.
GOD gives his people peace.
PSALM 29:11 MSG

At the center of life's storms, how do we find peace? If we're tossed about, struggling and hopeless, where is the peace? Don't worry—peace can be ours for the asking.

You see, *God* is our peace. He is ready to calm our storms when we call on Him. He will comfort and strengthen us each day.

The Bible tells of Peter and the other disciples, who were rowing their small boat against strong waves on the way to Capernaum. They knew Jesus was planning to join them, but they'd drifted out into the sea and left Him far behind. When they saw Jesus walking on the water, they were terrified—but He spoke and calmed their fears.

Impulsive Peter asked to meet Jesus on the water. He stepped out of the boat and, briefly, walked on the waves like his Lord. As long as Peter's eyes were on Jesus, he stayed atop the water—but the moment he looked away, he sank. Peter learned a valuable lesson.

The lesson works for believers today: Keep your eyes focused on the problems and you'll have mayhem. Focus on Jesus and you'll have peace.

Dear Lord, I thank You for Your protection. Help me
to keep my eyes on You. Please grant me peace.

In His Time

*He has made everything beautiful in its time. He has
also set eternity in the hearts of men; yet they cannot
fathom what God has done from beginning to end.*
ECCLESIASTES 3:11 NIV

When we're in the midst of a struggle, it's difficult to picture how
things could possibly end well. Maybe you're going through a
situation where a happy ending looks impossible. But in spite of how
things appear, God promises to make all things beautiful in His time.

That means there's a day coming when all of this hardship—the
work, the hours spent caring for one in need, the pain—will be a
priceless treasure to you. The memories will be precious.

It's good to remember that the Lord views everything in light
of *eternity.* He isn't limited by time. So when He sees your life, He
views it as a "forever" story. He knows this season you're walking
through—and it *is* a season—won't last forever. He also knows that
one day you will look back on this time of life and view it as a gift.

Ask for God's perspective on this season, and thank Him for
making it beautiful. . .in His time.

*Dear Lord, please give me Your perspective.
Help me to see that my situation—tough as it is—
will one day be a thing of great beauty to me.*

She Gave, and He Gave Back

Then Peter arose and went with them. When he was come,
they brought him into the upper chamber: and all the widows
stood by him weeping, and shewing the coats and garments
which Dorcas made, while she was with them.
ACTS 9:39 KJV

Dorcas had spent her life as a servant. She was a follower of Christ who was "full of good works and almsdeeds" (Acts 9:36 KJV) that she did continually. Scripture does not itemize her works, but we do know that she sewed coats and garments and took care of many widows.

She was the type of woman who could have "worked herself to death." People like Dorcas are often so busy caring for others that they fail to care about themselves. Of course, we can't say that for sure about Dorcas.

But we definitely know that when she died, many people grieved. And when they heard that the apostle Peter was nearby, they asked him to come—apparently believing he could raise the dead.

That's exactly what Peter did. Through his prayer, he raised Dorcas and returned her to service.

Dorcas had given her life to serve God, and God had given it back.

"For whosoever will save his life shall lose it: and whosoever will lose his life for my sake shall find it" (Matthew 16:25 KJV).

When you give your life to serve others, you are honoring God— and finding life.

Lord Jesus, I don't understand why You would give Your life for me.
There is nothing greater that I can do on Earth than to give my life for
You in service to others. Please strengthen me for this joyful task.

Don't Forget Me, Lord!

Think upon me, my God, for good,
according to all that I have done for this people.
NEHEMIAH 5:19 KJV

After the people of Judah lived for decades in exile, Nehemiah spent many busy years helping his people regroup. As governor of Judah, he helped rebuild Jerusalem's walls torn down by the Babylonians. It was an incredible feat that required every mental, physical, and spiritual resource Nehemiah could muster.

Nehemiah planned all the necessary stages of the work and figured out the finances with the Persian king, Artaxerxes. Although an aristocrat, Nehemiah labored alongside his people, doing the "heavy lifting" of the project. When enemies threatened to disrupt the work, Nehemiah turned "general," directing workers in military strategies. Even after the wall was completed, Nehemiah took responsibility for the people's spiritual welfare—contributions they did not always appreciate. He settled squabbles and even roughed up men who had foolishly married foreign wives. Exhausted after more than a decade of intense service, Nehemiah asked God to remember everything he had done for this needy group.

Nehemiah possessed excellent leadership abilities—but his faith in God proved to be the factor that pulled him through. When Nehemiah couldn't take it anymore, he ran to God.

Sometimes the sacrificial roles God asks us to assume last for days, months, even years. When no one seems to appreciate us, we, like Nehemiah, will find the support and affirmation we need in our heavenly Father.

Lord, when I feel I've poured my life out for nothing, please help me
care for others with Your heart. I thank You for Your faithful love.

Embracing Change

May the Lord direct your hearts into
God's love and Christ's perseverance.
2 THESSALONIANS 3:5 NIV

Most people don't like change. Change can fill us with fear. It can take away our sense of security. Self-doubt and feelings of powerlessness can invade our mind and emotions. We want our old lives back—those days when we knew the rules. But in many situations, everything feels uncertain and unpredictable.

God has promised, though, to direct us through all the twists and turns of life. That guarantee should give us hope and strength. Knowing that, we can step away from our situation momentarily, take a deep breath, and proceed. Then, with the courage He offers, we can move forward on our new path. Even if our direction is unclear, we know we can take at least the first step. As we put one foot in front of the other, the path will eventually be revealed.

And God's love will continue to guide our steps along this new road.

Direct my way, Lord. Give me strength to embrace the
changes in my life. I don't see where I am going or how
I will do this, but I know that Your guidance and
Christ's perseverance will lead my way.

Grab Hold of Hope

*We. . .have every reason to grab the promised
hope with both hands and never let go.*
HEBREWS 6:18 MSG

Martin Luther is quoted as saying, "Everything that is done in this
world is done by hope."

God created us to hope—and then communicated hope to us
in many different ways. The eternal hope we have in Christ is what
keeps Christians moving forward rather than wallowing in self-pity.
Caring for a dying loved one can rob us of hope, unless we hang on to
our hope of eternal life through Christ.

God promised that He would never leave us or forsake us. He
gives strength to the weak. And to those who are brokenhearted, He
promises comfort. Even on the darkest days, in the midst of the most
difficult trials, His promises shine forth as beacons lighting our way.
He is the same God who gave provided deliverance, protection, and
comfort to His people, Israel.

Don't give up. Jesus died and rose again to give us an eternal
hope. Rest in His promises today!

*Lord, sometimes the days and nights are so long. I see no change in
my loved one or the change steals even more of life away. Yet You
have promised to sustain me, to stay with me, to walk with me even
through the valley of the shadow of death. Help me to keep my eyes
on You and hold tightly to Your promises. Help me to never let go!*

God's Strength

Be my strong refuge, to which I may resort continually;
You have given the commandment to save me,
for You are my rock and my fortress.
PSALM 71:3 NKJV

What in your life is completely zapping your strength? Whether it's relational, emotional, or physical (or all of the above), we all have issues in life that drag us down.

So where do we seek the strength we need? From an energy bar? A jolt of caffeine? A quick nap? Those things might supply energy, but energy is not strength. The strength we need is found in God alone.

God's strength is never generic. He knows where we hurt and what lies ahead for us, and the strength He provides matches up to our very personal needs.

When we wearily step out of bed, God is there to supply the physical strength we need to get us through the day. When bitter words are about to escape our mouths, He supplies the spiritual strength to stop and consider what we're about to say. When our feelings are raw, He gives the emotional strength to avoid weariness and hopelessness.

Let's go to God in our weakness and exchange it for His mighty strength. His strength has no end!

Gracious Father, You know how weak I can become.
Thank You for supplying me with the strength
to face all that will happen each day.

Anxious Anticipations

*I am not saying this because I am in need, for I have
learned to be content whatever the circumstances.*
PHILIPPIANS 4:11 NIV

Have you ever been so eager for the future that you forgot to be
thankful for the present day?

We anxiously await the weekend, our next vacation, retirement,
or some other future event. Maybe we're eager to start a new
chapter in our life because we've been frustrated with our caretaking
responsibilities.

Those of us who have raised children have felt a similar pull. We
looked ahead to their first steps, their school days, their weddings.
In all the daily responsibilities, we sometimes wished the kids would
"just grow up." Then they did—and we missed those little ones and
their mischievous antics, wishing we could turn back the clock.

Humans have a tendency to complain about the problems and
irritations of life. It's much less natural to appreciate the good things
we have—until they're gone. While it's fine to look forward to the
future, let's remember to reflect on all of *today's* blessings—the large
and the small—and appreciate all that we do have.

*Thank You, Lord, for the beauty of today.
Please remind me when I become preoccupied
with the future and forget to enjoy the present.*

Acceptable Words and Pleasing Thoughts

*May the words of my mouth and the meditation of my heart be
pleasing in your sight, O Lord, my Rock and my Redeemer.*
PSALM 19:14 NIV

We've all heard the saying "Sticks and stones may break my bones,
but words can never hurt me." Unfortunately, the latter portion of
that saying isn't always true. Words *do* have the power to hurt others.
In the Bible, James describes our tongues as very difficult to tame.
Without God's help, it can't be done.

King David also knew the power of words. In Psalm 19 he praises
God for revealing Himself in nature and through His Word. Verses
7 through 13 extol the wonders of God's Word and declare that it
reveals not only God but also man's condition. David ends the psalm
with a plea that his words, both spoken and unspoken, be acceptable
and pleasing to God.

Often, we're tempted to speak before we think—especially in
times of stress and tiredness. Rather than bringing blessing to those
around us, we might even curse those we love. We can rip into their
weaknesses and tear down their character instead of lifting them up
with encouragement.

Today, let's make David's prayer our own, by meditating on the
truth of God's Word. Then our words will truly be acceptable and
pleasing—to the Lord and to our loved ones.

*Father, please cleanse my mind of negative thoughts so
that the words I speak today are words of encouragement
and comfort to my loved ones and praise to You.*

Is Anyone Listening?

*And I will ask the Father, and He will give you
another Comforter (Counselor, Helper, Intercessor,
Advocate, Strengthener, and Standby), that He
may remain with you forever.*
JOHN 14:16 AMP

Christians have the assurance that God will hear them when they call.
In turn, we can hear God's voice of love when *we* listen.

People who love each other spend time together. They share their
dreams and hopes. So it is with our heavenly Father, who wants to
hear from us. He cares so much that He sent the Holy Spirit to be our
Counselor, our Comforter.

The Greek translation for "comfort" is *paraklesis* or "calling
near." When we are called near to someone, we are able to hear his
or her whisper. It is this very picture scripture paints when it speaks
of the Holy Spirit. God sent the Spirit to whisper to us and to offer
encouragement and guidance, to be our strength when all else fails.
When we pray—when we tell God our needs and give Him praise—
He listens. Then He directs the Spirit within us to speak to our hearts
and give us reassurance.

Our world is filled with noise and distractions. Look for a place
where you can be undisturbed for a few minutes. Take a deep breath,
lift your prayers, and listen. God will speak—and your heart will hear.

*Dear Lord, I thank You for Your care. Help me
to recognize Your voice and to listen well.*

A Fresh Perspective

*"Listen now to me and I will give you
some advice, and may God be with you."*
EXODUS 18:19 NIV

Moses was doing too much.

Exodus 18:2–3 tells us that the great leader of Israel sent away
his wife Zipporah and their sons. Though the Bible doesn't elaborate,
it appears that Moses was working too hard—possibly even neglecting
his family. Maybe he sent them away because he couldn't work as
hard as he was working and care for the family at the same time.
Whatever the reason, his father-in-law Jethro decided to visit.

The next morning as usual, Moses got up to go to work. After
observing Moses' exhausting routine, Jethro sat down with his son-
in-law. "Why are you doing all the work yourself?" he asked. "You
need to start delegating."

Moses was working so hard that he had lost his objectivity. Jethro
provided him with a different—and helpful—perspective.

It's easy to get caught up in the "tyranny of the urgent" and lose
perspective. When we take a step back and look at our lives more
objectively, we often see alternative ways of doing things. Such
insights can come from a trusted friend or relative.

What is there about your present situation that might require
perspective from someone else? Is there something you could be
doing differently? Is there a task you could be delegating or an option
you haven't considered? Learn from Moses—take the advice of
someone who could offer you a much-needed perspective.

*Heavenly Father, I thank You for the perspective that others can
bring. Teach me to listen to and heed wise advice.*

Unchained!

For you did not receive a spirit that makes you a slave
again to fear, but you received the Spirit of sonship.
And by him we cry, "Abba, Father."
ROMANS 8:15 NIV

Imagine how difficult life would be inside prison walls. No sunlight. No freedom to go where you wanted when you wanted. Just a dreary, dark existence, locked away in a place you did not choose, with no way of escape.

Most of us can't even imagine such restrictions. As Christians we have complete freedom through Jesus Christ, our Lord and Savior. No limitations. No chains.

Ironically, many of us build our own walls and choose our own chains. When we give ourselves over to fear, we're deliberately entering a prison the Lord never intended for us. We don't always do it willfully. In fact, we often find ourselves behind bars after the fact, then wonder how we got there.

Do you struggle with fear? Do you feel it binding you with its invisible chains? If so, then there's good news. Through Jesus, you have received the Spirit of sonship. A son (or daughter) of the most-high God has nothing to fear. Knowing you've been set free is enough to make you cry, "Abba, Father!" in praise. Today, acknowledge your fears to the Lord. He will loose your chains and set you free.

Lord, thank You that You are the great chain-breaker!
I don't have to live in fear. I am Your child,
Your daughter, and You are my Daddy-God!

Leading the Way

*"The LORD himself goes before you and will be
with you; he will never leave you nor forsake you.
Do not be afraid; do not be discouraged."*
DEUTERONOMY 31:8 NIV

Does life sometimes feel like a walk in a dense fog?

Fog prevents us from seeing what lies ahead—just as our fears
and worries can. Will we be able to handle the stress or make the right
decisions? Will people offer to help us? Will the boss understand if we
aren't able to make it to work? There are so many unknowns—and
when we can't see beyond our present situation, it's easy to feel lost.

Whatever our struggles, we have Someone who sees our path
clearly. God's Word says that He goes ahead of us. The first step on
this path isn't really ours because God Himself has already taken it. He
can lead us through whatever lies ahead because He knows the way.

There is no better guide or companion for life's journey than our
all-knowing heavenly Father.

*Dear Lord, thank You for going ahead of me. Thank You
also for being ever-present with me. With You having
paved my way, I can walk in confidence, not fear.*

First Things First

*"Get up and eat, for the
journey is too much for you."*
1 KINGS 19:7 NIV

Elijah's work had dragged him down physically. One time, he was so exhausted that he begged God to take his life.

It's interesting to note what God *didn't* do for Elijah in response to that prayer: God didn't kill Elijah, nor did He say, "Stop your whining and get back to work." The first thing God did was send an angel to attend to Elijah's physical needs. In His wisdom, God knew that Elijah wouldn't see his situation clearly until he was nourished and well-rested.

When the demands of our lives become too much, it's tempting to stop right where we are and beg God to release us from our circumstances. And on those days, the best prescription may well be a nourishing meal or a good night's sleep. It's amazing what those things can do to revive our souls.

As women, caring for our own physical needs should be high on our priority list. Are there extra things in the schedule we can eliminate so we can get more sleep? Would a little planning allow us to eat more healthily?

Ask God for wisdom to evaluate your lifestyle and, if necessary, the steps you should take to sustain your physical well-being. It may take some up-front effort, but the dividends will be well worth it.

Father, I thank You for the relief You provide when the journey is too much for me. Teach me to eat well and get enough rest and to care for this physical body You've given me.

Did God Say. . . ?

For we walk by faith, not by sight.
2 CORINTHIANS 5:7 NASB

The more complex life becomes, the easier it is to lose our perspective.

Maybe we begin to feel overwhelmed with everything we are responsible for. There must be someone else who can do a better job, who can handle all the stuff that comes up, who can do it more graciously than we can. Did God really say *we* should do this?

This is the time faith really comes into play. God *has* given us the task—and we must believe that not only has He asked us to do this job, He's also given us an abundance of mental, emotional, and physical supply. And not just once, but over and over every morning.

Rarely can we see our way clear, but we can believe that God has the situation under His perfect control. We can believe that He will work it for His glory and for the good of ourselves and those around us.

As we learn to become more and more dependent on God, we trust Him more and more. Our faith, though it may have begun as the size of a mustard seed, will grow into a mighty tree.

Lord, I thank You for choosing me to work with You.
Give me the faith I need to see Your hand in everyday circumstances
and to ask You for the help I need.

Life Preservers

My comfort in my suffering is this:
Your promise preserves my life.
PSALM 119:50 NIV

It's the law for boaters in many states: Always wear your life
preserver. The purpose is simple. A life preserver keeps people
afloat—and their heads above water—should they accidentally fall
overboard. The device's buoyancy can even keep an unconscious
person afloat in a face-up position as long as it's worn properly.

God is our life preserver in this life. When we are battered by the
waves of trouble, we can expect God to understand and to comfort us
in our distress. His Word, like a buoyant life preserver, holds us up in
the bad times.

But the life preserver only works if you put it on *before* your boat
sinks. To get into God's life jacket, put your arms into the sleeves
of prayer and tie the vest with biblical words. God will surround
you with His love and protection—even if you're unconscious of His
presence. He promises to keep our heads above water in the storms
of life.

Preserving God, I cling to You as my life preserver.
Keep my head above the turbulent water of life
so I don't drown. Bring me safely to the shore.

Witnesses

*Therefore, since we are surrounded by such a great
cloud of witnesses, let us throw off everything that
hinders and the sin that so easily entangles, and let
us run with perseverance the race marked out for us.*

HEBREWS 12:1 NIV

A few days before she died, a godly woman was granted a view into
heaven. When asked what she saw, she said, "People. Lots of people."

When asked what they were doing, she replied, "They are waiting
to welcome me."

"Who are they?" was the next question. The woman started
telling of family members who had gone on before. Then she named
several whom she'd led to the Lord during her lifetime. Before long
she stopped, tired of talking and awed by the number of people who
were awaiting her arrival.

This story reminds us of the "great cloud of witnesses" a Bible
writer describes in Hebrews 11 and 12. It's so easy for us to feel
unnoticed, unappreciated, even forgotten by our friends, family, and
fellow church members. We forget that we have an invisible crowd
of believers who have gone on before us, many of whom suffered
persecution and horrible deaths for doing right, for staying faithful to
the tasks the Lord had given them to do. They are encouraging us to
keep on, to throw aside everything that weighs us down and keeps us
from running the race marked out for us.

*Father, help me to remember that I am not alone in this
task. Many have gone on before me, leaving an example
of faithful service. May I one day hear You say, "Well done,
good and faithful servant!" (Matthew 25:21 NIV).*

Laying Down Your Life

Greater love hath no man than this,
that a man lay down his life for his friends.
John 15:13 KJV

God-breathed love is sacrificial. It continues to give even under the most difficult of circumstances, never keeping track of the cost. As indicated in today's scripture, the ultimate expression of love is one's willingness to lay down his or her life for another.

We wonder if such love is really possible—and if we have it in ourselves to love so sacrificially. Does this scripture refer only to literal death, or is there a deeper message?

Sacrifice, by its very definition, is the ability to place another's needs before your own—to continue pouring out, even when you're tapped out. Every instance you give of your time, energy, or resources to care for a loved one in need, you demonstrate your willingness to lay down your life. You're expressing the heart of God.

Your ability to continue giving day in and day out pleases the heart of your heavenly Father, who perfectly understands the principle of "laying down" one's life. After all, that's what He did for us at Calvary.

Dear Lord, please create Your heart within me—a heart ready to give
sacrificially no matter the cost. When I feel I'm "given out,"
remind me of Your great sacrifice on the cross for me.

Constant Prayer

Be unceasing in prayer.
1 Thessalonians 5:17 amp

Paul's statement concerning prayer seems impossible. Nonstop prayer? How can we ever achieve that in our hectic world?

By our awareness of God. Through it, we become conscious of Him and discern His active involvement in our lives. God wants to have a relationship with us, and prayer demonstrates our faith in Him. His Word tells us to stay in constant contact.

Nineteenth-century preacher Charles Spurgeon described the Christian's prayer life as follows: "Like the old knights, always in warfare, not always on their steeds dashing forward with their lances raised to unhorse an adversary, but always wearing their weapons where they could readily reach them. . . . Those grim warriors often slept in their armor; so even when we sleep, we are still to be in the spirit of prayer, so that if perchance we wake in the night we may still be with God."

Prayer strengthens us for any battle. It's our armor and our mightiest weapon against fear, doubt, discouragement, and worry. Prayer changes our perspective and allows us to face the cares of each day. When our whole world is falling apart, prayer can keep us together.

That's why constant prayer is so important.

Dear Father, I want to be in the center of Your will.
Please help me to "be unceasing in prayer."

The Power of Gratitude

*It is a good thing to give
thanks unto the LORD.*
PSALM 92:1 KJV

Gloria's friends often feel sorry for her—she provides seemingly tireless care for her ailing husband and doesn't have time for outings or special events. But when her friends ask her about it, Gloria tells them, "I don't have time to feel sorry for myself. I have too much for which to be thankful!"

"Being thankful" doesn't mean we live in denial of our problems—nor does it minimize the fact that life can sometimes be very hard. But God's Word does tell us to give thanks—in all circumstances. Gloria knows that the purpose of gratitude is transformational. It gives us perspective on our situation, keeps us from feeling sorry for ourselves, teaches us to rely on God, and reminds us that all we have comes from Him.

Hardships help us to grow. Even when we feel we have nothing else for which to give thanks, we can be grateful that God loves us enough to want to make us more like Him.

Let's take a moment today to count our blessings. We may find we're so busy being grateful that we won't have time to feel bad.

*Father, I thank You for the ways that You reveal yourself to me.
Thank You for the many blessings You have given me and that I can
always think of something for which to be grateful.*

In Step

Since we live by the Spirit,
let us keep in step with the Spirit.
GALATIANS 5:25 NIV

Early one morning, members of a traveling family stopped at a rest area. After eight more hours of driving in a hot, cramped car, they stopped to stretch their legs at a very similar-looking rest area. One of the young boys exclaimed, "I know this place. This is where we ate breakfast!"

"Oh, I hope not," muttered the travel-weary mom. But as she looked around, she could understand how her son had reached that conclusion. Everything—the buildings, the landscaping, the picnic tables—looked the same.

Sometimes, we see our lives like that young boy perceived the roadside rest area. We spend time and effort completing all those routine tasks—but when we take stock, we conclude that we aren't getting anywhere. Like the weary mom, we hoped that our efforts would always propel us toward our destination.

Good news: The mom had read the map and road signs and knew she and her family were *not* where they had started. They hadn't just been spinning their wheels.

By reading our map (the Bible) and the signs (God's Spirit speaking to our hearts), we can know that we, too, are moving in the right direction.

It might not look like it. We might not get to our ultimate destination quickly. But we *will* get there—in God's time and in His way. Just keep in step with His Spirit!

Lord, as I complete my routine, help me to keep in
step with Your Spirit. You know where I'm headed,
and You will get me there on time.

Renewable Source of Energy

To this end I labor, struggling with all his energy,
which so powerfully works in me.
COLOSSIANS 1:29 NIV

Wind, sun, water, and geothermal are all examples of renewable energy sources. These abundant and powerful assets supply our power needs to fuel our homes and businesses.

As women, we also need energy to complete our tasks. Our daily labor drains our strength when we try to complete our work solely in our own power. A lack of energy can be a symptom of trying to do too much on own rather than relying on God. Think of it this way: Have you ever tried to move furniture by yourself? When others help out, we draw on their energy and power to share the load.

When our energy runs low, where can we turn for renewal? To God. But before doing so, we must admit that we are trying to work all by ourselves. We must also recognize that negative emotions, like anger and disappointment, sap our energy.

When we then take stock of ourselves and ask God for help, He promises us access to His unlimited source of energy. His bottomless supply is ready for tapping. All we need to do is plug into His power by pausing in His presence, soaking up His love and comfort.

God will sustain us in our struggles when we refuel with prayer, reading His Word, and basking in His presence. His energy works within us as an abundant and powerful asset to renew our strength.

Energetic Father, work within me with Your renewable
power. Thank You for being my source of strength and
energy. Your power is abundant and knows no limits.

Missing the Mercy in the Mayhem

*For the LORD will not cast off for ever: But though
he cause grief, yet will he have compassion
according to the multitude of his mercies.*
LAMENTATIONS 3:31–32 KJV

The days are too busy. The nights, too long. The pain, too great. The sorrow, too overwhelming.

And yet, somehow, you go on caring for those the Lord has put in your life.

How is this possible?

It comes through the infinite, renewable mercy of God. Every new morning comes with a new mercy.

Sometimes, though, we miss the mercy in the mayhem. Because we tend to be brilliant multitaskers, we can easily reduce life to a set of activities and errands that we think we can control.

As we move from one task to the next, we may start thinking that we are managing things pretty well by ourselves—and we might fail to see the hand of God in our lives.

Let's slow down, step back, and look at the bigger picture. We can do nothing apart from God's mercy. Let's acknowledge His hand on our lives and stop trusting our own strength.

If we're managing at all, it's because God is upholding us, bearing our burdens, and sustaining us with His compassion and grace.

*Father, how often I think I'm managing life well on
my own. But I couldn't care for these people without
Your help. I thank You for Your compassion and mercy
each day. Without You, I could do nothing.*

Arm in Arm

*The LORD is my strength and my song; he has become
my salvation. He is my God, and I will praise him.*
EXODUS 15:2 NIV

Accompanied by his son, an older gentleman began his daily walk.
Side by side, the two strolled down the sidewalk, the son adjusting his
steps to match his dad's. When they approached a crossroad, the older
man turned toward an incline. His son suggested the level grade.
Shaking his head, the gentleman said, "Walking uphill strengthens
me." The son took his father's elbow and they began to climb.

How often we turn to level ground and try to avoid the hills. Yet
it's the hard path that strengthens us. Through our difficult times,
God draws near and takes us by the arm. He becomes our guide and
companion—and strength.

Moses and the children of Israel faced undeniable peril. With
warriors behind and the Red Sea before, where could they turn? In
the nick of time, God saved them by parting the waters. Shadrach,
Meshach, and Abednego stepped into the fiery furnace, believing that
God would rescue them. He didn't let them down.

Whatever we face, God is bigger than the circumstances. With
God, all things are possible. Choose today to believe that He will
move in a mighty way. Choose today to cling to His arm and walk up
the mountainside.

*Dear Father, help me to learn to depend on You daily.
Show me Your mercy and grace, I pray.*

A Fragrant Offering

Be imitators of God, therefore, as dearly loved children and
live a life of love, just as Christ loved us and gave himself
up for us as a fragrant offering and sacrifice to God.
EPHESIANS 5:1–2 NIV

Have you ever walked into a place that smelled beautiful? Scented candles, potpourri, or fresh cookies in the oven can be very inviting, drawing us in and making us want to stay for a while.

In a similar way, if we carry the scent of Christ in our daily walk, people will be drawn to us and want to "stay for a while." But how do we give off that amazing, inviting fragrance?

There's really only one way—by imitating God. By patterning our actions after His. By loving others fully. By seeing them through His eyes. By looking with great compassion on those who are hurting, as Jesus did when He went about healing the sick and pouring out His life for those in need.

As we live a life of love in front of those we care for, we exude the sweetest fragrance of all—Christ. That's one aroma that can't be bottled!

Dear Lord, I long to live a life that points people to You.
As I care for those in need, may the sweet-smelling aroma of
You and Your love be an invitation for people to draw near.

Beans or Steak?

*Each of you must bring a gift in proportion to
the way the LORD your God has blessed you.*
DEUTERONOMY 16:17 NIV

At the harvest celebration, every Jew was to thank God with a
sacrifice according to the blessings He'd given. God's Word assumes
that every believer would receive a blessing of some sort. At the
very least, His people were alive because He provided food for them.
Those who didn't have much more than that would bring a small but
heartfelt offering. Others, blessed with physical abundance, brought a
generous offering of much greater value.

Our blessings may not be the kind we'd like: We may look for
extra money to pay off bills while God sends us spiritual strength. But
just as God provided for His Old Testament people even in the years
of lean harvests, He provides for us.

We may be eating more beans and rice than steak and lobster,
but isn't the former better for us in the long run? While we're looking
for the good life, God's looking at what's good for us. Sometimes that
means physical blessing—but other times it's a spiritual challenge.

No matter what our circumstances, God is blessing us—if we're
following Him with steadfastness. Let's bless Him in return with our
thanksgiving.

*Lord, I thank You for the many blessings You give.
In exchange, I offer You the gift of my heart and life.*

Does Anyone Hear?

And it shall come to pass, that before they call, I will answer;
and while they are yet speaking, I will hear.
Isaiah 65:24 KJV

Pam hurried out the kitchen door with her to-do list clenched between her teeth. As she slid behind the wheel of her car, she wondered how she could accomplish everything. With an eight-to-five job on weekdays, Saturday was supposed to be less structured—a time for laundry, housekeeping, groceries, and maybe, just maybe, a little time for fun. *Fun?* Pam had almost forgotten that word.

Pam's cell phone interrupted her thoughts. *What now?* She sighed.

"Mom," her seventeen-year-old daughter said, "could you pick up that book on hold at library for me? And don't worry about dinner—I'm making the Crock-Pot recipe we talked about yesterday. Stay as long as you need and give Gram a hug, okay?"

Pam smiled as she pulled into the nursing home parking lot. She and her mom could have an unhurried visit now. In fact, with dinner taken care of, she just might have a few minutes for some fun at the mall.

It's true. Sometimes God does answer before we call!

Dear God, You are the perfect Father,
seeing and meeting my every need. Thank
You for providing rest, relief, and recreation.

Contagious Hope

*[Jesus] died for us, a death that triggered life. Whether we're awake
with the living or asleep with the dead, we're alive with him!
So speak encouraging words to one another. Build up hope so
you'll all be together in this, no one left out, no one left behind.
I know you're already doing this; just keep on doing it.*
1 THESSALONIANS 5:10–11 MSG

What do we have to lose? Alive here on earth or dancing on heaven's
streets of gold, we have life with Jesus. Do you see the power of that?
When we can wrap our hearts and minds around that concept, we can
make a real difference for others. Fleshed out, this hope provides a
contagious encouragement that warms others with its radiance.

We are in a position to give that hope to others in great need.
Our well-placed words of encouragement can build up our loved
ones, transferring the Life that's within us to their hungry hearts.
In a world often narrowed by confinement or pain, their positive
perspective can dwindle—so they need our wider vision of abundant
life in Christ.

Bring them along on this joyful journey. Smile, look them square
in the eyes, and speak the truth of God's love to them. As we minister
daily to their needs, we build them up in ways that no one else could
possibly do.

*Father, please give me specific words of encouragement for those
I serve today. May the hope within me be contagious,
infecting them with Your abundant life.*

Create a Festive Atmosphere

A joyful heart is a good medicine,
but a broken spirit dries up the bones.
PROVERBS 17:22 NASB

Loneliness—it can creep up on us, even when we're busy caring for our loved ones.

Haven't we all felt the burden of isolation at one time or another? But we don't have to stay in that lonely place. Sometimes even a minor change in our routine can lift our spirit and the spirit of our loved one. With just a little effort, ordinary days can become extraordinary.

Lighting a candle can brighten the gloomiest of days. The aroma of an apple pie or chocolate-chip cookies baking has a comforting effect. We might play some pleasant background music or pop a lighthearted comedy into the DVD player.

Lonely days are perfect for inviting friends or neighbors over for an impromptu visit. It's fun to hear about the unusual experiences of our friends' lives—invite them to share stories of their childhood, describe some of the funniest people they've met, or tell about their most embarrassing moments. Such get-togethers are often sprinkled with humor and surprises.

God knows that a joyful heart is good medicine, helping both us and our loved ones to feel better.

Dear Lord, sometimes I feel lonely. I need Your touch.
Thank You for filling the void in my heart with Your joy.

When God Redecorates

God is the builder of everything.
HEBREWS 3:4 NIV

While planning to renovate the living room, a husband and wife most wanted to change two large rectangular posts that stood floor-to-ceiling in the middle of the room.

But the couple's cautious contractor didn't remove the posts. He explained that, without the posts as support, the room's ceiling could come crashing down.

Unlike that contractor, God—the renovator of hearts—doesn't work cautiously. When He begins renovations, He removes (or allows the removal of) all existing supports. Maybe that "support" is health—ours or a loved one's. Maybe it's our savings. Maybe it's something else. Our lives, as we know them, crash. We hurt. We don't know how we can go on.

But God knows. If we let Him, He'll replace the temporary supports we'd relied on—health, independence, ability, you name it—with eternal spiritual supports like faith, surrender, and prayer. Those supports enable us to live a life of true freedom, one abounding with spiritual blessing.

Lord, I am tempted to cling to the supports I've erected. When my life crashes, I'm tempted to despair. Please help me to be still and place my trust in You, the great builder of all lives.

What We See Is Not What We Get

*God. . .gives life to the dead and calls those
things which do not exist as though they did.*
ROMANS 4:17 NKJV

Disaster after disaster overwhelms us: Our loved one's health deteriorates. Medical bills pile up. Insurance balks at paying. Our spirits plummet.

Then the car won't start.

The circumstances of life seem to crash in on us like enormous waves over a small fishing boat. We feel like Jesus' doused disciples on the stormy Sea of Galilee—deserted by a sleeping Lord.

We desperately scamper to solve our own problems. We try to keep our heads above water on the tumultuous sea of life. We pray like the frantic disciples prayed: "Lord, don't you care that we are perishing?"

Or we say, like Martha did after her brother, Lazarus, died, "Lord, if you were here, things wouldn't be like this."

God understands our perspective. Sure, the circumstances look bad. But He's the God who asks us to exercise faith. With faith, what we see is *not* what we get. With faith we get *God*—His company and every spiritual blessing.

Stop looking at circumstances. Start looking at God. He is in control. Have faith!

*Lord, please grow faith in my heart so that I will know with
certainty that You are in charge—that You are arranging
my circumstances for my good and Your glory. Let me be
fully convinced—like Abraham was—that You are able
and willing to keep Your promises to me.*

Quiet Hope

It's a good thing to quietly hope,
quietly hope for help from God.
LAMENTATIONS 3:26 MSG

Hope is essential to life. Without it, life has no meaning, no purpose.

How much truer that is in our spiritual lives. The hope of eternal life in heaven grows more powerful the longer we live in our earthly bodies. Hope keeps us going in the midst of trouble and heartache. It allows us to live in expectation of life with no pain, no sorrow, no trouble of any kind to mar our eternal existence.

Jeremiah is often called the "weeping prophet." Yet even in his lament over Judah's sin and turning away from God, he wrote these words: "It's a good thing to quietly hope. . .for help from God." Dwelling on the confusion and chaos of his day only added to Jeremiah's distress. The prophet knew that keeping his focus on the Lord was essential to seeing the hope of his people's salvation that God had promised.

God calls us to "cease striving" (Psalm 46:10 NASB), so that we can know Him and understand the hope of His calling (Ephesians 1:18). He wants us to quietly hope and wait on God's promises for strength (Isaiah 40:31), for endurance (1 Corinthians 10:13), for peace (Romans 15:13), for salvation (1 Thessalonians 5:8), for eternal life in heaven (Titus 1:2)—for others as well as for ourselves.

Lord, help me to be quiet before You today no matter
what is going on around me. I look to the hope I have
in Christ Jesus for all I need to do Your will today.

Take Time to Sit

And Jesus answered and said unto her, Martha, Martha,
thou art careful and troubled about many things: But one
thing is needful: and Mary hath chosen that good part,
which shall not be taken away from her.
LUKE 10:41–42 KJV

Martha, the busy sister of the devoted Mary, has had a lot of bad press over the centuries. "Don't be a Martha," we're told. "Be a Mary."

But while she's often criticized, Martha had many good qualities. She was a diligent worker. She was a natural leader with a passion for serving.

The problem is that Martha didn't take time to sit. And because she didn't, she missed out on a deeper relationship with the One she served.

As we serve others, it's so easy to be on the run. But we must take time to sit. Certainly, we want to sit at the Lord's feet, to be quiet before Him. But we should also sit with those we serve.

Sitting gives us a chance to breathe—and to gain perspective. It gives us time to develop relationships with those we serve.

When the toddler decorates the bedroom with baby powder, clean it up, hug him, and thank God for his energy. Then play a game with him—even if you don't have time.

After cleaning up a bedridden parent, sit by his side, hold his hand, and talk.

The goodness of these times—the love, respect, and joy—will never be taken away.

Father, I am drained from being on the run.
Help me to sit more, both with those I serve and with You.

Building Trust

*Trust in the LORD with all your heart and lean not on
your own understanding; in all your ways acknowledge
him, and he will make your paths straight.*
PROVERBS 3:5–6 NIV

Many corporations send their employees to leadership training
courses in the hope that they will develop better working
relationships. One exercise takes place on a rope course. A person is
buckled into a harness on a high platform then falls into open space,
trusting their team members to guide them safely back to the ground.

If we can trust people with our lives while dangling in midair,
why is it so difficult to put our trust in a loving heavenly Father?
Perhaps it's because we can't see God. Trust—what some call "blind
faith"—is not easily attained. It comes after we've built a record with
others over time.

To trust God, we have to step out in faith. The adage "let go and
let God" sounds simple. It isn't—but it works. Try this: Challenge
yourself to trust God with one detail in your life each day. Build that
trust pattern and watch Him work.

He won't let you down. He holds you securely in His hand. He is
your hope for the future.

*Dear Father, I want to rely on You.
Help me learn to trust You this day.*

Discerning Hearts

*I am your servant; give me discernment
that I may understand your statutes.*
PSALM 119:125 NIV

Discernment is the ability to listen for God's guidance and wisdom
when making decisions. As Christians, this is one of our most valuable
tools—and one of our most important prayers should be, "Give me
discernment, Lord."

We are bombarded by important questions that deserve
thoughtful answers. Our decisions affect many people, both now and
in the future. Which of the overwhelming issues should we address
first? Who needs to be involved with those decisions? What are
the financial ramifications? How do we find the answers to these
problems?

We pray for wisdom. We involve others in the process by
consulting with family, friends, and professionals. We explore our
options by getting all the information available to us, and we simply
give the process time. Ultimately, we let it rest in God's hands.

Then we remember to be gentle with ourselves over the
situations that don't turn out as we had hoped. None of us is perfect—
but if we listen for God's wisdom, we'll find the answers we need.

*Guiding Father, You know what is best at every crossroad of decision.
As Your servant, I ask for Your guidance and wisdom.
Please give me the discernment I need.*

Faithful God

He who calls you is faithful, who also will do it.
1 THESSALONIANS 5:24 NKJV

When Moses encountered God in the burning bush, he wasn't thrilled with the assignment God had for him: to go to Pharaoh and seek the freedom of the Israelites.

Moses posed several questions to God in Exodus 3 and 4: "Who am I to go before Pharaoh?" "Who shall I tell the people of Israel sent me?" "What if they don't believe me?" "Why me, since I am slow of speech and slow of tongue?"

The Lord patiently reminded Moses that He would always be with him—that Moses wouldn't have to face Pharaoh alone. God told Moses His name: the great I AM, the God of Moses' ancestors. Then God equipped Moses with special signs to prove that he had been sent of the Lord. When Moses raised his last objection, God reminded him that He had made Moses' mouth and given him everything he needed to accomplish the task at hand. God was never angry with Moses until Moses said, in effect, "God, this sounds wonderful, but I'm not the man for the job. Find someone else."

Have you been called to a job you feel totally inadequate to accomplish? That's okay. God is faithful to fulfill His calling for you. All He wants are willing vessels.

Father, I thank You that You always equip us to
do the work You have called us to do. Help us
to go forth in Your strength today.

Unresponsive? Maybe Not

He said: "In my distress I called to the LORD,
and he answered me. From the depths of the
grave I called for help, and you listened to my cry."
JONAH 2:2 NIV

In the hallway of the nursing home, Amy sat beside Kate, who slumped sideways in her wheelchair.

"Your hair looks nice today," Amy began. No response.

"Can you hear the music? That is one of your favorite songs." Silence.

"I have a funny story to tell you. . . ." Still no response.

Amy looked around in embarrassment to see if anyone was watching the one-way conversation.

Kate no longer recognized Amy's voice, said her name, or squeezed her hand. Most of the time Kate's eyes were shut. Even when they opened, a bland, dull stare was all that was visible.

What's the use? Amy thought. *I can't get through to her anymore.*

Discouraged, Amy ended the visit in her usual manner, reciting the Lord's Prayer. Holding Kate's hand, Amy whispered, "Our Father, who art in heaven. . ."

Surprisingly, Kate's weak voice continued, "Hallowed be thy name. . ."

With tears streaming down her cheek, Amy thought, *I can't get through to you anymore—but God can.*

Lord, we call and You answer us. You never forget us when
we cry out to You, even the silent prayers of our hearts.

Martyr or Servant?

Let nothing be done through strife or vainglory; but in lowliness
of mind let each esteem other better than themselves.
PHILIPPIANS 2:3 KJV

As we minister to those around us, we must constantly be on guard
against the flesh.

While our spirit delights in serving, sometimes our flesh fights
against it. We can easily slip from humility to pride; from being
servants to thinking ourselves martyrs:

"Why must I always be the one to do this? Why can't anyone else
help?"

"Where is this person's family, Lord? Why aren't they helping?"

"Go on without me—I'll just stay here alone *again* with
Grandma."

Let's be vigilant to keep the selfish martyr's complex from
gaining a root in our hearts. It leads only to bitterness and
resentment.

The antidote, of course, is to remember the example of Jesus and
allowing the Spirit to put His mind in us.

"Let this mind be in you, which was also in Christ Jesus: who. . .
made himself of no reputation, and took upon him the form of a
servant, and was made in the likeness of men: and being found in
fashion as a man, he humbled himself, and became obedient unto
death, even the death of the cross" (Philippians 2:5–8 KJV).

Let us always serve as Christ served, for the benefit of others.

Father, I have not served to the point of blood as Jesus did.
Nothing I can do will ever come close. Strike down my pride
and let me always minister with a humble and cheerful heart.

Password, Please

Now if we are children, then we are heirs—heirs of
God and co-heirs with Christ, if indeed we share in his
sufferings in order that we may also share in his glory.
ROMANS 8:17 NIV

Passwords are required everywhere, it seems: ATM machines, computer settings, bill paying. Passwords identify the user. They are intended to keep others out of our business. We're urged to change them frequently to protect our identity.

Christians have but one password: *Jesus.* Once we acquire this password through salvation, we become heirs of God with Him. We're children of the king. Precious saints. The Father gives us His own name to set us apart from the world.

Unlike computer or ATM passwords, this special name can never be compromised. We are safe and secure in the Father's arms, able to access every gift promised. Read the scriptures to see all that is available to you as a believer: eternal life, provision, promise after promise, blessing upon blessing.

Do you have your password, ready to swing open the gates of heaven? It's *Jesus.* Jesus, *period.* No other name is needed, no other combination.

You can take that to the bank.

Dear heavenly Father, today I choose to follow You. I give You my life,
my all. Teach me Your ways and guard my heart.

Give It All

Jesus looked him hard in the eye—and loved him! He said,
"There's one thing left: Go sell whatever you own and give it to
the poor. All your wealth will then be heavenly wealth. And come
follow me." The man's face clouded over. This was the last thing he
expected to hear, and he walked off with a heavy heart. He was
holding on tight to a lot of things, and not about to let go.
MARK 10:21–22 MSG

It wasn't the response the rich young ruler wanted to hear. Things usually went his way. His position and prestige afforded him that.

But these straightforward, piercing words, blended with the love in Jesus' eyes, troubled the man's soul. It just was too much. He understood just what was being asked of him—everything! The pain in his heart was reflected on his face and in his posture as he slumped away. The truth was, this ruler was not ready to relinquish his all for Jesus.

What has Christ asked *you* to let go of? What are you holding tightly to? Most of us don't have great wealth (we might wish for that kind of "problem"), but are we willing to give up what we *do* have to serve Him?

Outwardly, we may look fine. But inwardly? Are our motives pure? Do we have an "underground" thought life? Is there anger bubbling beneath our calm surface?

The stresses of life can bring such trouble spots to light in our lives. Today let's face the truth of exactly who we are and give up those things that prevent us from wholeheartedly serving Jesus.

Lord, show me what I need to relinquish to You. Help me
to abandon everything to freely and joyfully serve You.

Seeing the Light

"I am the light of the world."
JOHN 9:5 NKJV

Let's be honest with ourselves. We've all faced those "dark" moments that life can bring. We've experience bouts of self-pity, frustration, anger, envy, doubt, confusion, even despair.

Like people deep within a cave, we've found ourselves surrounded by a blackness that seems overwhelming. Doubts assail us. We question ourselves and the decisions we're making. We may even doubt God's concern for us, wondering if He's totally unaware of how badly we hurt.

Jesus doesn't want this darkness to swallow us. Have you ever noticed the light that a full moon gives off? Far more powerful than that is Jesus' light. It cuts through the darkness, sending it fleeing away. His light shows us the path we should travel, a path filled with encouragement and hope.

Don't stumble around in the darkness of despair. When gloom and shadows try to overtake you, call on Jesus. The darkness is no match for His true light.

Dear God, it's easy to get caught up in discouraging thoughts or feelings of helplessness. May I see Your light in all my situations— and may it guide me safely home.

Cease Striving

"Cease striving and know that I am God."
PSALM 46:10 NASB

In the midst of trouble and the chaos of daily living, our souls cry out for quiet, for peace, for calm. We are weak, pulled in every direction by our responsibilities and by the expectations of others. Often we forget that there is great power in *quiet.* In fact, our souls demand a zone of silence. Our God calls us to cease striving against all that would distract us from Him, to be still and learn to depend on Him to straighten out the tangles of our lives.

Many of the churches of post-Reformation Germany lapsed into ritualism after the vibrant change that had characterized the reformers. To counteract this, the Pietist Movement emphasized the need of being quiet before God in order to experience His peace. One of the more popular hymns to come from that movement emphasized the reality of the Christian life versus external show. According to Katharina von Schlegel, the writer of "Be Still, My Soul," recognizing who God is and what He can do goes a long way toward calming our inner spirit:

Be still, my soul: thy God doth undertake
To guide the future, as He has the past.
Thy hope, thy confidence let nothing shake;
All now mysterious shall be bright at last.
Be still, my soul: the waves and winds still know
His voice who ruled them while He dwelt below.

Father, You desire the best for me. Today may I cease
striving against the trouble and turmoil and allow
You to guide my future as You have my past.

God—Our Constant Companion

When I remember You on my bed, I meditate on You
in the night watches, for You have been my help,
and in the shadow of Your wings I sing for joy.
My soul clings to You; Your right hand upholds me.
PSALM 63:6–8 NASB

Worry. All too often, it robs us of precious sleep. The future is uncertain. Finances trouble us, especially when those big, unexpected costs pop up. Sometimes it's hard to release our troubles to the Lord. It's hard just to relax.

If you find you can't sleep, make good use of that wakeful time in the night hours—talk to God about your fears. He hears every prayer of His needy children, and He fills them with His peace.

Sometimes it helps to write our problems on paper and set them aside to deal with in the morning. God may surprise us with creative ideas while we sleep, showing us His divine way to handle our concerns.

Worried chicks, fearful of the world around them, run to their mother hens, who lift their wings to protect their little ones. In the same way, God invites us to hide under His wings. There we find shelter and joy, knowing that we're never alone.

Thank You, Lord, for helping me release my burdens and
trust You for the outcome. Help me to get a good night's
sleep so that I feel strong and well during the day.

He Is Your Confidence

For the LORD will be your confidence,
and will keep your foot from being caught.
PROVERBS 3:26 NKJV

Sometimes we wish for more confidence. A job interview or a social situation we are facing may make us nervous. A new situation we're thrown into may cause us to worry. Will we be dressed appropriately? Will we know what to say?

Those are the times to remember that the Lord is always with us. He has promised never to leave or forsake us. He tells us we are His little lambs and He is our great Shepherd. He upholds us with His righteous right hand. He leads us along still waters and restores our soul. These are just a few of the promises of God regarding the care He provides for His children.

The next time you need some confidence, instead of worrying or trying to muster it up on your own, seek God. Read 2 Corinthians 12:9 and remember that in your weakness, God shows up to be your strength. He will be your confidence.

God, be my confidence when this world brings situations
in which I feel insecure or inadequate. Thank You.

People Pleaser vs. God Pleaser

We are not trying to please men
but God, who tests our hearts.
1 THESSALONIANS 2:4 NIV

Much of what we say and do stems from our desire to be accepted by others. We strive to make a certain impression, to shed the best light possible on ourselves. Wanting to be viewed as successful, we may decide to exaggerate, embellish, or even lie. It's difficult to be true to ourselves when we care so much about the acceptance and opinions of others. Impression management is hard work, so it's good to know God has a better plan!

Rather than being driven by the opinions of others, strive to live your life for God alone and to please Him above all else. God knows our hearts. He perceives things as they truly are. We cannot fool Him. When we allow ourselves to be real before Him, it doesn't matter what others think. If the God of the universe has accepted us, then who cares about someone else's opinion?

It is impossible to please both God and man. We must make a choice. Man looks at the outward appearance, but God looks at the heart. Align your heart with His. Let go of impression management that focuses on outward appearance. Receive God's unconditional love and enjoy the freedom to be yourself before Him!

Dear Lord, may I live for You alone. Help me transition
from a people pleaser to a God pleaser. Amen.

Guilt-Free

So now there is no condemnation for
those who belong to Christ Jesus.
ROMANS 8:1 NLT

Every one of us has messed up—some of us big-time. Fortunately, we serve the God of second chances.

He tells us in 1 John 1:9, "If we confess our sins, he is faithful and just and will forgive us our sins and purify us from all unrighteousness" (NIV).

When we confess our failures, repent, and move on, God wipes those mistakes away—He sees the child He created, who is washed in the blood of Jesus.

"Therefore," Romans 8:1 says, "[there is] now no condemnation (no adjudging guilty of wrong) for those who are in Christ Jesus, who live [and] walk not after the dictates of the flesh, but after the dictates of the Spirit" (AMP).

Whatever we've done wrong, let's stop condemning ourselves. If we've confessed those sins, there is no need for our feelings of guilt.

Guilt has held back the blessings of God long enough! Let it go! Have faith in the blood that cleanses *all* sins—past, present, and future.

"Even if we feel guilty, God is greater than our feelings, and he knows everything" (1 John 3:20 NLT).

Father God, I thank You that You have forgiven me.
Help me to forgive myself—and to let go of the guilt that keeps
me from becoming the person You say that I am. Your Word
is true, and I choose to believe what You say over what I feel.

Burden-Bearing

*"For I satisfy the weary ones and
refresh everyone who languishes."*
JEREMIAH 31:25 NASB

What kind of burdens are you carrying today? Finances, health, work, family cares, children—they're all burdens we take on, thinking we have to work out all the problems and find the solutions.

Jesus tells us, "If you are tired from carrying heavy burdens, come to me and I will give you rest. Take the yoke I give you. Put it on your shoulders and learn from me. I am gentle and humble, and you will find rest. This yoke is easy to bear, and this burden is light" (Matthew 11:28–30 CEV). While these verses primarily refer to the burden of guilt and shame over sin and our inability to release that burden on our own, a secondary meaning applies to the burdens we take on ourselves—by not trusting God's sovereignty in every area of our lives.

Several times in scripture, we humans are compared to sheep. Sheep are not burden-bearing animals. You don't see shepherds loading them up like mules, camels, and horses. Neither are we required to take on burdens. The fact is that many times in God's Word we're encouraged to roll every burden onto *Him.*

The promised result is God's rest—His peace, His refreshing of our spirits—in spite of any problem we face. When we submit to His yoke, we find that the burden truly is light and easy to bear. No longer languishing, we find ourselves refreshed, walking forward in His strength.

*Father God, may we heed Jesus' invitation today, knowing that
Your desire is to do all things for our good and Your glory.*

"Perfect Peace and Rest"

For thus said the Lord G OD, the Holy One of Israel,
"In returning and rest you shall be saved; in quietness and in
trust shall be your strength." But you were unwilling. . . .
ISAIAH 30:15 ESV

Some of the saddest words in the Bible are found at the end of
Isaiah 30:15: "But you were unwilling." Here the Lord sets before
His people a simple formula to the extreme difficulties of life they
were experiencing. By returning to God's ways and resting in Him,
they could be safe from the enemies who sought to destroy them. In
quieting their spirits and trusting in God, they could be strengthened
for the battles ahead. But they were unwilling. Instead they wanted to
flee God's presence.

Frances Ridley Havergal's devotion to God throughout her short
life is seen in her many hymns. The nineteenth-century English
woman's life was riddled with pain and sickness, yet she sought the
Lord through it all. In her hymn "Like a River Glorious," she depicts
the peace and rest God offers as a mighty river, growing fuller and
deeper each day. The refrain summarizes God's promise to each of us:
"Stayed upon Jehovah, hearts are fully blest; finding, as He promised,
perfect peace and rest."

Father, I'm tired of trying to outrun my problems.
May Your peace flow through me like a mighty river,
bringing rest to my soul.

Make a Choice

"Do not let your hearts be troubled.
You believe in God; believe also in me."
JOHN 14:1 NIV

Some days are full of joy and peace; others are not. When we face the inevitable difficult days in life, we must choose how we respond. We bring light to the darkest of days when we turn our face to God. Sometimes we must let in trusted friends and family members to help on our journey toward solving our problems.

David knew much distress and discomfort when he cried out, "God is our Refuge and Strength" (Psalm 46:1). Matthew Henry's commentary says of Psalm 46, "Through Christ, we shall be conquerors. . . . He is a Help, a present Help, a Help found, one whom we have found to be so; a Help at hand, one that is always near; we cannot desire a better, nor shall we ever find the like in any creature."

Knowing that Christ is at the center of our battles—and that we can trust Him—lends peace and stills the weakest of hearts. Rely on Him to lead you through the darkest days.

Oh Lord, still my troubled heart. Let me learn to rely on You in all
circumstances. Thank You, Father, for Your everlasting love.

Firm Footing

The Sovereign Lord is my strength; he makes my feet like
the feet of a deer, he enables me to go on the heights.
HABAKKUK 3:19 NIV

Violence and destruction surrounded the prophet Habakkuk as
his disobedient nation, Judah, fell under the heel of the warlike
Chaldeans. Though he called out to God, the faithful prophet seemed
to get no answer.

Habakkuk recognized God's judgment in this attack by a pagan
people, yet he still looked to his Lord for mercy. This verse of hopeful
words declares that Habakkuk's strength still came from the same Lord
who used His power to humble His people.

Are we feeling tired today? Drained spiritually and financially? Do
the warriors of disease, depression, or despair attack us? Let's follow
in Habakkuk's footsteps: When destruction stares us in the face, let's
make God our strength.

Our Lord's power offers us a firm footing, no matter what
dangerous places we travel through. He will carry us safely over high
mountain trails or through deep swamps.

Though He sometimes sets a difficult path before us, God does
not leave us to walk alone. In His strength, wherever we go, we
cannot fall.

Lord, in my own power I'm extremely frail. I stumble daily.
Help me to cling to You, trusting that You'll safely lead
me through. Your strength alone gives me firm footing.

A Sure Foundation

*Now faith is being sure of what we hope
for and certain of what we do not see.*
HEBREWS 11:1 NIV

This definition of faith is not "wishing upon a star." No, Hebrews 11 describes faith as a firm confidence in God's promise and provision. He can—and will—perform a work in us for our good and His glory, whatever trials or heartaches occur along the way.

People speak of "blind faith," but real, biblical faith has three important elements. First, true faith is grounded in the knowledge of God that we discover in scripture. As we study God's Word, the facts become clear and we move to the second element: acceptance of the evidence, or belief. The third element of faith is trust, including repentance from our sins and reliance upon our God. As our understanding grows, we actually realize that, from start to finish, our faith and repentance are gifts from God.

Are you certain of God's design for your life amid any assignment? If not, try to view your duty from God's perspective, as an opportunity to become more like your Savior. Jesus fulfilled the role of servant every day, ultimately giving His life to bring us into His kingdom.

Today you can stand in faith, being sure of what you hope for and certain of what you do not see. It's the only way to live.

Lord, You are full of mercy and grace. I thank You for this gift of faith. Increase it, I pray, and make me more fruitful for You.

I'm Weary, Lord

The LORD is the strength of my life.
PSALM 27:1 KJV

All of us have moments in our journey when we feel drained—when we can't take another step. We have difficult days, trying times, and perplexing periods in life. But we can be thankful that our God stands ready and willing to give us comfort and strength—if we'll just open our hearts and let Him.

We're tempted to "burn the candle at both ends," sapping our energy to the breaking point. But then we're of no use to anyone. We're spent, poured out. Now is the time to learn to place first things first.

We might have to say no to something we simply cannot do or, as hard as it may be, delegate responsibilities to others. Then we rest our weary frames in the hands of the Almighty. He knows our limits, though there are times we wonder if He's overestimating our abilities. But our faithful Father sees the big picture and shoulders our yoke with us.

Focus on the Lord. Ask Him for wisdom to prioritize the duties you have. Ask Him for the strength to fulfill your responsibilities. Send up a silent plea for rest and rejuvenation then rejoice when He answers.

Dear Lord, let me find my strength in You.
Teach me to rest in Your love and leadership.

Secure

*"For I hold you by your right hand—I, the LORD your God.
And I say to you, 'Don't be afraid. I am here to help you.' "*
ISAIAH 41:13 NLT

Like children, we can lift up our hands and grasp our Father's firm hand whenever fear threatens to overtake our lives. It doesn't matter whether we have a sin to conquer or an unsolvable crisis. God always stands there for us.

When our troubles lie beyond human solution, we are not cast adrift on a sea of woes. Nor when we face purely practical, ordinary troubles are we left to our own devices. Jesus walks at our side, ready to intervene or comfort us. Though any problem may toss us around a bit, anxieties need not overwhelm us completely.

No fear permanently damages us when our Father stands beside us. Let's grab His hand, knowing He will protect and love us. He never fails.

Do we need more security than that?

No matter how protective my earthly father was, I know, Lord, that I can trust You to help me as I face so many overwhelming challenges. You control the whole earth and every life on it, including mine. I trust that You will never fail me.

Don't Give In

But you'll welcome us with open arms when we run for
cover to you. Let the party last all night! Stand guard over
our celebration. You are famous, God, for welcoming
God-seekers, for decking us out in delight.
PSALM 5:11–12 MSG

From time to time, we can lose hope and become discouraged despite
all the blessings surrounding us. When this happens, we need to
remember Paul's words about the certainty of God's promises and
realize that our God will never forsake us.

When we have those down-in-the-dumps days, we should
encircle ourselves with encouragers, Christian friends who can hold
up our arms, like Moses, when we're unable to continue the journey.
We can reach for God's Word, which breathes life into our spirits.
Moments of prayer will connect us to the Life-giver and refresh us.

Worry and discouragement are spiritual traps that sap our energy
and cover us with a cloud of gloom. These evil twins can be dispelled
by praise. Turn on the radio, hum an old hymn, read a psalm aloud.
We can choose to praise and look for joy in spite of our circumstances.
David did. Paul and Silas did. We can, too.

God has promised to give us peace and joy in spite of our trials
and struggles. Let's reach out to Him and shed our veil of darkness
for a mantle of praise.

Heavenly Father, I lift my eyes to the heavens and
ask for Your peace. Thank You for Your love and care.
Thank You for standing by my side. I praise Your name.

Nourishment

*So then, just as you received Christ Jesus as Lord,
continue to live your lives in him, rooted and built up
in him, strengthened in the faith as you were taught,
and overflowing with thankfulness.*
COLOSSIANS 2:6–7 NIV

Dana's neighbor peeked over the fence, trying to figure out the strange contraptions next door. Three-tiered towers of cone-shaped containers holding. . .what? A limp, spindly plant of some kind. Whatever they were, they didn't look like they were going to make it.

Turns out they were strawberry plants growing in a fluffy artificial soil. Dana fed them through tubes delivering fertilized water directly to the roots of each plant. In time, the plants grew healthy and productive, with roots deep and strong. The continual input of nutrients strengthened the once-scrawny plants. An overflow of plump red berries resulted.

We're a lot like those strawberry plants, strengthened and built up in the Lord when we dig deep into His Word. Like that fluffy artificial soil, our surroundings may seem unstable—but God's sustaining living water is what makes all the difference.

His power, His influence, His dynamism girds us up to accomplish the tasks at hand each day. Our anemic efforts, our weary bodies, and our lackluster minds receive the needed vitality and vigor to meet each day's demands with power and enthusiasm. And an overflow of thanksgiving is the result.

*Lord, please nourish my inner being with Your Word
and Your presence. Gird me up for today's tasks,
and help me to be thankful.*

Day Writer

*All the days ordained for me were written in
your book before one of them came to be.*
PSALM 139:16 NIV

*Why does Almighty God, a being with unlimited health at His
disposal, write pain into today?*

*Why does God, initiator of various infinite excitements, write
drudgery—the tedious repetitive routine of caring for someone who
can't care for himself—into this day for me?*

These questions nettle us.

In John 9:1–3, Jesus' disciples saw a desperate blind man and
asked the question that nettled them. "Rabbi, whose sin caused this
suffering?"

"This happened so the glory of God might be displayed in his
life," Jesus replied.

Jesus' answer shifted the conversation's focus from a perplexing
human question to a satisfying divine answer. Then Jesus acted to
display God's glory.

Like the disciples, we ask questions rooted in human perspective.
God's answer helps us look at life from His perspective. Maybe God
wrote our pain so His glory could be displayed in our lives today.

Allow God to shift your focus from pain to His glory. He promises
to show up and arrange circumstances—so He is your hero. Pain may
lead to a cascade of spiritual blessing. Drudgery may be the backdrop
for extravagant compassion.

The God who writes the pain is with us. He writes with purpose
and love—and with our supreme benefit in mind.

*Dear God, Author of life and each day, help me trust You with my
pain. I beg You to take it away—but if my pain brings You glory, I ask
You to take my focus off myself and help me turn my thoughts to You.*

Blessing to Others

From the day Joseph was put in charge of his master's household and property, the LORD began to bless Potiphar's household for Joseph's sake. All his household affairs ran smoothly, and his crops and livestock flourished.
GENESIS 39:5 NLT

Joseph was a man who honored the Lord in all he did. Everything Joseph did was done "heartily, as to the Lord, and not unto men" (Colossians 3:23 KJV).

The household of Potiphar, an Egyptian official, was blessed because of Joseph. His own brothers, who had sold him into slavery, were blessed. The entire nation of Egypt—the world power of the day—was blessed.

Joseph lived centuries before Paul wrote his letter to the Colossians, but he clearly knew in his heart that he was to serve with all his might. That brought glory to God—and, as a result, Joseph became the second-in-command of all Egypt. He literally rose from prison to palace.

There's a lesson here for us. Whatever we do should be done "heartily, as to the Lord, and not unto men." Just as God blessed Joseph and those around him, God will be faithful to bless us and those we care for.

Father, I thank You for the blessings You bestow not only on me, but also my loved ones as I faithfully seek You. Help me to be the very best I can be. Let Your faithfulness shine through me.

He Enjoys You

The LORD your God is in your midst, a mighty one who will save;
he will rejoice over you with gladness; he will quiet
you by his love; he will exult over you with loud singing.
ZEPHANIAH 3:17 ESV

Memory is a powerful part of each one of us. Perhaps you can see your father cheering you on in a sports event or you remember your mother stroking your feverish forehead while you lay sick in bed. With those mental pictures comes a recollection of emotion—how good it felt to be cheered and encouraged—how comforting it was to be loved and attended.

Zephaniah's words remind us that God is our loving parent. Our mighty Savior offers us a personal relationship, loving and rejoicing over us, His children, glad that we live and move in Him. He is the Lord of the universe, and yet He will quiet our restless hearts and minds with His tender love. He delights in our lives and celebrates our union with Him. We can rest in His affirmation and love, no matter what circumstances surround us.

Lord, help me remember that You are always with me
and that You delight in me. Remind me that I am
Your child and that You enjoy our relationship.

Actively Wait on Him

Wait on the LORD: be of good courage, and he shall strengthen thine heart: wait, I say, on the LORD.
PSALM 27:14 KJV

Do you feel overwhelmed with the demands of your life?

Are you frustrated by your circumstances or weary in your service?

Then think of David.

Having already been anointed king by Samuel, David was running for his life. David's foes, followers of the murderous, disobedient King Saul, were out for his life.

But David didn't fear. He knew that God would hide him, protect him, and eventually set his feet on a rock. In the midst of the trouble, David praised God.

David ended this confident psalm by saying we should "wait on the Lord."

Notice he says "wait *on*," not "wait *for*." Sometimes we miss the difference. "Waiting on" someone is active, like waiting on tables. "Waiting for" someone is passive, like waiting for a package to be delivered.

As we "wait on" the Lord, we need to actively seek Him, behold Him, and praise Him. As we do this, we'll gain confidence and strength in Him.

Father, my life is so busy that I sometimes think I need to stop so You can catch up. But I know I never have to "wait for" You. You're always with me. Let me wait on You. In this I will find the strength to go on.

A New Day

The faithful love of the LORD never ends!
His mercies never cease. Great is his faithfulness;
his mercies begin afresh each morning.
LAMENTATIONS 3:22–23 NLT

Did you have a rough day yesterday?

Sometimes it feels like we have more than our share of things that go wrong. Often we just don't handle those problems the way we wish we would. Then more doubt and concern loom on our horizon.

But this is a new day, full of grace and promise. One day is separated from another by night, and with the morning light comes a renewal of God's grace and strength to carry on. We might use all our human resources—all our grace, our strength, our patience, our ability—in a single day. But don't worry. The Lord is faithful, and He'll give us a whole new supply of every good thing for the new day.

Before this day even began, God knew what we would face, what we would need to get through—and He provided for that. Drawing on *His* assets—His grace, His faithfulness, His gifts for us—we'll have plenty of strength.

As we trust and praise God, we are able to draw on all His blessings for today—and all the days to come.

Thank You, Lord, that Your mercies are new every morning.
I thank You for providing me with all I will need for this day.
Please remind me to rely on You.

Holy Spirit Prayers

> *We do not know how to pray as we should, but the*
> *Spirit Himself intercedes for us with groanings too*
> *deep for words; and He who searches the hearts*
> *knows what the mind of the Spirit is, because He*
> *intercedes for the saints according to the will of God.*
> ROMANS 8:26–27 NASB

Many times the burdens and troubles of our lives are too complicated to understand. It's difficult for us to put them into words, let alone know how to pray for what we need. And unless we know someone who has been through similar circumstances, we can feel isolated and alone.

But we can always take comfort in knowing that the Holy Spirit knows, understands, and pleads our case before the throne of God the Father. Our groans become words in the Holy Spirit's mouth, turning our mute prayers into praise and intercession "according to the will of God."

We can be encouraged, knowing that our deepest longings and desires, maybe unknown even to us, are presented before the God who knows us and loves us completely. Our names are engraved on His heart and hands. He never forgets us; He intervenes in all things for our good and His glory.

> *Father, I thank You for the encouragement these*
> *verses bring. May I always be aware of the*
> *Holy Spirit's interceding on my behalf.*

Above the Clouds

"The engulfing waters threatened me, the deep surrounded me. . .
but you brought my life up from the pit, O LORD my God.
When my life was ebbing away, I remembered you."
JONAH 2:5–7 NIV

As a plane ascended, passengers peered out the windows at the swirling gray mist shrouding their jet. Nothing was visible; all was barren and bleak. In a few minutes, though, the plane broke through the clouds, startling passengers' eyes with shafts of light. Above the clouds the sun shone brightly.

Sometimes we have our heads in the clouds. All we see is the swirling gray mist, the gloom and sadness. We become myopic and focus on our circumstances, forgetting that above it all, our God sits upon the throne, shining light and piercing the darkness.

Remember Jonah inside the belly of the great fish? He saw no light. He saw no way out of his circumstances. Yet Almighty God delivered him and used him for His glory. There was light despite the darkness, hope instead of despair.

When life knocks us for a loop, we must focus on God's promises. We must rely on His words. Evil exists and hard times can envelop us, but our heavenly Father still reigns. He is the Light.

O Lord, bless Your name. Thank You for
Your watch-care even when I don't see it.

Answering God's Call to Care

*And she went and did according to the saying of Elijah:
and she, and he, and her house, did eat many days.*
1 Kings 17:15 kjv

Before God sent Elijah from the brook Cherith, He had already commanded a widow in Zarephath to sustain the prophet.

We don't know if God did that by a specific revelation or by some inner prompting. But we can tell from the account in 1 Kings that the woman recognized Elijah as a Jew who followed Jehovah.

As Elijah arrived at the gate of Zarephath, the widow seemed unaware of God's full plan. She was preparing to make her last meal, but the stranger offered her a choice: She could feed herself and her son first, or she could feed *him* first, believing that he was speaking the truth when he said her oil and meal would last until the drought ended.

The woman chose to serve Elijah first—and God blessed her. He kept her alive through the famine and eventually gave her back her son's life.

Like that widow, we often have a choice in caring for the people God sends into our lives. They may be members of our family or our church—or they might be total strangers, the people most easily overlooked.

Like the widow of Zarephath, we receive unexpected benefits when we choose to serve. Answer God's call to care for others—even strangers—and be blessed.

*Father, give me ears to hear Your command to serve.
Let me be discerning, so I can be a minister
to all those You want me to help.*

An Extravagant God

Change your life, not just your clothes. Come back to God,
your God. And here's why: God is kind and merciful.
He takes a deep breath, puts up with a lot, this most
patient God, extravagant in love.
JOEL 2:13 MSG

There are times when we are exhausted and discouraged and we allow our minds to roam to dark places. Despair and disappointment set in. A woe-is-me attitude prevails. How do we rise from the doldrums? How do we continue? We turn our faces toward the Lord God and know that He is in control.

Scripture tells of God's mercy and loving-kindness. It speaks to us to come back to God. This doesn't necessarily mean a change of circumstances, but a change of heart. And this change is a choice we intentionally make. It's not necessary to be in a church building or revival tent. While many changes happen there, ours can be in our closet, our car, our office. We reach inwardly to the Highest and ask for His mercy. And scripture says He is merciful.

Focusing on the negative—choosing despair—doesn't bring life. Voluntarily focusing on Jesus will. Praise Him for all your blessings: They are there, look for them! Some might be tiny, others magnificent. But they're all because of our Lord Jesus Christ. He is a most patient God and extravagant in His love.

Heavenly Father, I praise Your name. You are
extravagant in Your love, filling me to overflowing!
I am grateful for all You've done.

Be a God-Pleaser

Am I now trying to win the approval of men, or of God?
Or am I trying to please men? If I were still trying to
please men, I would not be a servant of Christ.
GALATIANS 1:10 NIV

Sometimes we work ourselves to the bone because we have no choice.
Other times, we do it to win the approval of others.

Today, let's be honest with ourselves. Are we run down? Worn
out? If that's the result of situations we can't control, let's ask the
Lord to give us the strength we need to keep going. But if we're
exhausted because we're afraid of letting someone down or hurting
his or her feelings, it might be time to reassess. If we're up to our
eyebrows in work, overlooking other options for the people under our
care, then we might be caught up in the "man-pleaser" game.

Here's how the game works: We do our best to make others
happy—at any expense. Our health, our finances, our time. We
sacrifice in unbalanced ways because we're concerned about what
people will think of us.

Today, let's aim to be God-pleasers. Let's do the things *He* calls
us to—nothing more and nothing less.

Lord, You see my heart. You know what struggles I
have in accomplishing these tasks. Redirect my thoughts,
Father, to pleasing You rather than men.

The Best-Laid Plans

In his heart a man plans his course,
but the LORD determines his steps.
PROVERBS 16:9 NIV

Why is it so hard to do the things we intend to do? We create to-do lists and plan our agendas, but the next thing we know, life interrupts. The reality is that we don't *have* any control—God does.

When all our intentions for the day are turned upside down, what can we do? Why not pause and turn your heart to God in prayer? We can set aside our own agendas and trust Him to show us the way. We can recognize that He is in charge of our next steps.

Sure, we should still make plans to accomplish the things that need to be done. But we need to leave enough flexibility in those plans for God's ultimate direction. He's the only One who really knows what lies ahead. And He will lead us in our daily steps.

God of our steps, You know my plans, hopes, and dreams
for each day. I rely only on You to shine Your light on
each of my steps on the path laid out before me.

Look Around

*Come and see the works of God; He is awesome
in His doing toward the sons of men.*
PSALM 66:5 NKJV

We tend to think of encouragement as coming in the way of cards,
phone calls, gifts, or efforts performed on our behalf. Isn't it
wonderful how God uses people to encourage us? But when the cards
or calls don't come, we're wise to look at the other ways God can send
us encouragement.

First, He uplifts us through His Word. Just by reading the Bible,
we're reminded of the grace and love God has for us. Then there's
His creation. Watching a bird fly, seeing a squirrel scramble up a tree,
and observing a beautiful flower or a wonderful sunrise are just a few
ways God reminds us of His power. Encouragement can also be found
by remembering what God has done for us.

If it's been a while since you received a phone call, visit, or card,
don't grow discouraged, thinking that God isn't aware of your needs.
He's creative in His encouragement—just take the time to look for it.

*Dear God, I thank You for all the ways You encourage
me. May I not overlook Your blessings because
they didn't come in the form I expected.*

Chosen

"Before I formed you in the womb I knew you, before you were born I set you apart; I appointed you as a prophet to the nations."
JEREMIAH 1:5 NIV

What an awesome thought! God said that before He formed Jeremiah in his mother's womb, He knew him. He *chose* Jeremiah. God separated him from everyone else to perform a specific task, and He consecrated him for that purpose. Wow!

We can be sure that if God did that for Jeremiah, He did it for each one of us. In fact, the apostle Paul said, "He chose us in Him before the foundation of the world, that we would be holy and blameless before Him. In love He predestined us to adoption as sons through Jesus Christ to Himself, according to the kind intention of His will, to the praise of the glory of His grace, which He freely bestowed on us in the Beloved" (Ephesians 1:4–6 NASB).

Nothing about us or our circumstances surprises God. He knew about everything before we were born. And He ordained that we should walk in those ways because we are uniquely qualified by Him to do so. He approved us, because He chose us for our specific situation. And He equipped us for every trial and difficulty we will ever face in life. What an awesome God we serve!

Father, the thought that You chose me before the foundation of the world and set me apart for a specific calling is humbling. You are so good. May I go forward with a renewed purpose in life.

Do Good and Do Well

*Trust in the LORD, and do good; so shalt thou
dwell in the land, and verily thou shalt be fed.*
PSALM 37:3 KJV

It's a fact of life: Once you start meeting the needs of the people around you, you'll always find more people around you with needs.

This is no surprise, of course. Jesus Himself said, "The poor you will always have with you" (Mark 14:7 NIV). There will always be people who need financial, physical, or spiritual help.

As much as we may want to help everyone with a need, we can't. We can't provide food to every hungry person in our town. We can't keep every disabled child from the world's cruelty. We can't care for every widow and orphan we meet.

And we aren't called to do so. Paul wrote, "As we have therefore opportunity, let us do good unto all men, especially unto them who are of the household of faith" (Galatians 6:10 KJV).

We must have faith that the Lord will bring those who need us most into our lives. And we must trust Him to provide for us. As we do good to those around us, He will meet our needs. "He that giveth unto the poor shall not lack" (Proverbs 28:27 KJV).

Open your eyes to the needs around you and trust in the Lord. As you care for others, He will care for you.

*Father, sometimes I don't think I can take care of one
more person! My resources are already stretched.
Please give me the faith to stretch out my hands to the needy,
knowing that You will provide my needs as I minister.*

Kick Back—Refresh

"Ask and you will receive,
and your joy will be complete."
JOHN 16:24 NIV

Is your life the American norm: hustle and bustle and stress-laden?
Do you find yourself "coming and going"? In a rat race? Then you
need to find a way to kick back and relax. It might only be a three-
minute break in your busy schedule, but you have to stay healthy.
One of the best ways to relax is through laughter.

Studies show that belly laughs result in muscle relaxation. While
you laugh, the muscles that do not participate in the belly laugh relax.
After you finish laughing, those muscles involved in the laughter start
to relax. So the action takes place in two stages. Laughter also aids
in diminishing pain, if by nothing more than providing a distraction.
Laughter is free and has no negative side effects. The dictionary
defines *laugh* this way: to find amusement or pleasure in something;
to be of a kind that inspires joy.

Joy! The word *joy* or *joyful* is used over two hundred times in the
Bible. Find those passages and mediate on one each day. Seek out a
source of joy. Look for things that are joy-producing: a funny sitcom
with Lucy and Ethel or Moe and Curly. A joke in a magazine. A child's
laughter can be contagious. Ask God for laughter to relax.

Dear Lord, so much in my life is hectic.
Give me the opportunity to take a breath,
slow down, and rejoice. Thank You.

Celebrate God's Greatness

"Our LORD, we are thankful. . . . Because of your wonderful
deeds we will sing your praises everywhere on earth."
Sing, people of Zion! Celebrate the greatness of the
holy LORD of Israel. God is here to help you.
ISAIAH 12:4–6 CEV

Intimately acquainted with physical difficulties since birth, a woman named Ruth learned early in life to rely on God for strength. She was normally a quiet, reserved woman, but when the opportunity rose to praise her Savior, she boldly proclaimed His mighty acts in her life. Her life was a celebration of praise to the glory and greatness of her God.

In today's scripture passage, the people of Israel were facing the most powerful army in the known world. Sennacherib boldly proclaimed what he would do to those who foolishly put their trust in God. But the inhabitants of Jerusalem chose to follow their king and trust wholly in their God to deliver them. And He did! Soon this prophecy proclaimed by Isaiah became fact.

How about you? Are you thankful for life? For your circumstances? For the blessings God bestows on you daily? For the difficulties? Today, let's celebrate God's greatness because He "is here to help you."

Father God, I thank You for saving me, for delivering
me from sin's penalty and power and—one day soon—
from sin's presence. Thank You for Your grace to live
each day, to serve You in my humanness. May I sing
of Your wonderful deeds to all the world.

The Blessings of Waiting

Blessed is the man who listens to me,
watching daily at my doors, waiting at my doorway.
PROVERBS 8:34 NIV

We wait for other people. We wait in line at the grocery store. We wait to see what the next medical test will show. We wait quietly for our loved ones.

Waiting is part of life—but it isn't easy. When nothing seems to be happening, we can become impatient and anxious. We want things to start moving!

But waiting can be a form of activity. Waiting creates a pause that, if used correctly, can help us to linger and to listen. We can stop and collect our thoughts. We can take a few deep breaths and rest in God's care, even if we can't find the words or the energy to talk with Him.

Waiting allows us time to absorb our surroundings and enjoy a quiet moment. We can savor the sights, listen intently to the sounds, and touch base with our emotions. We can drink in all that is occurring around us instead of gulping it down.

The down times allow us to open our hearts to be with God. Each wait-and-see moment holds His promises and blessings, because God waits and watches with us.

Lord, waiting is so difficult. Be with me as I wait,
and open my eyes to see the blessings in these pauses of life.

Out of the Pit

God rescued us from dead-end alleys and dark dungeons.
He's set us up in the kingdom of the Son he loves so much,
the Son who got us out of the pit we were in, got rid of
the sins we were doomed to keep repeating.
COLOSSIANS 1:13–14 MSG

It was as if he'd fallen into a deep, dark hole. Sleep, withdrawal, and numbness were his coping mechanisms. Going through the motions, trapped in despair, stuck in the ugliness of his sin—he seemed helpless to make the necessary changes within himself. He'd dealt with these same battles years before, thinking he'd conquered them. Yet here they were again, creeping through the chambers of his heart and mind and wreaking havoc on his spirit.

The message of the gospel doesn't leave any of us there, trapped in sin and misery with no hope of rescue. God sent His Rescuer, Jesus Christ, who plucks us out of the dungeon of despair, transferring us into His kingdom of light. It's a message of hope that says we are not consigned to our habitual ruts.

Have the struggles of life led you into bad, even sinful, habits? Those dead-end alleys, so void of purpose, aren't the place to be. We walk in God's bright and beautiful kingdom. Get out of that pit, striding confidently toward Him, enjoying life to its fullest.

Glory to You, Jesus! You have rescued me from
the pit and lifted me to Your kingdom of real life
and victory. Help me to walk in that truth today.

To Rest, Keep Going

*And he said, My presence shall go
with thee, and I will give thee rest.*
EXODUS 33:14 KJV

If you think your lot in life is difficult, imagine being Moses, stuck in the desert with a million people, whom you must lead to the Promised Land.

And if that's not tough enough, God has just told you that although you are supposed to get all those rebellious people marching again, He is not going to go in their midst, because He's ready to consume them for their resistance.

Moses knew he couldn't proceed. He couldn't take care of all those people without God's guidance and provision.

So Moses did what any wise person would do: He communed with God. He humbly appealed to God's character and reputation.

The Father relented and promised Moses His presence and His rest. And Moses went.

While our jobs are not as great as the one Moses had, we can learn from his example. When faced with a difficult situation, instead of complaining, we must *commune.*

And then we must go. God goes with us as we are going.

As we go with His guidance, He will give us rest. His rest is more than just a chance to put our feet up. It's a quiet confidence and inner peace, knowing that we are doing what God wants us to do.

Find rest today—commune, then continue, keeping a peaceful pace with Him.

*Dear Father, You work in amazing ways—with You
the strength comes in weakness; the rest, in activity.
Refresh me today as I care for those around me.*

Do Not Be Afraid

*"Do not be afraid, for I have ransomed you. I have called you
by name; you are mine. When you go through deep waters,
I will be with you. When you go through rivers of difficulty,
you will not drown. When you walk through the fire of oppression,
you will not be burned up; the flames will not consume you."*
ISAIAH 43:1–2 NLT

Trials are inevitable, a part of life. God uses them to refine us, to
burn up the dross, to mold us into the image of Jesus Christ. Even He
was not immune to the difficulties of life. Jesus faced persecution,
mocking, and death on the cross.

But in the midst of all trouble, Jesus walks beside us. He holds
our noses above the water; He wraps us in flame-retardant clothing.
We will not drown, nor will we be consumed in the fiery furnace.
Why? Because He ransomed us. He paid sin's penalty, He delivered us
from the slave market of sin, and He calls us by name.

So when you feel like you're drowning in a flood of trouble and
difficulty, breathe deeply and relax. Bodysurf across those waves.
Even if the fire of oppression singes you, remember that His promise
says you will not be consumed. He will satisfy your desires in the
"scorched places" (Isaiah 58:11 NASB).

Face life with no fear—you are God's.

*Father, may I keep my focus on You today, not on
the water that threatens to drown me or the fire that
threatens to engulf me. I am Yours, and You will enable
me to walk through the dangers that surround me.*

Without Love, I Am Nothing

*If I had such faith that I could move mountains,
but didn't love others, I would be nothing.*
1 CORINTHIANS 13:2 NLT

If I can communicate effortlessly with doctors and nurses, comprehending difficult medical terminology, but have not love, I am only an annoying know-it-all.

If I claim to understand exactly how other people feel and can anticipate their needs without them having to say anything—even if I consider myself to be a mature Christian—when I do it without love, my service is meaningless.

If I give of myself daily, sacrificing my own needs and doing everything I can to help others, but have not love, my sacrifice is empty.

Love is patient when the person I love is impossibly slow. *Love is kind* when the one I love snaps at me. *It does not envy* those who seem better off than me. *It does not boast, it is not proud* of all the things I do for others. *It is not rude* even when I'm at the end of my rope. *It is not self-seeking* in spite of the fact that I give so much of myself. *It is not easily angered* when I'm sleep-deprived or feel taken advantage of. *It keeps no record of wrongs* no matter how unfair my situation seems. *Love does not delight in evil but rejoices with the truth* even when I am unable to see my circumstances clearly. *It always protects, always trusts, always hopes, always perseveres* even when I feel helpless, hopeless and afraid.

Love never fails.

*Dear God and Author of love,
please teach me to love as You do.*

Demonstrate Righteousness

"I, the Lord, have called you to demonstrate my righteousness.
I will take you by the hand and guard you."
Isaiah 42:6 nlt

It is often difficult to live a life that demonstrates Christ's righteousness before those we are closest to—our family members. Yet they may be the ones most needful of the Savior.

Living a consistent, righteous life before our spouses, our children, and our parents and siblings is challenging. We look at our homes as places we can relax, be "ourselves," and regroup for another day of stress. Yet it is in this environment that we are most tested. As we get older, our parents need help and support. Many of us may also have children still at home who require much of our attention. The stress of the "sandwich generation"—those caring for both oldsters and youngsters—is great.

But God is faithful. He doesn't require us to demonstrate Christ's love and righteous living without His help. Jesus told His disciples that when He left earth for heaven after His resurrection, God would send the Holy Spirit, our Comforter (John 14:26 kjv), to enable each of us to live righteous, godly lives. The apostle Peter declares that when we accept salvation through Jesus Christ, we are equipped with all we need to live a godly life (2 Peter 1:3–4). Because of this we are able to demonstrate righteousness in the most stressful circumstances.

Father, You are so good! You allow trial and difficulty, stress, and pain to enter our lives, but not without equipping us with the strength and abilities to live righteously before our families. Thank You, Lord.

Overwhelmed by Life

*"The waves of death swirled about me; the torrents
of destruction overwhelmed me. . . . In my distress I
called to the LORD. . . . From his temple he heard
my voice; my cry came to his ears."*
2 SAMUEL 22:5, 7 NIV

Some days the "dailyness" of life seems like a never-ending grind.
We get up, eat, work, rest—and do it again the next day. Then when
tragedy strikes, we're swept up in grief. What once seemed doable
now seems a huge challenge. Depression sinks its claws deep into our
spirit. Fatigue sets in, and we are overwhelmed: Life is hard. We may
be tempted to question, "Is this all there is?"

Here's the good news: There's more. God never meant for us
to simply exist. He created us for a specific purpose. He longs for
us to make a difference and show others His love and grace. What's
more, He never asked us to do life alone. When the waves of death
swirl around us, and the pounding rain of destruction threatens to
overwhelm us, we can cry out to our heavenly Father, knowing that
He will not let us drown. He will hear our voice, and He will send
help.

So, next time you feel that you can't put one foot in front of the
other, ask God to send you His strength and energy. He will help you
to live out your purpose in this chaotic world.

*Lord, thank You for strengthening me when the "dailyness"
of life, and its various trials, threatens to overwhelm me.*

Unexpected Rewards of Mercy

Then she fell on her face. . .and said unto him, Why have I found grace in thine eyes. . .seeing I am a stranger? And Boaz answered. . . It hath fully been shewed me, all that thou hast done unto thy mother in law since the death of thine husband.
RUTH 2:10–11 KJV

When Ruth, the Moabitess, married into a family of Israelites, she had no idea what trials and blessings were ahead.

Her marriage was brief. Her husband died, as did her father- and brother-in-law. And then her grieving, bitter mother-in-law, Naomi, decided to return to Israel.

Would Ruth go home, or would she live among strangers with Naomi? Although she had seen sorrow in Elimelech's household, she had also seen faith. She knew Naomi's God was the true God, and she chose Him.

So she remained with Naomi, serving her as a faithful daughter.

Her mercy did not go unnoticed. The people of Bethlehem talked. By the time she arrived in Boaz's field, he already knew of all she had done for Naomi, so he offered her food and protection. He also blessed her saying, "a full reward be given thee of the LORD" (Ruth 2:12 KJV).

Ruth had a fuller reward than she could have imagined. She married Boaz and became part of the lineage of Christ.

Our acts of mercy are never ignored by our Lord. In His time, He will give a full reward. As we sow, so shall we reap.

Father, sometimes I sense no honor or reward as I serve. But I know there is a greater reward coming. Let me remain faithful.

Calmed by His Love

"The LORD your God is in your midst, a mighty one who will save;
he will rejoice over you with gladness; he will quiet you
by his love; he will exult over you with loud singing."
ZEPHANIAH 3:17 ESV

What is causing you unrest today? Inadequacy? Lack of strength?
Poor finances?

God wants you to know that He is with you. He sees your
circumstances, your concerns, your worries. And He wants you to
know that He's the mighty one who will save you. He is rejoicing over
you with gladness, exulting over you with loud singing. Why?

Because He loves you. And He wants to wrap you in His love
that's like a thick comforter on a cold winter evening. He wants us to
rest in His love. For only His love can calm the fear that hinders you
from doing what He's tasked you to do.

God's love sent His Son to die for you, that you might receive
everything you need pertaining to life and godliness. His love enables
you to keep on going even when you're ready to give up. His love
allows you to rest, to gain strength, to be still in the midst of the
storm that is raging all around you. The waters will not rise enough to
drown you, nor will the raging fire consume you.

Father, I thank You for the gift of Your love. It calms me,
it soothes me, it gives me peace in the middle of the storm.
Please fill me with Your love and peace today.

Lasting Strength

Finally, be strong in the Lord
and in his mighty power.
EPHESIANS 6:10 NIV

Where do we draw our strength? Do we think it comes from a good workout? Do we believe we'll be strong if we get enough sleep at night? Or eat a hearty breakfast? Those are all healthful energy boosters, but they do not provide the *real* strength that daily life requires.

Sometimes we need physical strength. Other times it's the strength that allows us to hold up under stress or sorrow. Or perhaps we need strength to battle feelings of frustration and impatience we find ourselves experiencing.

Whatever the reason for our need, the source of strength is always the same: God. His strength isn't temporary; it won't wear out over time. There's no waiting for Him to order in a fresh supply or worrying that He won't have enough. His strength is there continually, an outgrowth of His mighty power.

Stop reaching for the energy that fades, asking instead for the strength our God supplies.

Heavenly Father, from Your power You
provide me with the strength I need each day.
Help me to remember to call upon You.

Joy in the Morning

All who seek the Lord will praise him.
Their hearts will rejoice with everlasting joy.
PSALM 22:26 NLT

How grand God is! He knows how dependent we are on Him for the everyday joy we need to carry on. And every day, He provides us with beauty all around to cheer and help us.

It may come through the beauty of flowers or the bright blue sky—or maybe the white snow covering the trees of a glorious winter wonderland. It may be through the smile of a child or the grateful face of the one we care for. Each and every day, the Lord has a special gift to remind us of whose we are and to generate the joy we need to succeed.

In our own pain and frustration, there are times when our eyes don't see the beauty God sends. But if we'll ask, He'll show us. God is faithful to build us up with everything we need to serve Him with joy. What an awesome God we serve!

Lord God, I thank You for Your joy; I thank You for
providing it every day to sustain me. I will be joyful in You.

A Cheerful Heart

Happy is he. . .whose hope is in the LORD his God.
PSALM 146:5 KJV

When we walk the road of life, cheerfulness is often a foreign feeling. Our responsibilities lay heavily on our hearts, miring us in the dark. That's when we need an attitude check. We have to consciously make a choice to be cheerful. That doesn't mean our circumstances are any less difficult or trying. But we can choose, every day, to rise above them and smile.

In Proverbs 15:15, Solomon wrote, "The cheerful heart has a continual feast" (NIV). Solomon had probably gleaned this bit of wisdom from his father, King David. Who better than David, living in fear of constant pursuit, would know the importance of choosing happiness? In the midst of his darkest hours, he called on his God of hope. His obedience connected him with the Life-giver, the Lifeline, his Lord.

In His word, God promises lives of abundance and joy—but we need to claim these promises. When we do, Jesus fills our spirits with His power and His love, which enable us to journey forth with hope. We receive this gift by giving Him the gift of our lives and hearts—a conscious choice. A choice that will change our lives.

This day let's choose joy. Let's choose to be cheerful.

*Dear Lord, today help me choose an attitude of
cheerfulness. Fill me with Your joy, hope, and peace.
Help me to celebrate today.*

Calming the Storm

The disciples went and woke him, saying, "Master, Master, we're going to drown!" He got up and rebuked the wind and the raging waters; the storm subsided, and all was calm.
LUKE 8:24 NIV

Ever feel like you're in over your head? Like you might go under at any point? Are the waves crashing? The winds howling? The thunder rumbling? Take heart—Jesus is in the business of calming storms. Even the most frightening ones.

It's not unusual to feel overwhelmed, especially when the boat of their lives is rocking out of control. But Jesus stands at the helm, speaking with great authority to the wind and the waves. "Peace, be still!" He commands.

And as the realization sets in, peace like a river washes over you. He is with you! When you pass through the waters, you will not drown. The storm you're experiencing will subside. . .in time. Even while the thunders roar, know that His holy calm is coming.

He's more than able to calm whatever storm you're facing.

Dear Lord, I feel like the boat of my life has pitched back and forth. So many times I've felt like I might drown! Father, I ask You to calm this raging storm. Bring peace, Lord, as I rest in Your arms.

A Quiet Place

At daybreak Jesus went out to a solitary place.
LUKE 4:42 NIV

Don't you find it interesting that Jesus, the Savior of the world, took time to slip away to a quiet place? He knew that this quiet, intimate time with His Father was absolutely essential.

With all the hustle and bustle of caring for someone in need, it's tough to sneak away for quiet time. But it's worth it! In those peaceful moments, we gain the strength we need for the tasks ahead. There, in the arms of our loving Savior, we find comfort, peace, and rest. We garner the courage and the tenacity to keep on keeping on, even when things are tough.

So when can *you* manage a few minutes of respite from the world? And where will it be? In the quiet of the morning in your bedroom? Soaking in a warm bubble bath? On a leisurely walk through a nearby park? In the car as you scurry from one place to another? Whenever and wherever, be sure to get away as often as you can. God will meet you in that place.

Dear Lord, remind me that when I draw near to You, You draw near to me. Woo me daily into that quiet, solitary place— away from the chaos and confusion. Let me rest my head on Your shoulder and feel Your strong arms around me.

God's Proving Ground

*God said to Moses, "I'm going to rain bread down from
the skies for you. The people will go out and gather
each day's ration. I'm going to test them to see if
they'll live according to my Teaching or not."*
EXODUS 16:4 MSG

It seemed like such a simple test. The directions were clear; the time
frame was easy enough to handle. No study for the exam was needed.
All the preparatory work was done.

Yet many failed.

With God fighting the battle, the people of Israel had escaped
the tyranny of Egypt. Now they were a free people—but faced with
nothing to eat, they wouldn't live to enjoy it. Or so they thought.

God told Moses that *He* would provide bread, manna from
heaven. All the people had to do was gather it up each morning. A
specific amount—no more, no less. And therein lay the test: Would
the people follow the specific instructions each day? Or would they
allow greed, laziness, or unbelief rule their response?

God has promised to provide *our* every need—strength,
wisdom, ability, daily bread. But many of us fail when it comes to
appropriating the gift. We allow greed (desiring more than we need),
laziness (trying to cut out the necessary exercise of prayer and the
food of God's Word), or unbelief ("I need to help God out or it won't
be enough") to keep us from His promises.

Today, let's purpose to succeed on God's proving ground.

*Father, please help me to follow Your instructions carefully so that I
may experience the best You have for me today.*

It's All Good

*For the LORD God is a sun and shield: the LORD
will give grace and glory: no good thing will he
withhold from them that walk uprightly.*

PSALM 84:11 KJV

Our God is so much more than we can imagine. To help us understand Him, He gives us simple word pictures of Himself.

In this passage, God is a sun. Like the sun, He makes things grow, so we are sustained. But also like the sun, His rays can burn, purging our lives of evil.

God is also a shield. Although His glance could turn us to ash, He is able to protect us from Himself, as well as from other things that could harm us.

As part of His protection, He gives us grace. He gives us favor and kindness. We are precious to Him; so precious that He makes us partakers of His glory (2 Corinthians 3:18).

This is our God! And He is good.

His goodness leads Him to give good things to His children. As we walk in obedience, we can trust that the difficulties of our lives are good, because they come from the hand of a good God who sustains and protects us.

If a situation in your life doesn't seem good, don't doubt. That crisis or trial really is good, because God promises to cause all things to work together for good.

Because God is in control, it's all good.

*Father, sometimes the trials of my life don't look very
good to me. But I must trust You, because You are good.
Thank You for always working for my good.*

Exercise! Five Reasons Why

*Don't you know that you yourselves are God's
temple and that God's Spirit lives in you?*
1 CORINTHIANS 3:16 NIV

You're busy. So trying to squeeze exercise into your day seems to be an impossible task. But physical activity is an investment that pays immeasurable dividends. Here are five reasons why daily exercise is a wise idea:

1. It's a great stress reliever. Exercise helps fight depression, in part because it releases chemicals in our brain that make us feel good.

2. It's good for your body. Obesity, heart trouble, diabetes, high blood pressure. . . . Being ill is no fun—plus it's expensive, time-consuming, and robs joy from your life. Squeeze in just three ten-minute sessions of exercise every day to help ward off disease.

3. It's easy. Getting enough exercise can be as simple as parking farther away from the grocery store, taking the stairs instead of the elevator, or doing some crunches in front of the television. With a little creativity and resourcefulness, your exercise options are virtually unlimited.

4. It improves your energy level and your quality of sleep. People who exercise have more energy when they're not exercising and sleep better when their head finally hits the pillow. Who wouldn't benefit from that?

5. It honors God. God's Word calls our bodies "temples." He has entrusted these temples into our care, and when we care for our bodies, we are being good stewards. We demonstrate our thanks for this magnificent creation.

*Father, I thank You for my body that enables me to do
so much. Help me to make caring for it a top priority.*

Giving Thanks

*It is good to proclaim your unfailing love in the
morning, your faithfulness in the evening.*
PSALM 92:2 NLT

Do you feel like giving thanks today? Do you recognize your many
blessings? Your eyes may have opened this morning to situations and
circumstances that don't inspire joy, but in spite of the worry and
uncertainty, this day is a treasure. You're alive; you drew a breath
when you awoke. Praise God!

Each day is a special gift to be savored and celebrated. God has
created this time for us—and He's given us too many blessings to
count. An attitude of praise and celebration will lift our spirits and
help us commune with Him.

So look for the good things this day, the treasures. Sing a song
in the shower or hum a tune over the washing machine. Whisper a
prayer of gratitude before you turn out the light. Recognize the Lord.
Show Him your gratitude.

Despite the mundane, everyday tasks we encounter, there is
something special about each day. God has ordained that. He is in
control. Praise and rejoice, for this *is* the day He has made (Psalm
118:24).

*Heavenly Father, I thank You for another day of life.
Let me celebrate this day and use it according to Your plan.*

Personal Choice

*Truly no man can ransom another, or give to
God the price of his life, for the ransom of
their life is costly and can never suffice.*
PSALM 49:7–8 ESV

There are some things no person can do for another. For example, none of us can make a decision to accept Christ for another. Every soul makes its own choice.

That truth hurts many of us, because we love people who have resisted the gospel message. Though we seek to share the joys of Jesus, some will never come to Him.

God does not hold us accountable for another's decision. He only tells us to bear the news. We should do that gently, with respect, because we all know those who have irritated others by coming on too strong. Pushing doesn't work. It causes resentment, not faith.

If a loved one refuses God, perhaps it's time to stop talking and start praying. Maybe another messenger will open that hard heart to the truth. Perhaps it's time to *live* our faith as much as speaking it.

Ultimately, that decision lies between one person and God. Give them the truth, let your loved ones choose, and trust God for the outcome.

*Lord, help me to share Your love with others in an
attractive way. You say each must make the choice.
Help me be fervent in prayer instead.*

Well-Aged Wisdom

Hearken unto thy father that begat thee,
and despise not thy mother when she is old.
PROVERBS 23:22 KJV

Our culture seems allergic to age. Book, movie, and television plots rarely portray heroes and heroines above the age of thirty. Advertisements avoid older actors unless the product involves disease. Instead, the media presents young, healthy people as experts in every situation, despite their lack of experience.

It's easy for Christians to absorb this attitude, especially when aged parents need help in managing their everyday lives. God does not expect us to agree with them all the time. The years take a toll on decision-making abilities, and sometimes we must make unpopular choices for our parents. But as we provide medical, financial, and household assistance, we should offer them as much independence as possible.

The Bible also urges younger believers to look to older Christians for advice and prayer. An eighty-five-year-old saint may use a walker, but the lifetime lessons of faith she has learned remain strong and steady. Her prayers for her children are no less powerful than when she prayed at their bedside; in fact, they have grown up with her sons, daughters, and grandchildren. An old man may seem at the mercy of his hearing aids; but his spiritual ears have sharpened with the years. He hears God clearly, and God always hears him.

Shouldn't we listen, as well?

Father, You are the Ancient of Days. Help us to welcome
the wisdom You share with Your people, old and young.

Overwhelmed? Cry Out

[Prayer of the afflicted, when he is overwhelmed, and poureth
out his complaint before the Lord.] Hear my prayer,
O Lord, and let my cry come unto thee.
PSALM 102:1 KJV

If any word describes life in the twenty-first century, it's *overwhelming.*

It doesn't matter if we are single or married or if we stay home or have an outside job. Even with all of our modern conveniences, we never seem to get on top of things.

There's always one more thing to do; always one more hug to give, one more call to answer, one more crisis to solve.

Life never lets up.

It's overwhelming.

And it becomes more overwhelming when we get so busy that we forget our Source of strength and sanity. When we forget to pray.

May we never overlook this vital connection with God!

Our Lord loves us. He is not surprised when we are overwhelmed; He is not afraid of our complaints. He is ready to answer when we cry out for mercy and strength.

While God hears silent prayers, it is the cry of His people that seems to get the ear of God and move His hand more dramatically. When we cry out, we admit that we cannot help ourselves and we need His help.

God is there. And He does not want us to be silent.

Father, HELP! I have more than I can handle. Help me to say
yes to the best things and no to those less-important things that
tend to overwhelm me. Thank You for hearing my complaint
and answering, for turning my plea into praise!

White or Whole Wheat?

*You shall love the LORD your God with all your heart
and with all your soul and with all your might.*
DEUTERONOMY 6:5 ESV

Nutrition experts tell us to eat whole-grain breads because they're better for us. While white bread tastes good and is often easier to chew, it doesn't carry the whole-wheat loaf's nutrition.

Eating white bread is the physical version of loving God with only part of our hearts. Spiritually, we need the sustenance of a wholehearted faith; a deep, fruitful commitment that encompasses all our lives. We need to feed our minds with the Word, our hearts with an intimate relationship with Christ, and our spirits with prayer.

God is most gracious. He understands when responsibilities keep us from church—and He doesn't look poorly upon us. But that doesn't mean our faith life should die out entirely. Can we reprioritize a few things and go to an evening service? We need to meet with God's people. If that is utterly impossible, do we make the most of other methods that feed our souls?

Life can be a school of faith, but are we supporting it by fellowship with saints? Let's not live white-bread lives when we can enjoy whole wheat.

*Lord, help me to love You with all my heart
and do all I can to get spiritual nutrition.*

Stressed Out?

God, the one and only—I'll wait as long as He says.
Everything I need comes from him, so why not?
He's solid rock under my feet, breathing room for
my soul, an impregnable castle: I'm set for life.
PSALM 62:1 MSG

In our modern day, we invite stress into our lives. Busy schedules, financial strains, being overburdened with caring—it all adds up.

How do we handle the inevitable stress? Just let it go. Relinquish control to a loving God and realize that the reins are in His hands.

Give up control? we might think. *Isn't that dangerous?*

When we give our lives to Christ and accept His will—instead of vainly seeking to impose our own—we discover an inner peace. We can rest assured that His plans are the best. God is omnipotent; full of love, grace, and mercy. He knows what is best for us. His eyes roam the future He's planned for us.

Elisabeth Elliot said, "If my life is surrendered to God, all is well. Let me not grab it back as though it were in peril in His hand but would be safer in mine." Let go. Trust. Be less stressed.

Dear Jesus, it sounds so simple: Let go. But it isn't.
Help me trust in You and recognize that You're in control.
I thank You for the plan You've established for my life.

24/7

He will not allow your foot to be moved;
He who keeps you will not slumber.
PSALM 121:3 NKJV

Are you old enough to remember when most stores were *not* "open twenty-four hours"? If you needed something but the store was closed, you just had to wait.

Some of the hardest waiting comes with medical or health issues: waiting for a surgery to be over, waiting for a chemo treatment to end, or waiting for a doctor to show up. Waiting to see a specialist, get into the lab, or experience the effects of a new medicine. It's easy to become discouraged when it seems that nothing we need is immediately accessible.

God, however, is always available. He doesn't hang out a CLOSED sign. He doesn't work a nine-to-five day then go off to do whatever He wants. With confidence, we can call on Him and know that He's listening.

Jesus showed us real accessibility: People came to Him during the day, at night, while he was eating, and when He was on His way to help someone else. A convicted criminal even called upon Jesus while they both hung on crosses.

The expression "24/7" is relatively new—but it describes perfectly how God takes care of us.

Gracious God, I'm so thankful I can come to You at
any time of the day or night and know that You're there.

Generous Sowing

*Remember this: Whoever sows sparingly will
also reap sparingly, and whoever sows
generously will also reap generously.*
2 CORINTHIANS 9:6 NIV

The concept of sowing and reaping is pretty simple. If you want a garden filled with colorful flowers, you start by planting seeds. If you want a large, fruitful garden, you've got to sow lots of seeds!

Blooming flowers attract people with their colorful petals and fragrant aromas. Well-kept gardens draw us in with their tasty variety of fruits and vegetables. Do you want to attract others to yourself and the God you serve? Want them to recognize the "fruit of the Spirit" residing in you? Want to win them with your fragrant aroma? Then sow seeds!

What seeds have you planted today? Kindness? Joy? Gentleness? Self-control? Goodness? If you drop those seeds into fertile soil—and what soil is more prepared than those you care for on a daily basis?— God will cause them to spring to life.

As you begin each day, ask the Lord to show you which seeds to plant. . .and how. Follow His lead. Then watch the blossoms of a fruitful life spring forth!

*Heavenly Father, I want to bear fruit in my life. I want
others to be drawn to me so that I can effectively minister to them.
Please help me to plant good seeds. Show me when and where to do
the planting so that the harvest will be plentiful!*

Forever Love

Can anything ever separate us from Christ's love?
Does it mean he no longer loves us if we have trouble
or calamity, or are persecuted, or are hungry, or destitute,
or in danger, or threatened with death?
ROMANS 8:35 NLT

What does it take to make you doubt God's love for you? Financial difficulties, poor health, or job loss? A sick child, Alzheimer's, or cancer? The death of a parent, spouse, or child?

In Romans 8:28, Paul declares that God makes all these things work for our good because He uses them to mold us into the image of His Son. But when we experience these things, it can feel as though God has forgotten us. Satan would have us believe that God withdraws His love from us in order to punish us. So we draw back from loving Him; we build walls against the hurt of rejection and betrayal.

But God never promised to keep us or our loved ones from trouble. He loves us with an everlasting love. We are never out of His thoughts. He has graven our names on His heart and His hand. In our trouble, God reveals Himself.

In *My Utmost for His Highest*, Oswald Chambers said, "Either Jesus Christ is a deceiver and Paul is deluded, or some extraordinary thing happens to a man who holds on to the love of God when the odds are all against God's character. . . . Only one thing can account for it—the love of God in Christ Jesus."

Father, may my love for You grow stronger in the trials,
knowing that Your love never fails.

The "Wait" Room

God, the one and only—I'll wait as long as he says.
Everything I hope for comes from him, so why not?
PSALM 62:5 MSG

Waiting doesn't fit today's immediate-results world. Technology and time-saving gadgets have conditioned us to be impatient people. We rush from place to place, from appointment to appointment. We fidget when we find a line blocking us from our goal or when the stoplight is red for more than a couple of minutes or when the preacher goes on "too long" with his sermon.

Yet much of life is learning to wait. The dictionary defines *waiting* as a time of stillness with an attitude of readiness or expectancy. Some Bible versions translate *waiting* as "resting."

God's timetable cannot be rushed. He is not bound by time, nor does He run on man's schedule. So He gives us warm-up exercises of short waits or delays in our schedules—a light that stays red longer than we think it should or lines at the bank, grocery store, or pharmacy—to prepare us for the more intense times of life, such as wait times in doctor's offices and hospital testing rooms or beside a loved one's deathbed. These are the times He calls us to rest in His time schedule, not anxious of the outcome, not striving for our own way, agenda, or deadline.

Take advantage of the "wait" training God has for you today. He will reward you with so much more when you do.

Father, please help me wait on You today,
resting in the knowledge of who You are and
knowing that Your plan, Your timetable, is perfect.

Just God's Name

We give thanks to you, O God, we give thanks,
for your Name is near; men tell of your wonderful deeds.
PSALM 75:1 NIV

We trust certain names. There are products with particular brand names we buy over and over. We rely upon a certain repair company that we know provides quality services. Someone shares a good report about her doctor and we see if he's taking new patients. Hearing the name of an old friend brings a smile.

"What's in a name?" William Shakespeare asked. If it's a reliable, honest name, we know we can put our faith in that name. Hearing that name brings peace and hope. We are thankful that name is present whenever a need arises.

Sometimes the reliable, honest name of God becomes a one-word prayer. We don't have the clarity or the energy to say much more. Just God's name.

We can't explain how we are feeling or what the next day will bring, so we call out His name. Just God's name.

The pain of grief may be so deep that repeating His name is our only comfort. Just God's name.

Friends and family may let us down, making us feel all alone. God's name goes with us through our dark times. Just God's name.

We can trust God's name. It's all we need. Just God's name.

Almighty God, I thank You for being near. You know
what I need, and I trust You with my present and
my future. You are my Lord, my God, and my Savior.

Have the Compassion of Christ

But when he saw the multitudes, he was moved with
compassion on them, because they fainted, and were
scattered abroad, as sheep having no shepherd.
MATTHEW 9:36 KJV

What's your day like today—busy?

In Matthew 9, Jesus was very busy. He healed a crippled man;
invited a tax collector to be His disciple; gave a brief lecture on
the new covenant; healed a woman, two blind men, and a demon-
possessed man—and even raised a girl from the dead.

If we had been in Christ's sandals, we might have found a tree,
sat down beneath it, and said, "Now that was good work—I did a
good job today." But Jesus shows us that that's not enough.

After all He had done, He looked at the people and was "moved
with compassion"—not because of their physical needs, but because
they were spiritually lost.

If we serve others without directing them to the Good Shepherd
who can save their souls, our service to them is in vain. And if we
serve without compassion and love, we will not profit (1 Corinthians
13:3).

For fruit to abound, we must have the compassion of Christ, to
lead men and women to Him.

Father, let me see the true needs of those around me.
Fill me with compassion for their souls. Use me
to meet the greatest need in their lives—You.

Knee Mail

The prayer of a righteous
man is powerful and effective.
JAMES 5:16 NIV

We've all had those inevitable days when we're exhausted or discouraged and it seems too hard to carry on. We feel as dry as the desert sand, with nothing left to give. This is a time when we could use nourishment for our souls.

The prophet Zechariah said, "Ask the LORD for rain in the spring, for he makes the storm clouds. And he will send showers of rain" (Zechariah 10:1 NLT). Commentator Matthew Henry explained this scripture by saying, "Spiritual blessings had been promised. . . . We must in our prayers ask for mercies in their proper time. The Lord would make bright clouds and give showers of rain. This may be an exhortation to seek the influences of the Holy Spirit, in faith and by prayer, through which the blessings held forth in the promises are obtained."

When these times occur, use "knee mail." Carve out some time to pray, to praise, and to petition our heavenly Father for the strength to carry on. He is faithful to answer our pleas and send refreshment to our hearts—maybe in the form of a restful night's sleep, a friend to encourage us, or a stranger's greeting.

We never know just how the Lord will answer our prayers, but answer He will. God's inbox is never too full.

Lord, how we long for Your presence. Father,
hear our prayers; extend Your hand of mercy to me.

Such as We Have

Then Peter said, Silver and gold have I none;
but such as I have give I thee: In the name
of Jesus Christ of Nazareth rise up and walk.
ACTS 3:6 KJV

Our modern materialism often skews our spiritual thinking. When called upon to do a task, we often think we need to have all the money, equipment, and personnel we'll need in the end before we begin.

This is not God's methodology. God operates through us with "such as we have."

Peter and John didn't have money—but they did have the healing power of Jesus, which they offered in faith to the crippled man.

The little boy didn't have enough lunch to feed a multitude. But when he gave such as he had to Jesus, it multiplied.

The widow of Zarephath had only enough grain and oil for one meal, but she gave such as she had to Elijah, and she survived the famine.

When God gives us a job to do, He doesn't require our resources. He has everything He needs to accomplish His will. As Hudson Taylor said, "God's work done in God's way will never lack God's supply."

All God needs is such as we have—a willing heart and a willing body. He can—and will—take care of the rest.

Father, You have given me this task of caring for others,
and it seems too big for me. I don't have all the things I
need to do the job. Yet I know that You do. Father, I am
willing to serve. Work through me as You desire.

Hidden Things

> " 'Call to me and I will answer you. I'll tell
> you marvelous and wondrous things that
> you could never figure out on your own.' "
> JEREMIAH 33:3 MSG

Life has a way of perplexing us. Just as we think we've got it all figured out, something happens to change everything. Chaos and confusion reigns.

That's where Jeremiah found himself. God had called him to be His prophet to Israel. He gave him a specific message to preach. And Jeremiah obeyed when God promised to make him a strong tower against the evil that prevailed in the land.

Now Jeremiah is confined in the court of the guardhouse to the palace in Jerusalem. God's deliverance is seemingly nonexistent. Here God meets with Jeremiah and encourages him to pray for revelation. In a situation beyond Jeremiah's comprehension, God promises to reveal what has been previously hidden.

Again Jeremiah obeyed—though it made no sense—and God gave him a fresh vision of His purposes, far beyond what Jeremiah could have imagined.

God's promise holds true for us today. While we are only a small part of God's overall plan, He will reveal what we cannot see when we call on Him.

> *Father, I thank You that when I call on You,*
> *You answer. You reveal Your way to me in terms*
> *that I can comprehend. One day I will see the*
> *whole picture and marvel at Your wonderful ways.*

Still My Troubled Heart

*"Peace I leave with you; my peace I give you.
I do not give to you as the world gives. Do not
let your hearts be troubled and do not be afraid."*
JOHN 14:27 NIV

We can call upon the Lord to give us peace: a peace that passes all understanding despite our circumstances. It's the same peace that calmed Peter on the open sea, Paul and Silas in prison, and Stephen as he faced martyrdom—the undeniable, indescribable calm from the Holy Spirit.

The peace that God extends to us can be accepted or ignored. In the frustrations of everyday life, it's entirely possible to turn our backs on this incredible gift—bringing on ourselves worry, stress, and loss of sleep. But accepting Jesus' gift of peace quiets our inner spirit and helps us to calm down.

When frets and worries assail, take a few moments to read the Bible. Turn to the psalms, read some out loud, and copy a line or two to stick in your pocket or on the bathroom mirror. Find words of praise penned by a man on the run, King David. He knew to pursue the heavenly Father for peace. We should do the same.

*Father, please still my troubled heart.
I need an extra measure of peace this day. Thank You.*

The Prayer Map

Be joyful in hope, patient in affliction, faithful in prayer.
ROMANS 12:12 NIV

Did Paul get the cart before the horse here? No. But sometimes it helps to rearrange the words and ideas for a clearer look. We could paraphrase this verse as, "When we are faithful (and fervent) in prayer, we will become more joyful and patient in affliction."

It's easy to become so focused on particular situations or crises that we lose sight of God's ultimate purpose for us and the person in our charge. We want to finish our tasks, return to our own agendas, and move on. But in His love, God keeps drawing our eyes and hearts back to a better destiny, a journey of the soul, a journey home.

Isn't *home* a beautiful word? It certainly is for God's children, who Paul wrote to in Romans. Throughout his letter, he explains how Christians can, and do, reside in God's family by Christ's finished work on the cross. Then he calls them to abide in this family as faithful and fruitful sons and daughters.

Since affliction will come, he exhorts us all to faithful prayer, which always draws believers back to a sure hope—back to a trust in God's love and provision until the journey's end.

Father, as a believer, my ultimate destination is heaven.
Keep me from grumbling when You have me take a
bumpy side road rather than the interstate. Help me
see how a rocky road may bring me closer to You.

The Son Is Shining

*Then Jesus again spoke to them, saying,
"I am the Light of the world; he who follows Me will
not walk in the darkness, but will have the Light of life."*
JOHN 8:12 NASB

It is dark and dreary outside—and it seems that way inside, too.
Everything feels cold and uncomfortable. It's hard just to get out of
bed, let alone muster the energy to provide the care that God has
called us to give.

But there is a bright light on the horizon! Jesus Christ, the Son,
shines every day, regardless of the weather in our soul. Nothing can
stop Him from shining—and He is waiting for us to come and bask in
His light.

Jesus will brighten each day and give us the strength and energy
to do His will. He will shine on us every minute, if only we'll ask
Him to, and He can make what seems gloomy bright and full of His
presence.

The Lord's light will shine in the darkness and cheer every corner
of our world. The Son is shining in our lives today, with a light that
gives us the courage and strength to any circumstance.

*Thank You so much, Lord, that You are the spiritual
Sun in my life—and You are there for me every
single day. I praise Your holy name!*

Getting It All Done

*"But seek first his kingdom and his righteousness,
and all these things will be given to you as well."*
MATTHEW 6:33 NIV

Have you ever thought of Jesus as a caregiver?

His disciples did—they followed Him everywhere and depended on Him for, well, everything. Then there were the sick people, who constantly tugged at His robes and asked for healing. And there were those other people who came to Jesus for the healing of *others*. . . . You get the idea.

Jesus definitely qualified as a caregiver. Even with all those demands, Jesus used His time perfectly. Not a moment was wasted. His Father approved of every single thing that He did. What was His secret? He shared it in Matthew 6:33: "Seek first his kingdom and his righteousness" (NIV).

It seems miraculous that Jesus could find time to heal the sick, raise the dead, teach His disciples, feed hungry crowds, even enjoy a meal with friends on occasion. But He was able to do all that because He had His priorities in order. Always. God came first—God's kingdom, God's righteousness. This was the single most important priority in Jesus' ministry. Everything else followed.

What would your day look like if God came first? What would happen if you *only* did the things He wanted you to do? Give it a try— you'll be amazed at the results.

*Jesus, I thank You for Your example as the perfect
Caregiver. Teach me how to put You first and to
trust You with all that I need to accomplish.*

Blind Skier

For this God is our God for ever and ever;
he will be our guide even to the end.
PSALM 48:14 NIV

Attached to each other by harnesses and a pole, a pair of skiers slid in
tandem down a slope. The one in back wore a large orange sign that
said, in black letters, BLIND SKIER. Zooming sightless down a snow-
covered slope, he exuded personal courage and trust in his guide.

Sometimes life is that hill. Our path is steep, scary, and
potentially dangerous.

We are the blind skier—our limitations prevent us from seeing or
successfully weaving our way through the challenges of life.

But God is the front skier—expert, all-seeing, completely in charge,
and totally caring. He carefully guides us through each day's obstacles.
We can't see Him; we can only trust that He'll bring us through. On the
brink of our "hills," we could sit down in the snow and refuse to budge,
crying over our limitations, the scary circumstances, and the fact that
we can't see God.

Or, using His Word as our harness and pole, we can securely
follow Him down the hill. We can exercise courage and faith, clinging
to His promise to safely maneuver us through the challenges ahead.

As you go about your day, remember that blind skier. Cling to
the pole. Rest confidently in the harness, knowing that God is on the
other side.

Lord, when I can't see You, when circumstances obscure Your
goodness, help me to remember Your Word to me. Enable me to
follow You closely through the frightening course of my life.

No Afternoon Picnic

Take everything the Master has set out for you,
well-made weapons. . . . This is no afternoon athletic
contest that we'll walk away from and forget about in
a couple of hours. This is for keeps, a life-or-death fight
to the finish against the Devil and all his angels.
Ephesians 6:11–12 msg

The first major land battle of the American Civil War was fought near Manassas, Virginia, on July 21, 1861. Certain of a Union victory, many of the Washington D.C. elite rode out in their carriages to watch the battle. Untrained and undisciplined, the battle soon turned into a rout that had the Union forces scattering in retreat. The panicked civilians added to the confusion as they attempted to flee both armies.

We, too, are in a battle. Even though our opponent is invisible, this battle is no less real than any other fought in the many wars in the history of the world. It isn't an afternoon picnic in the park, complete with volleyball or softball, where we vie for athletic superiority. It's a lifelong fight to the death.

The only way to be successful against Satan and his evil forces is to take up the armor God has given us, utilizing the weapons of prayer and scripture in order to successfully parry the darts and sword thrusts the enemy sends our way. The battle is fierce, even though the war is won.

Father, please give me wisdom, strength, and determination to stand
firm in the battle raging about me. Help me use all the armor and
weapons You have given me to their fullest extent.

Serve with the Soul in Mind

*To the weak became I as weak, that I might
gain the weak: I am made all things to all men,
that I might by all means save some.*
1 CORINTHIANS 9:22 KJV

As an apostle, Paul had the right—and the power—to preach the gospel with no holds barred. He could have thundered the gospel from his pulpit without regard for the minds and hearts of those in his audience.

But that wasn't Paul's style. As a Jew, he reasoned with the Jews, showing them that the Law was given to lead them to Christ. Using his great intellect, he reasoned with the Greeks at Mars' Hill, declaring the true identity of their "UNKNOWN GOD" (Acts 17:23 KJV). Acknowledging his own weaknesses, he showed the weak the strength of Christ.

In other words, Paul met people where they were. He empathized and identified with them so they could see how Christ could work in their lives.

As we interact with those around us, we must know them as they are, without prejudice, so we can show them how Jesus can take them from their sinful state to His holy heaven.

Our goal is not to be honored for our sacrifices, but to honor the Father by gaining the lost. Serve with the soul in mind, so that through you, God will save some.

*Dear Jesus, please help me to understand the deep needs
of the people around me, so I can show them how You can make a
difference in their lives. Please save some today.*

Borrowing Trouble

Why are you down in the dumps, dear soul? Why are you crying
the blues? Fix my eyes on God—soon I'll be praising again.
He puts a smile on my face. He's my God.
PSALM 43:5 MSG

One evening a man found himself staggering alone under a burden
heavy enough to crush a half dozen strong men. Out of sheer
exhaustion he put down his entire load and took a good look at it. He
found that it was all borrowed: Part of it belonged to the following
day; part of it belonged to the following week. Yet it was crushing
him *now*.

Sound familiar? We often find ourselves carrying a load of
responsibility, worry, and grief. Ignored, the burden soon grows too
heavy to bear, robbing us of the joy of life.

Take a good look at your burden. Is it borrowed from tomorrow,
next week, or even further down the road? Jesus said, "Do not worry
about tomorrow, for tomorrow will worry about itself. Each day has
enough trouble of its own" (Matthew 6:34 NIV).

Fix your eyes on God, the great burden-bearer. Roll all the care,
the worry, the responsibility, and the grief on Him. Allow Him to
manage every detail. He wants to put praise in your heart and a smile
on your face.

Father, give me the wisdom not to borrow trouble
from the future. When I trust You to help me bear only
today's problems, the load lifts and the praise begins.

God's Formula for Happiness

Is any one of you in trouble? He should pray.
Is anyone happy? Let him sing songs of praise.
JAMES 5:13 NIV

Humanity's formula for happiness is vastly different from God's. We most often live to please ourselves, and when things don't go our way, we grumble. The Lord wants us to live for Him. And whether we're happy or sad, He longs for us to lift our voices in praise.

So what *is* God's formula for happiness? Prayer and praise. Sounds simple, right? Not necessarily. Imagine that you're in the throes of caring for someone who doesn't seem to be improving. You've cried out to God, but silence on His end has you boggled. So you stop praying. You stop asking. You give up. Oh sure, you still offer up some basic, generic prayers. But praise? No way.

God longs for us to keep on knocking, keep on seeking. When you're going through rough times, slip into your prayer closet and spend time with your heavenly Father—praying *and* praising. When you're faced with times of silence from God, don't take it as apathy on His part. While you're waiting, continue in a hopeful mind-set of prayer and praise.

Lord, I don't like to wait. And it's hard for me to imagine
praying and praising my way through a situation when I
don't have the answer yet. Help me to learn Your formula
or happiness. Teach me to wait patiently. . .hopefully.

Faithful, Not Famous

The Lord give mercy unto the house of Onesiphorus;
for he oft refreshed me, and was not ashamed of my chain.
2 TIMOTHY 1:16 KJV

Onesiphorus is mentioned only twice in the Bible. Paul introduces him in his letter to Timothy as a person who went out of his way to refresh and encourage him—a sharp contrast to Phygellus and Hermogenes, who had deserted Paul (2 Timothy 1:15). We might view these fair-weather friends with scorn. But in that volatile political climate, those who associated with the apostle put themselves at risk. After all, the Romans had imprisoned Paul, and they often did not hesitate to jail a convict's friends.

Onesiphorus, however, did not let that stop him. He not only helped Paul nurture the fledgling church in Ephesus but determined to help and encourage his friend when the Romans imprisoned him. Onesiphorus went to Rome and searched the city until he tracked Paul down and met his needs.

While few Christians in North America languish in prisons because of persecution, many suffer from illnesses and old age, which distance them from the believing community. Fortunately, modern-day encouragers like Onesiphorus seek out these needy Christians with a refreshing ministry that blesses lonely, hurting hearts. Jesus, who commanded His followers to visit the prisoners, honors those who serve shut-ins with love like His.

Lord Jesus, even though my contributions to Your
kingdom seem insignificant, You never forget a cup of
cold water or a smile given in Your name. Thank You!

At Rope's End

*We were under great pressure, far beyond our ability to endure,
so that we despaired even of life. Indeed, in our hearts we felt the
sentence of death. But this happened that we might not rely on
ourselves but on God, who raises the dead. He has delivered us
from such a deadly peril, and he will deliver us. On him we
have set our hope that he will continue to deliver us.*
2 CORINTHIANS 1:8–10 NIV

Some people have said that when they reached the end of their rope,
they tied a knot and hung on. Others have said that living through
great difficulty showed them that they didn't know as much as they
thought they did but they were stronger than they imagined they
were.

Still others say that God's children endure suffering until they
realize that circumstances are far more difficult than they can handle.
At that point, each person has a choice: He or she can curse God
like Job's wife recommended, or embrace God like Job did. Who can
forget Job's moving affirmation, "I know that my Redeemer lives, and
that in the end he will stand upon earth" (Job 19:25 NIV)?

When we focus intently on God rather than our difficult situation,
He sustains and fills us with hope and joy—helping us to continue
our journey. Eventually, He delivers us. When we are saved, we know
who saved us.

When you reach your rope's end, count on God. He will deliver you.

God, life is too much for me today. Help!

The Blessings to Come

*You know that you will receive an inheritance from
the Lord as a reward. It is the Lord Christ you are serving.*
COLOSSIANS 3:24 NIV

Even city folk know that if we plant a kernel of corn, it produces
several ears of corn, loaded with many more kernels. A single
sunflower seed grows into a tall, sturdy stalk with a heavy golden
head holding hundreds of seeds. It's amazing how great the return we
get when we plant seeds in a garden or field.

We are sowing good things into other peoples' lives. It may
sometimes seem like a thankless job, but God sees all that we do—
and, in time, He will reward us with a great "crop" for our efforts.

That's another thing about sowing seeds: They produce their fruit
in a future season. A day or week after we sow, it looks like nothing
is happening. But with the appropriate sun, rain, and time, tender
plants rise up from the ground. As the weeks continue, the plants
grow stronger, become fruitful, and produce a harvest.

Whenever we serve others, God rewards us. It may not be as
quickly as we'd like—but it will certainly be good. We can count on
the Lord!

*I am grateful, dear Lord, that You love me and notice the things
I do for others. Thank You for rewarding me—in Your time.*

Sing a New Song

Everything has happened just as I said it would. . . .
Tell the whole world to sing a new song to the LORD! . . .
Join in the praise.
ISAIAH 42:9–10 CEV

Jeremiah loved his people, but the message God called him to preach was a harsh one—judgment was coming. Along with God's call to Jeremiah came a caveat: "I have put My words in your mouth. But, Jeremiah, they're not going to listen to you. In fact, they are going to persecute you, punish you, and even try to kill you. But you continue to speak My words to them, and I will protect you and deliver you."

When the high priest, Pashhur, heard Jeremiah preach against Judah's sin and proclaim the coming judgment, he put Jeremiah in the stocks. But as soon as Pashhur released him, Jeremiah spoke judgment against Pashhur himself (Jeremiah 20).

Later, Jeremiah complained to God that every time he opened his mouth to speak His Word, he was made a laughingstock, a mockery to his people. His obedience resulted in reproach and derision. But in the midst of his complaint, Jeremiah burst forth in a song of praise to God for delivering him from the hands of his persecutors.

When you are misunderstood and your motives are questioned, sing to the Lord a new song of deliverance and praise. He will deliver His people, no matter how impossible the circumstances are.

Father, I lift up my song of praise to You today,
for You alone can deliver me from the enemy's clutches.

Deeds of Wisdom

Who is wise and understanding among you?
Let him show it by his good life, by deeds done
in the humility that comes from wisdom.
JAMES 3:13 NIV

Have you ever met someone who seems to have the gift of
"understanding"? Such a person is genuinely compassionate because
they relate to the other person. They connect on a deep level.

How much more wonderful would it be if we walked in
understanding with God, especially during the tough seasons of our
lives? We would think His thoughts, have His heart for people, act the
way He would act, and respond the way He would respond. In short,
we would be His hands and feet in action.

If you're struggling to have genuine compassion, if you're trying
your best to make something work that doesn't seem to, ask God to
give you His kind of understanding. Once you catch a glimpse of His
heart for another person, then your deeds will arise from a place of
godly sincerity. And those deeds, which spring from your relationship
with Him, will be evident to everyone you come in contact with.

Dear Lord, I want to genuinely care for those You've
entrusted to me. Not just tolerate them. Not just serve them
Give me Your understanding, and motivate me to act—
and react—only as You would.

Secret Petitions

Take delight in the LORD, and he
will give you the desires of your heart.
PSALM 37:4 NIV

We all have them. Things that are so dear to us we can't share them with others. Feelings and desires that we don't want to reveal for fear of being judged insensitive, unloving, selfish, or ambitious.

Only God knows these desires. In many cases He's the One who has placed them in our hearts. The longing to see our loved ones well, happy, and fulfilled. Knowing God and following Him completely. The longing to be freed of certain responsibilities because they are hard to bear.

When we find ourselves in circumstances not of our own making and opposite of what we expected from the realization of our desires and dreams, it's easy to turn away from God. Yet we're told to *delight* in Him—to take joy in the circumstances in which we find ourselves, to rejoice in every situation, to praise Him because He is good and faithful and loving.

Delight in the knowledge that He is proving Himself to you as you deal with that special-needs child or dependent parent or spouse. Delight in knowing that God's love never fails, His grace is always sufficient, and His presence is always near. He will grant us our deepest desires in ways we don't expect.

Father, remind me to focus on You—on Your
characteristics and attributes—as I walk the path You
have set before me. Help me to experience Your love and
grace, Your strength and wisdom, as I need them today.

Hope

*Why are you downcast, O my soul? Why so
disturbed within me? Put your hope in God,
for I will yet praise him, my Savior and my God.*
PSALM 42:5–6 NIV

If you've ever been depressed, you're not alone. Depression can be caused by circumstances, biology, environment, or a combination of all of those things. Research indicates that as many as 25 percent of Americans suffer from depression at some point in their lives.

We are blessed with scriptural accounts of godly people like David and Jeremiah who struggled with depression. These stories let us know that it's a normal human reaction to feel overcome by the difficulties of life.

While feeling this way is normal, it doesn't have to be the norm. As Christians, we have hope. Hope that our circumstances will not always be the way they are right now. Hope that no matter how dismal the world situation seems to be, God wins in the end. Hope that eternity is just on the other side.

Hope is like a little green shoot poking up through hard, cracked ground. When you're depressed, do what David and Jeremiah did— pour out your heart to God. Seek help from a trusted friend or godly counselor.

Look for hope. It's all around you, and it's yours for the taking.

*Father, even when I am depressed, You are still God. Help me to find
a ray of hope in the midst of dark circumstances. Amen.*

Fear-Free

You will not fear the terror of night,
nor the arrow that flies by day.
PSALM 91:5 NIV

Were you afraid of the dark when you were a little girl? It's hard to be comfortable when you can't see what's out there, right? Even as a big girl, the nighttime hours can still be a little scary. Seems like we're most vulnerable to fears and failures in the wee hours, when the darkness closes in around us.

So, how do you face the "terror of night" without fear? You have to grasp the reality that God is bigger and greater than anything that might evoke fear. He's bigger than financial struggles. He's bigger than job stress. He's even bigger than relational problems. Best of all, He can see in the dark. He knows what's out there and can deal with it. All it takes is one sentence from Him: *"Let there be light!"* and darkness dispels.

We serve an awesome and mighty God, One who longs to convince us He's mighty enough to save us, even when the darkness seeps in around us. So don't fear what you can't see. Or what you *can* see. Hand over that fear and watch God-ordained faith rise up in its place.

Father, I'm glad You can see in the dark. Sometimes I
face the unseen things of my life with fear gripping
my heart. I release that fear to You today.
Thank You for replacing it with godly courage.

My Thirsty Soul

O God, you are my God, earnestly I seek you;
my soul thirsts for you, my body longs for you,
in a dry and weary land where there is no water.
PSALM 63:1 NIV

Let's face it—life provides us little leisure time. Days slip away from us until we find ourselves falling exhausted into bed—often, without having spent any time with the Lord. But our connection with God through prayer and Bible study is an absolute necessity.

God doesn't expect us to spend three hours a day in intense prayer or devote an entire evening to an in-depth study of the Bible's original Hebrew and Greek words. But He does ask for a little of the time we have. If the only "alone moments" we can offer Him are during our drive time to work, He'll take them!

Finding quiet time with God is crucial for our spiritual, mental, even physical health. Let's think of our alone-time with Him as a period of refreshing for whatever strength, wisdom, or encouragement we'll need to succeed in the day before us.

The psalmist describes a "dry and weary land," ready to absorb an evening rain or morning dew. What a picture of our lives, eagerly awaiting our Lord's life-giving sustenance.

Lord, though I truly need You, I'm not always quick to
recognize that truth. Cause me to see that You alone meet
my deepest needs. Then shower me with Your living water
and refresh my spirit until my cup overflows.

Time Clocks

Is not the LORD your God with you?
and hath he not given you rest on every side?
1 CHRONICLES 22:18 KJV

The time clock is a wonderful invention. You clock in and (here is
the best part) you clock out! While we're "on the clock," we're aware
that our time is not our own. Whether cooking for a hungry throng of
customers, typing on a keyboard, or emptying trash, for a set time we
must do another's bidding. Then we go home, off the clock at last.

At home, there is no time clock. No way to "punch out" for the
day. Our duties seem endless: picking up dry cleaning, rushing to a
soccer game, folding the millionth load of laundry, trying to find an
interesting way to use hamburger *again,* reading to the kids, helping
with homework. . .Where's the time clock to put an end to this work?

God promises to give His people rest. The laundry will be there
tomorrow. We can occasionally live with cereal for dinner. The
vacuuming can wait for the weekend. Algebra will always be hard.

Slow down. Rest. Catch your breath. Allow God to renew you.
You have His permission to clock out for the day.

Father God, teach me how to slow down. There are
so many pressing needs, yet I know I must find a way
to clock out for my day. Enable me to rest in You.

Christ, My Identity

"The LORD your God is with you, he is mighty to save.
He will take great delight in you, he will quiet you
with his love, he will rejoice over you with singing."
ZEPHANIAH 3:17 NIV

As women, we love to love. We tend to trust easily. If we were married, we expected our husbands to look after our children and us, to admire and desire us as wives, always to be our protectors. Even if we've never been married, most of us have dreamed of such relationships.

But when our expectations fall short and we find ourselves parenting alone—whatever the reason—our spirits shatter into a million little pieces. Often, we lose our identity. Any self-esteem we may once have had evaporates along with our dreams.

But God Himself, the maker of all creation, the very One who hung the stars in space and calls them by name, looks at each one of us with love. In His eyes are delight and joy. Because the Father has created us in His own image, He knows every hurt we feel—and He will quiet us with His love. He rejoices that we are His daughters and He delights in us – not because of anything we do but simply because we are His.

Lord Jesus, though I sometimes feel alone and without
an identity, I trust that You are with me. I ask that You
will quiet my spirit with Your mighty peace and allow
me to know the depth of Your love for me.

Hurt by Others' Choices

God heard the boy crying. The angel of God called from
Heaven to Hagar, "What's wrong, Hagar? Don't be afraid.
God has heard the boy and knows the fix he's in."
GENESIS 21:17 MSG

A slave during early biblical times, Hagar had little say in her life decisions—others made them for her. Because of the infertility of her mistress, Sarah, Hagar became the concubine of Sarah's husband, Abraham, and gave birth to Ishmael.

At first, Hagar's hopes soared. Her son would become Abraham's heir, rich and powerful beyond her wildest dreams! However, the surprise appearance of Isaac, the late-life son of Sarah and Abraham, destroyed Hagar's fantasies of a wonderful future. Sarah wanted Hagar and Ishmael out of their lives. Abraham, though upset, loaded Hagar with water and food and told her to take Ishmael into the unforgiving desert.

When their water supply failed, Hagar laid her dehydrated son under a bush and walked away crying because she could not bear to watch Ishmael die. But God showed Hagar a well of water. Quickly she gave her child a drink. Both survived, and "God was on the boy's side as he grew up" (Genesis 21:20 MSG).

God is also on our side when we suffer because of others' choices. Even when we have lost hope, God's plan provides a way for us and those we love.

Heavenly Father, when my world seems out of control,
please help me love and trust You—even in the deserts of life.

Commitment Challenges at Church

*Remember me for this, my God, and do not blot out what I have so
faithfully done for the house of my God and its services.*
NEHEMIAH 13:14 NIV

Have you ever sacrificed precious "leisure" hours to serve on a church
committee, count offerings, or weed church flowerbeds? Despite
your work schedule and double duty at home, you agree to co-teach
Bible school—only to receive a phone call the night before from your
partner. She has decided to go on vacation instead! Now, surrounded
by hyper kindergarteners, you wonder what you did to deserve this.

Nehemiah felt the same way. A governor during Old Testament
times, he spearheaded the rebuilding of Jerusalem's broken walls,
then spent years encouraging his countrymen to worship Yahweh.
He organized priests and Levites and served as a spiritual lay leader.
He managed the practical affairs of the temple, including schedules,
payments, and distributions. Nehemiah fought enemies, settled
internal squabbles and—and—*and!* His days never seemed long
enough. He grew discouraged when trusted fellow workers in God's
house placed their priorities elsewhere. Between crises, Nehemiah
took a deep breath and prayed the above prayer.

More than twenty-five hundred years later, God tells the story of
Nehemiah's perseverance in the Bible. Like you, Nehemiah may not
have seen his reward as soon as he wanted. But now he is enjoying it
forever.

So will you.

*Lord Jesus, when I feel tired and unappreciated as
I serve others, let Your applause be enough for me.*

Clap Your Hands!

Clap your hands, all you nations; shout to God with cries of joy.
How awesome is the Lord Most High, the great King over all the
earth!. . . God has ascended amid shouts of joy, the Lord amid
the sounding of trumpets. Sing praises to God, sing praises;
sing praises to our King, sing praises.
PSALM 47:1–2, 5–6 NIV

In 1931, German theologian Dietrich Bonhoeffer spent a year at
a seminary in New York City. While there, he was introduced to
a church in Harlem. Astounded, then delighted, at the emotion
expressed in worship, he returned to Germany with recordings of
gospel music tucked in his suitcase. Bonhoeffer knew that the worship
he observed was authentic and pleasing to God.

King David would have loved gospel music! Many of the psalms
were meant to be sung loudly and joyfully. David appointed four
thousand professional musicians—playing cymbals, trumpets, rams'
horns, tambourines, harps, and lyres—for temple worship. We can
imagine they would have rocked the roofs off of our modern-day
church services!

Dancing was a part of worship in David's day, too. David angered
his wife, Michal, with his spontaneous dance in the street, as the Ark
of the Covenant was returned to Jerusalem (1 Chronicles 15:29). The
world, in David's viewpoint, couldn't contain the delight that God
inspires. Neither could he!

How often do we worship God with our whole heart? Do we ever
burst forth in a song of praise? Do we clap our hands, and lif them up
high? Probably not often enough. Let's try that today!

O Lord, great is Your name and worthy of praise!

God's Mirror

Charm is deceptive, and beauty does not last;
but a woman who fears the LORD will be greatly praised.
PROVERBS 31:30 NLT

A woman admitted that she spent much of her attention on how she looked and who was looking at her. She even watched her reflection in store windows to see how passersby reacted as she walked down the street.

Her overwhelming focus on appearance was driven by a fear of being alone. The woman was afraid that if she wasn't outwardly attractive, she might never find a husband. But she misunderstood what really determined her value.

Proverbs 31:30 shares a very important truth about charm and beauty: They fade. If a woman marries primarily on the basis of physical beauty, the couple will eventually be left wanting. Much more fulfilling to a marriage is the woman's spiritual focus.

May our minds be focused on the qualities that last: honesty, faithfulness, loyalty, and spiritual growth. Mr. Right will define beauty as God does—and will value good personal qualities above physical perfection.

Today, gaze into the mirror of scripture. Allow your true beauty to be that inner beauty of soul—a reflection of Christ—that never fades.

Father, thank You for the beauty that You reflect from
my soul. Help me to place less importance on my outward appearance
and more value on the inner qualities
that You are developing in me.

Ideal Place

*For consider your calling brethren, that there were not many
wise according to the flesh, not many mighty, not many noble;
but God has chosen the foolish things of the world.*
1 Corinthians 1:26–27 nasb

Once my life is running smoothly. . .
 If I didn't have toddlers under foot. . .
 As soon as I get this anger problem under control. . .
 When I get enough money. . .
 As soon as I (fill in the blank). . .then I can be used by God.
We are *where* we are, *when* we are, because our Father chose us
for such a time as this. Our steps are ordered by Him. Whether He
has called us to teach a Sunday school class, pray with other moms,
lead a Bible study, or sing in the choir—we need not wait for the ideal
time and place to serve Him. The only "ideal" is where you are right
now.

God delights in using His people—right in the middle of all that
appears crazy and wrong and hopeless. *Now* is the time to serve God,
not next week or next year or when things get better. He wants our
cheerful, obedient service right in the midst of—even in spite of—our
difficult circumstances.

> *Father, help me see that there is no "ideal" place
> or circumstance to serve You. You can, and will,
> use me right where I am. Thank You that I do not
> have to have it all together to be used by You.*

God in the Details

*"When we heard of it, our hearts melted and everyone's
courage failed because of you, for the LORD your God is
God in heaven above and on the earth below."*
JOSHUA 2:11 NIV

The people of Jericho had reason to be worried. They had seen
evidence of God's strength and support of His children   and knew
that Joshua planned to conquer Canaan. As residents of the key
military fortress in the land, they understood that Joshua would soon
be at their gates.

Yet only Rahab seemed to recognize the right course of action: to
embrace the Lord and open her home to Joshua's agents. In return,
they made sure she and her family survived the attack. Because of her
courage and faith, Rahab became an ancestor of Jesus.

Sometimes, when our own lives seem to be under siege from
the demands of work, bills, and other worries, finding the work of
God amid the strife can be difficult. Even though we acknowledge
His power, we may overlook the gentle touches, the small ways in
which He makes every day a little easier. Just as the Lord cares for
the tiniest bird (Matthew 10:29–31), so He seeks to be a part of every
detail in your life. Look for Him there.

*Father God, I know You are by my side every day, good or bad,
and that You love and care for me. Help me to see Your
work in my life and in the lives of those around me.*

Budget Breaker

Then the LORD said to Moses, "Behold, I will rain bread from heaven for you; and the people shall go out and gather a day's portion every day, that I may test them, whether or not they will walk in My instruction."
EXODUS 16:4 NASB

The month lasted longer than the paycheck. The grocery bill exceeded the budget. Childcare expenses surpassed the rent. It's not an easy road to travel, yet one that many of us walk.

Isn't it interesting that we can trust God for eternal life, yet find it harder to trust Him for help with the mortgage?

In the Old Testament, God told the wandering Israelites He would feed them "manna from heaven," but with one caveat: He would only allow them to gather enough food for one day. No storing food away for the dreaded "what if's" of tomorrow. They would simply have to trust their God to faithfully supply their needs.

They didn't always past the "trust test"—and neither do we. But thankfully, God is faithful in spite of us! He will meet our needs when we come to Him in simple trust. Then we can bask in His faithfulness.

Father, Your Word promises to supply all my needs.
I trust You in spite of the challenges I see. You are ever faithful.
Thank You!

Perfect Prayers

"This, then, is how you should pray: . . ."
MATTHEW 6:9 NIV

How many messages have you heard on prayer? Have you ever come away thinking, *Did you hear how eloquently they prayed? How spiritual they sounded? No wonder God answers their prayers!*

Sometimes we take the straightforward and uncomplicated idea of prayer—the simple give and take of talking with God—and turn it into something hard. How many times have we made it a mere religious exercise, performed best by the "holy elite," rather than what it really is—conversation with God our Father.

Just pour out your heart to God. Share how your day went. Tell Him your dreams. Ask Him to search you and reveal areas of compromise. Thank Him for your lunch. Plead for your kids' well-being. Complain about your car. . . . Just talk with Him. Don't worry how impressive (or unimpressive!) you sound.

Talk with God while doing dishes, driving the car, folding laundry, eating lunch, or kneeling by your bed. Whenever, wherever, whatever—tell Him. He cares!

Don't allow this day to slip away without talking to your Father. No perfection required.

*Father God, what a privilege it is to unburden
my heart to You. Teach me the beauty and
simplicity of simply sharing my day with You.*

Smiles Bring Joy

A cheerful look brings joy to the heart,
and good news gives health to the bones.
PROVERBS 15:30 NIV

The teenage girl nervously walked backstage. It was her turn next. She had practiced for hours. This song was perfect her teacher had said. But the butterflies in her stomach were telling a different story. Fear began to grip her throat. She couldn't breathe. It was then that she saw her mother sitting in the front row. There she was, eyes sparkling, smiling that goofy smile and proudly saying, "My daughter is next! She is so talented!" The young girl took a deep breath and closed her eyes. The fear melted and confidence took over. *I can do this,* she thought as she boldly walked on stage.

Smiles can say so many things in a quiet, gentle form. They can give comfort and support and bring joy and strength to someone who is weary. Courage and confidence are given by the love that smiles portray. They can simply remind a person that someone really does care. And more often than not, a smile is immediately returned to the giver.

Joy is contagious; spread it around. Smile at someone today. Go ahead and chuckle at that joke. Laugh with someone. Not only will you be blessing another, but will be blessed yourself.

Dear Lord, fill me with Your joy today that I may
bless others with my smile and laughter and
portray Your love to those around me. Amen.

Jesus' Wristwatch

Be very careful, then, how you live—
not as unwise but as wise, making the most
of every opportunity, because the days are evil.
EPHESIANS 5:15–16 NIV

Time is money, they say. Society preaches the value of making good use of our time—and the expense of wasting it.

In the Bible, Ephesians 5 speaks of using every opportunity wisely. But even though scripture teaches the value of time, Jesus never wore a watch. He didn't view His opportunities within the bounds of earthly time.

Have you ever ended a day with guilt and regret over the growing black hole of work yet to be completed? Or do you feel peace at the end of your day, having walked in the presence of the Lord?

Satan wants to consume you with endless lists of meaningless tasks. Fight back! Concern yourself less with the items you can cross off your to-do list, and more with those things the Lord would have you spend your time and energy on. You can strive to be a great multitasker or workhorse—but it's more important and fulfilling to be an efficient laborer for the Lord.

Father, help me to see where You are working and join
You there. Let me place my list of tasks aside as I seek
Your will for me today. Then give me the ability to show
myself grace over the things I do not get done.

Two Hopeless Sisters

Lot and his two daughters left Zoar and settled in the mountains,
for he was afraid to stay in Zoar. He and his two daughters lived
in a cave. One day the older daughter said to the younger,
"Our father is old, and there is no man around here to lie with us,
as is the custom all over the earth."
GENESIS 19:31 NIV

Those poor sisters. These girls had been raised in Sodom, a Canaanite city so corrupt that God sent angels to destroy it. Lot fled with his daughters and lived in a cave.

In that primitive culture, hope for a secure future rested entirely on a son's shoulders. Lot's daughters were out of luck. There were no bachelors hanging around the caves. Desperate, hopeless, and faithless, the daughters came up with an idea: get their father drunk, then sleep with him to conceive a child.

It's hard to feel anything but disgust for those two sisters. But how many times have we scrambled to find a man- (or woman-) made answer to our problems? How many times have we turned to God as an afterthought?

The Lord is faithful even when we are not. Scripture tells us that the older daughter had a son named Moab, father of the Moabites. Five hundred years later, a Moabite baby grew up to become Ruth, grandmother of Israel's great King David.

Heavenly Father, when will I learn to turn to You
to solve my problems? When I go my own way,
it ends in disaster. Thank You that even my poor
choices are not beyond Your ability to redeem.

One Thing Is Needed

"Martha, Martha," the Lord answered, *"you are worried and upset about many things, but only one thing is needed."*
LUKE 10:41–42 NIV

We are each given twenty-four hours in a day. Einstein and Edison were given no more than Joseph and Jeremiah of the Old Testament. The president and the paratrooper are all given an equal share. Even Mother Teresa and plain ol' moms are peers when it comes to time.

Time—we can't buy it, save it, or get a greater share no matter what we do. Its value is beyond measure. So we should learn to use it carefully. Do we tackle the laundry now or help the kids read *If You Give a Mouse a Cookie* one more time? Do we stay up late, cleaning the living room, or slip into bed early, knowing we need the rest? Do we fuss over our hair and makeup or find a moment to kneel before our Father?

Since God has blessed each of us with twenty-four hours, let's seek His direction on how to spend this invaluable commodity wisely giving more to people than things, spending more time on relationships than the rat race. In Luke, our Lord reminded dear, dogged, drained Martha that only one thing is needed—Him.

*Father God, oftentimes, I get caught up in the minutia of life
The piled laundry can appear more important than the precious
little ones You've given me. Help me to use my time wisely.
Open my eyes to see what is truly important.*

Ladies in Waiting

I will wait for the LORD. . . .
I will put my trust in him.
ISAIAH 8:17 NIV

Modern humans aren't good at waiting. In our fast-paced society, if you can't keep up, you'd better get out of the way. We have fast food, speed dialing, and jam-packed schedules that are impossible to keep. Instant gratification is the name of the game—and that attitude often affects us.

The Lord Jesus Christ doesn't care about instant gratification. Our right-now attitudes don't move Him. Maybe He finds the saying, "Give me patience, Lord, *right now*," humorous—but He rarely answers that particular prayer.

Do we want joy without accepting heartache? Peace without living through the stress? Patience without facing demands? God sees things differently. He's giving us the opportunity to learn through these delays, irritations, and struggles. What a wise God He is!

We especially need to learn the art of waiting on God. He will come through every time—but in *His* time, not ours. The wait may be hours or days, or it could be years. But God is always faithful to provide for us. It is when we learn to wait on Him that we will find joy, peace, and patience through the struggle.

Father, You know what I need, so I will wait.
Help me be patient, knowing that You control my
situation and that all good things come in Your time.

Blessing, Not Blasting

Bless the Lord, O my soul: and all
that is within me, bless his holy name.
PSALM 103:1 KJV

Many people in our country claim they do not believe in God; others shrug and say they don't know if He exists. But whenever a copier jams at work, or a dish is dropped in a restaurant, or a flight is delayed, atheists and agnostics include God in the midst of their misery. They yell His name as if *He* messed up on the job—even though they believe He doesn't officially exist.

We, as Christians, are called to invest all our emotional energy in blessing God, rather than blasting Him. When others demean their day as "god-awful," we can choose to experience a "God-wonderful" day. When others swear at traffic, we can sing praises along with a CD or radio. With His help—because no one can praise God without tapping into the power of His Spirit—we can develop spiritual radar that detects daily God-moments worthy of applause: rainbows and roses, clean water to drink, and belly laughs with our kids.

Every day God stacks His gifts around us as if it were Christmas. Like children, we can't give Him much. But we can offer all we are to bless His holy name. And that's the present He loves most.

Lord, each day I encounter thousands of opportunities
to bless You, the Lord of the universe. Help me
seize the day and praise You whenever I can!

Three Days without a Miracle

So the people grumbled against Moses,
saying "What are we to drink?"
Exodus 15:24 NIV

The Israelites were thirsty. Really, really thirsty. The kind of thirsty where they couldn't think of anything *but* water. Their tongues felt thick and their eyes burned under the relentless glare of the hot sun.

They had been wandering in the desert for three days without water and they were about to snap. Could anyone blame them? Three million people, wandering in the desert without a road map, lacking such basic supplies as food and water. They did what people do when under stress. They blamed their leader. "Moses!" they complained. "It's all your fault!"

In reality, the Israelites had gone three days without a miracle. A few days prior, the Lord had parted the Red Sea, allowing the Israelites to escape, then closed it up against to drown the pursuing Egyptian army. Just three days ago! How had they forgotten God's just-in-time provision?

Moses didn't forget. His first response was to turn to God. "Then Moses cried out to the LORD, and the LORD showed him a piece of wood. He threw it into the water, and the water became sweet" (Exodus 15:25 NIV).

God held the answer to the Israelites' basic needs. He responded to Moses' prayer immediately, as if He had just been waiting.

What if we turned to God immediately with our basic needs, instead of waiting until the thirst set in? What if we remembered His faithfulness before, or better still, instead of, panicking? Most likely, we would have our sweet water sooner.

Lord, thank You for supplying my every need.

Anxieties

Cast all your anxiety on him
because he cares for you.
1 PETER 5:7 NIV

Because He cares for you. Not because you have to. Not because it's the "right" thing to do. Not because it's what you're supposed to do. No. Read it again. . . Because He cares for you. That's right, He cares for you!

Our Father isn't standing there with His hand on His hip, saying, "All right, spit it out, I don't have all day," or worse. . .holding His hands to His ears, saying, "Enough! You have way too many problems."

The Amplified Bible puts it this way: "Casting the whole of your care [all your anxieties, all your worries, all your concerns, once and for all] on Him, for He cares for you affectionately and cares about you watchfully" (1 Peter 5:7).

Because He cares for you. How humbling and emotionally overwhelming it is to realize that our Lord and God, Jesus Christ, actually wants us to unburden our hearts to Him. Not just because He knows that's what's best for us but simply because He cares. To know He isn't just informing us of one more requirement we have to meet. No. He asks each one of us to cast all our cares and anxieties on Him because He cares for us.

Father, I am overjoyed at Your concern for me.
Thank You! Please teach me to cast my cares
into Your arms. . .and leave them there.

The Three R's

*Whoever gives heed to instruction prospers,
and blessed is the one who trusts in the LORD.*
PROVERBS 16:20 NIV

Not long ago, educators emphasized the three R's: reading, 'riting and 'rithmetic. We believed that if we could succeed at higher learning, we would obtain good work and thus prosperity. Education was perceived as the solution to all social ills.

The Bible suggests a different path to prosperity: Heed God's Word. The dictionary defines the verb *heed* as "to give consideration or attention to." In other words, we mind what God says.

There are three ways we can heed God's Word.

Read it. The options for systematic Bible reading vary more than ever before. We can choose among a plethora of versions and even among audio renditions. Most Bibles contain a plan for daily reading. Whatever we choose, we must read the Word in order to heed it.

Remember it. Review the verses we learned as children. Tape favorite verses to our mirrors, on our computers, in our cars. We heed the Word by meditating on it and memorizing it.

Respect it. We heed the Word when we obey it. God did not give us a list of suggestions but rather commands for daily living.

These three R's are the path to prosperity.

*Lord, in Your Word I find all that I need for peace
and prosperity. Teach me the discipline of time
spent in the Bible and then transform me through it.*

More Than Enough

Let us not become weary in doing good, for at the
proper time we will reap a harvest if we do not give up.
GALATIANS 6:9 NIV

How often do we become impatient and give up? We stand in line
at the coffee shop and find ourselves behind an indecisive person.
Frustrated, we give up—but before we get to our car, that person—
coffee cup in hand—walks past. If we'd only waited another minute,
we, too, could be sipping a steaming caramel latte.

Or maybe we have a dream that we can't seem to make a
reality—and rather than trying "just one more time," we give up. A
piece of who we are drifts away like a leaf on the sea.

The Word of God encourages us to keep going, to press on, to
fight off weariness and never give up. Jesus Christ has a harvest for
each of us, and He eagerly anticipates blessing us with it—but we
have to trust Him and refuse to give in to weariness.

We can only imagine what that harvest might be, because
we know that God is the God of "immeasurably more than all we
ask or imagine" (Ephesians 3:20 NIV). We can be recipients of His
"immeasurably more" if we press on in the strength He provides.

When you're tired, keep going—and remember that, in His
perfect timing, you will reap an unimaginable harvest.

Father, You know that I'm tired and weary in this
uphill struggle. Fill me with Your strength so I can
carry on. I long to reap the harvest You have for me.

This House Is Too Crowded

"Agreed," she replied. "Let it be as you say."
JOSHUA 2:21 NIV

Rahab and her family were crowded inside her tiny house situated on the walls of Jericho. They were waiting for those two Israeli spies to return with their army.

The spies had promised Rahab they would keep her safe from the coming siege. That's all she had to rely on—the word of spies. But Rahab had come to believe that the Israelites' God was the true God. She was willing to stake her life, as well as the life of her crowded household, on that belief.

Still, she faced an indeterminate wait—probably with irritable family members who doubted her story. On the day the spies had departed, Rahab had tied that scarlet cord outside her window, to tip them off to her house. Had the cord grown faded, like the patience of her family?

Where were the Israelites? What was taking them so long? Rahab could have no idea what was happening in the camp of the Israelites where, in obedience to God, Joshua had ordered all the men to be circumcised, in a day without anesthetics. Huge numbers of men, each one requiring time to heal!

Rahab didn't know any of that, but she still remained steadfast. Ultimately, she did see God act—saving herself and her family.

There are times when all we have to rely on is the Word of God. When that happens, remember Rahab's steadfastness! We can have confidence that His promises will come true: Let it be as He says.

Lord, may my faith in Your Word benefit my family as
Rahab's faith in the spies' word helped hers. Help
me to remain steadfast regarding Your promises.

Wise Guys

> *Who is wise, and he shall understand these things? prudent,
> and he shall know them? for the ways of the LORD are right, and the
> just shall walk in them: but the transgressors shall fall therein.*
> HOSEA 14:9 KJV

Have we read many headlines that include the words *wisdom* and
prudence? Few "Ten Ways to Succeed" lists feature them—especially
if we're talking about God's wisdom and prudence as defined in the
Bible.

"Don't be so narrow-minded!" Coworkers laugh when we refuse
to compromise Christian standards of honesty and diligence.

"The Bible? You've got to be kidding!" Friends roll their eyes.
"It's about a zillion years old! What's the Bible got to do with today?"
They pat us on the shoulder. "You need some fun in your life. Do
what works for you."

God loves us, and He cares about our individual needs—and our
fun! But His plan often stretches far beyond "what works" for each
of us. If we choose to believe God and walk in His ways, He helps us
deal with our weakness as we accept the scary challenges looming
before us. God makes safe paths for our feet. But those who rebel
against God stumble over His truth. The Word that heals us hurts
unbelievers—and no one can offer them true relief until they "get
wise" by turning back to God.

> *Father, even when I don't understand Your wisdom,
> help me believe Your loving heart. I pray for my friends
> who don't know You that they, too, may walk in safety.*

Sleep on It

It is of the LORD's mercies that we are not consumed,
because his compassions fail not. They are new
every morning: great is thy faithfulness.
LAMENTATIONS 3:22–23 KJV

"Sleep on it." Researchers have found that to be sound advice. They believe that sleep helps people sort through facts, thoughts, and memories, providing a clearer look at the big picture upon waking. Sleep also separates reality from emotions like fear and worry, which can cloud our thinking and interfere with rational decision-making. Scientifically speaking, sleep is good medicine.

For Christians, the biological effects of sleep are outweighed by the spiritual benefits of the new day God gives us. At the end of an exhausting day, after the worries and the pressures of life have piled high, we may lay down, feeling as though we can't take another moment of stress. But God's Word tells us that His great mercy will keep our worries and problems from consuming us.

Through the never-ending compassion of God, His faithfulness is revealed afresh each morning. We can rise with renewed vigor. We can eagerly anticipate the new day, leaving behind the concerns of yesterday.

Heavenly Father, thank You for a giving me a new measure of Your
mercy and compassion each day so that my concerns don't consume
me. I rest in You and I lay my burdens at Your feet.

Follow the Leader

I will instruct you and teach you in the way
you should go; I will guide you with My eye.
PSALM 32:8 NKJV

As children, most of us played the schoolyard game of "Follow the Leader." We ran around laughing, as others followed us wherever we went—down a sliding board, under a culvert, or maybe through poison ivy. It was fun to have control for awhile.

As grown women, the game isn't quite as enjoyable. It goes along well for awhile, but there's something exhausting about constantly being in charge. Of always being the go-to person, whether in our jobs or our homes. On occasion, it feels good to assign the role of leader to someone else.

In Psalm 32, God reminds us that He desires to be the real leader in our lives. He promises to instruct, teach, and guide us—always keeping His eye on us.

He doesn't casually toss out orders with His head buried in heavenly paperwork. God's eye is always on us as He guides us through both the mundane and major decisions of life.

Let's play "Follow the Leader" with God as our guide.

Father God, how I long to lay down the role of leader.
I am under daily pressure to make difficult decisions.
Thank You for the assurance that You are keeping an eye
on me and are guiding me through this maze of life.

Wimps for Jesus?

Wherefore lift up the hands which hang down, and the feeble knees; and make straight paths for your feet, lest that which is lame be turned out of the way; but let it rather be healed.
HEBREWS 12:12–13 KJV

God's discipline sometimes leaves us feeling limp—and not too bright.

"How could I do such a thing? Why didn't I stop to think, read the Bible, and pray about the situation?"

All Christians live through these humbling experiences, because we all make mistakes—sometimes big ones. Washed up and wiped out, we wonder why Jesus bothers with us. We want to give up.

Satan would like nothing better. "What's the use?" he whispers. "You've embarrassed yourself and God, and there's no way you will ever hold up your head again." We let our Bibles gather dust and stop going to church. When we see other Christians around town, we hide! We also find ourselves spending time and energy in paths that aggravate our pain rather than heal it.

As always, God presents better solutions for our problems. He disciplines us for the same reasons we correct our children: out of love. Ultimately, we want our kids to lead healthy, productive lives. How can we think God wants any less for us?

Lord Jesus, You gave Your life that I might be healed of my sin and weakness. Please help me to obey You, trusting that You know what You're doing in my life.

From Bitterness to Freedom

*Why do you say, "The Lord does not see what happens
to me; he does not care if I am treated fairly?"*
ISAIAH 40:27 NCV

Bitterness. . .even the sound of that word, when spoken aloud,
conveys unpleasantness. And we as single mothers are particularly
prone to this toxic form of resentment.

Though it's not always the case, the circumstances that brought
us to our single parent status often create a deep root of bitterness
in us. Perhaps we faced betrayal, deception, or broken promises.
Financial struggles, the emotional sorrow of loneliness, losing hope
over what might have been—so many things can lead to bitterness in
our lives.

We know bitterness is wrong, and our friends tell us to let go. But
it's not always that easy. Especially because, well. . .it can feel good to
be the injured party. For many people, there's a strange satisfaction in
being the "victim."

Bitterness, whether conscious or unconscious, is clearly not
a biblical feeling. It eats at us emotionally, spiritually, and even
physically. So what should we do?

Tell God how badly you hurt—then ask Him for the capacity
to forgive. Allow God to be your vindicator. Place all of your
mistreatment into His hands, because He cares. And He'll work things
out in the end.

*Father, I admit I've been bitter at times. Enable me
to forgive when I need to. I know that will set me free.*

The Gift of Receiving

"In everything I did, I showed you that by this kind of hard work we must help the weak, remembering the words the Lord Jesus himself said: 'It is more blessed to give than to receive.' "
ACTS 20:35 NIV

You probably already know that, like Jesus said, it is better to give to others than to receive for yourself. But what if everyone gave and no one received? That would be impossible, actually. In order for some to give, others have to receive. God designed it perfectly so that the body of Christ would work together and help each other.

Have you ever turned down help of any kind—tangible goods like money or groceries, or intangible things like babysitting or wise counsel—out of pride? Are you trying to keep a stiff upper lip to show the world how strong you are? Maybe you are fully capable of succeeding with no outside help. But in doing so, you might rob others of the joy of giving.

Next time someone offers help, consider graciously accepting the extended hand. By your willingness to receive, others might enjoy the blessings of giving.

Lord, thank You for the times that You have sent help my way. Please give me the wisdom and the grace to know when to accept help from others—and even the courage to ask for it when I need it.

Waiting

Blessed are all who wait for him!
ISAIAH 30:18 NIV

Some studies indicate we spend a total of *three years* of our lives just waiting!

That may seem hard to believe. But consider a typical day, with a few minutes stopped at traffic signals, a half hour in the doctor's waiting room, more time yet in a bottlenecked check-out line at the grocery store.

Some of us can handle that waiting through a natural patience. Others? Forget it.

Yet waiting is an inevitable part of everyone's life. And it's a necessary part, too. We wait nine months for a baby's birth. We wait for wounds to heal. We wait for our children to mature. And we wait for God to fulfill His promises.

Waiting for God to act is a familiar theme in scripture. Abraham and Sarah waited for a baby until a birth became humanly impossible. But it wasn't impossible to God. Joseph languished, unjustly accused, in Pharaoh's prison, while God ordained a far-reaching drought that would force Joseph's family to Egypt for survival. David spent years hiding from King Saul, but he matured into a wise and capable warrior during that time.

As frustrating as waiting can be, God is always at work on our behalf. Waiting time isn't wasted time. Whatever we might be waiting for—the salvation of our friends, provision for a physical need, a new job—we can wait with expectancy, trusting in God's timing.

By Your grace, Lord, help me to do the work You've called me to do and wait patiently for the good results You promise.

I've Fallen and I Can't Get Up

The godly may trip seven times,
but they will get up again.
PROVERBS 24:16 NLT

Years ago, a famous television commercial depicted an elderly women who had fallen, but, try as she might, she just couldn't get back up. Thankfully, she wore a device that connected her to an outside source of help. All she had to do was push the button! The dear grandma was just one click away from rescue.

In our lives, too, there are times when we fall down—not physically, but emotionally, spiritually, and relationally. We fall in our attempts to parent, we fall in our struggle with particular temptations. We may fall as we try to climb the ladder of success or in our effort to lead a consistently godly life.

But in whatever area we wrestle, however many times we fall, our heavenly Father never gives up on us. He never leaves us to ourselves, to stagger to our feet alone. God is always present with us, encouraging us to keep trying—regardless of past failures—picking us up, dusting us off, and setting us on our way again.

He is better than any button we could ever push!

Heavenly Father, it's such a comfort to know
You will never leave me or forsake me. You are
closer than the clothes I wear. I love You, Lord.

How Do I Love Thee?

This is what real love is: It is not our love for God; it is God's love for us. He sent his Son to die in our place to take away our sins.
1 JOHN 4:10 NCV

If the word *love* were banned from popular music, radio stations and songwriters would go out of business. Even the Internet would shrink without this word, so key to human existence. All around the world, people search for someone to care. They chat with strangers, post videos, pay for profiles—anything to find the real love they crave.

Few prove successful—because we human beings are hard to love! Even our charity often wears a disguise. We give so we will receive attention, prestige, or assurance that other people will respect us. Some of us even think our little five-and-dime "love" will obtain a place for us in heaven, as if God were a headwaiter to be bribed.

The Bible tells us He does not *need* our love. He *is* love. God the Father, God the Son, and God the Spirit love each other in perfect eternal unity and joy. If God had done the logical thing, He would have wiped out us troublesome humans and created a new race, one that would worship Him without question.

But He would rather die than do that.

Oh, Lord, when I presume on Your love, please forgive me. Open my eyes to Your magnificent generosity so I can worship with my whole heart, in a way that pleases You.

One Chapter

"In the future, when your children ask you, 'What do these stones mean?' tell them that the flow of the Jordan was cut off before the ark of the covenant of the LORD. . . . These stones are to be a memorial to the people of Israel forever."
JOSHUA 4:6–7 NIV

Faith boils down to a willingness to trust God without knowing the end of the story. It means we trust the promises of God even though we don't know how He's going to work them out.

Centuries ago, Joshua faced that very issue of trusting God without knowing the outcome. God told him to march the Israelite soldiers around the city of Jericho in complete silence, once a day for six days. On the seventh day, they were to march around the city seven times. Then the priests were to blow their rams' horns and the soldiers to shout.

That's all the information Joshua had to conquer Jericho. But that's not the only chapter in this story. Joshua had long history with God's interventions. He had seen God part the Red Sea for the wandering Israelites, and had just witnessed another watery miracle as the Israelites walked through the Jordan River to reach Jericho. Joshua knew, by experience, that God was trustworthy.

When his army did what God had instructed, Joshua saw Jericho's walls come tumblin' down.

It's easy to focus on a single chapter in our story, and to forget God's many provisions. But the Lord wants us to keep the big picture in mind, remembering His answered prayers.

Is it worth starting a journal, like Joshua's stone monument, that will remind you of God's trustworthiness?

Lord, Your compassion has never failed me. Thank You.

Microwave Faith?

*And so after waiting patiently,
Abraham received what was promised.*
HEBREWS 6:15 NIV

Pop a little bag into the microwave, and in two minutes you have hot, delicious popcorn. Unfortunately, faith doesn't always work the same way.

Imagine what Abraham wondered nine months after his conversation with God. He had been promised a son. Abraham believed God. His faith was credited to him as righteousness (Genesis 15:6). Nine months later, he was still waiting. Even nine years later, there was no sign of the promised child. Each passing day brought an opportunity for doubt. But Abraham "*considered him faithful who had made the promise*" (Hebrews 11:11 NIV). Abraham looked past the facts. He was not swayed by the circumstances. He simply believed God and many years later, received his son.

How many times have you given up on the promises of God because circumstances told you something different? It's not too late. Pick up your faith. Determine to see those promises come to pass.

Heavenly Father, I thank You that You are faithful. Your word does not return void. I ask You to forgive me for doubting You. I believe Your Word. I praise You and glorify You in advance for the promises You are bringing into my life.

Nobody's Fool

He who trusts in his own heart is a fool.
PROVERBS 28:26 NKJV

Ever heard one of these lines? "Follow your heart." "What's your heart telling you?" "Let your heart be your guide."

Today's world gives a clear message to look to our own hearts for direction. But are our hearts the best guide for making important life decisions? The Bible says our hearts are not to be trusted. In fact, God calls us *fools* when we trust our own hearts. Those are mighty strong words.

Think about it: we may so deeply desire a companion to share the joys and challenges of life that we allow our desperate feelings to lead us into hasty decisions—decisions we may later regret. Our hearts might persuade us to rationalize, "He'll be a good provider—he only needs help finding a job." Or worse, "He really *is* a Christian—he just doesn't like church."

Making choices based on heart leanings can lead us into a world of trouble, even danger. Though feelings are important, they should never be the sole basis of a choice we make.

Let's not be anyone's fool.

Heavenly Father, I am often tempted to allow my heart—rather than You through Your Word and Your people—to guide me. Teach me to trust You more than my own feelings.

Faith Eyes

*Now faith is being sure of what we hope
for and certain of what we do not see.*
HEBREWS 11:1 NIV

Think for a moment of things we can't see, but we know are there.

There's the wind, for one. Its effects are obvious, as golden grain sways to and fro or fall leaves blow into the sky. And there's gravity, which pulls our kids' cups—full of red Kool-Aid, usually—right to the floor.

It's the same with faith, as we simply believe in what do not see. God *says* He is faithful, and so His faithfulness exists. He gives us the signs of His unseen presence, and its effects surround us.

We read how the Israelites walked to the sea and, at Moses' command, the sea parted. They could have been killed—by the pursuing Egyptians or by the sea itself—but God made a safe way of escape for them.

What signs surround you, showing your God is real? Perhaps someone blessed you with money to pay a bill or purchase school supplies. Maybe your "guardian angel" caught your attention and helped you avoid a serious accident.

Those are all signs of the faithfulness of God. Look around with your "faith eyes" and see the signs surrounding you.

*God, I struggle to have faith. Show me where You have
been faithful so my faith can be strengthened. I know You
are faithful, but today I'm asking for a special sign that
You have not forgotten me. Thank You, Father.*

Swing and Miss

And though she spoke to Joseph day after day,
he refused to go to bed with her or even be with her.
GENESIS 39:10 NIV

Hardships? Joseph knew them.

Sold into slavery by his brothers, he was carried off to a foreign land. By God's grace, Joseph gained an opportunity to manage the household of an Egyptian official named Potiphar. He was still a slave, but he had impressed Potiphar tremendously.

Joseph also impressed Potiphar's wife. She had a lusty eye for the "well built and handsome" young man (Genesis 39:6 NIV), and she was determined to seduce him.

Was God tempting Joseph? Had the Lord set Joseph up to test his mettle? Maybe God was giving Joseph a chance to practice with temptation so he'd be more skilled at saying no when bigger temptations came later. You know—like a baseball player taking batting practice, hitting some balls, but occasionally swinging and missing.

That may seem logical, but scripture tells us God would *never* entice us to sin or fail. Since doing so would be contrary to His nature, He allows situations into our lives only for good. He wants us to succeed, each and every time. He wants us to hit a home run, by faith, every time we come to bat.

Joseph did. He told the woman, "How then could I do such a wicked thing and sin against God?" he said (Genesis 39:9). Then he ran!

Let's learn from Joseph's example.

Lord, help me to see every circumstance in my life as ordained by You
for my welfare. Teach me to respond in faith, every time.

Fill 'er Up—with Joy

We continually ask God to fill you with the knowledge
of his will through all the wisdom and understanding that
the Spirit gives, so that you may live a life worthy of the
Lord and please him in every way: bearing fruit in every
good work, growing in the knowledge of God.
COLOSSIANS 1:9–11 NIV

We've all had days when we feel exhausted on every level, when we've drained our emotional gas tanks bone dry. As Paul prayed for the Christians of Colosse, we need a filling of God's strength so we can keep going—and rediscover *joy.*

But when can we find time to refill our tank in a life of constant work and worry? We don't have enough time for the rat race itself, let alone a pit stop. But if we don't refuel, we'll stall out—and be of no use to anyone.

That means we have to learn to make time for ourselves. We can explore things that give us a lift. Some things, like listening to a favorite CD as we drift off to sleep, take no extra time. Others, like a bubble bath, may require minor adjustments to our schedule. Maybe we'll want to spend time in the garden or call a friend. There are any number of ways to recharge our spiritual batteries.

Every week—perhaps every day—we must set aside time to refill our tanks. The joy of the Lord will be our reward.

Lord of joy, we confess that we are tempted to work
until we fall apart. We pray that You will show us
the things that will give us the strength to go on.

Tucking an Octopus into Bed

*"Do not worry about your life, what you will eat
or drink; or about your body, what you will wear. . . .
Who of you by worrying can add a single hour to his
life? . . . God clothes the grass of the field. . . .
will he not much more clothe you, O you of little faith?"*
MATTHEW 6:25, 27, 30 NIV

Who among us doesn't struggle with anxiety?

Compare worry with trying to tuck an octopus into bed. One tentacle or another keeps popping out from under the covers. If we're not worried about one child, it's the other. If we're not worried about our kids, it's our aging parents. Or the orthodontist's bill. Or the funny sound under the hood of the car.

In the Bible, Jesus spoke much about worry. In a nutshell, He told us not to! Jesus never dismissed the untidy realities of daily life—He knew those troubles firsthand, having spent years as a carpenter in Nazareth, probably living hand-to-mouth as He helped to support His family.

But Jesus also knew that, without looking to God in faith, worry would leave us stuck in a wrestling match with the octopus. Only when we look to God to provide for our needs are we released from worry's grip. "Seek first his kingdom and his righteousness, and all these things will be given to you as well," Jesus promised (Matthew 6:33).

At that point, worry no longer has a hold on us. It is replaced by a liberating confidence in the power of God.

*Lord, with Your help we can live our
daily life free from the grasp of worry.*

Answered Prayer

Delight yourself in the LORD; and He
will give you the desires of your heart.
PSALM 37:4 NASB

Sometimes our heartfelt prayers receive a "yes" from God. Sometimes, it's a "no." At other times, we get back only a "not yet."

Have you heard anyone quote today's scripture, saying that God will give us the desires of our hearts? Some believe the verse means that a Christian can ask for anything—health, money, possessions, you name it—and get exactly what she wants. But this passage actually teaches something much deeper.

Note the first part of Psalm 37:4: "Delight yourself in the Lord." A woman who truly delights herself in the Lord will naturally have the desires of her heart—because her heart desires only God and His will. Our Father takes no pleasure in the things of this world—things which will all wither and die. Neither should we.

So what pleases God? He loves it when witness for Him, live right, and raise our children in His Word. If those are things that we also truly desire, won't He grant us the "desires of our heart" and let us see people brought into the kingdom? Won't we have a life rich in spiritual growth and children who honor His name?

Lord, please help me see where my desires are not in
line with Your will—so that the things that I pursue
are only and always according to Your own desires.

But Everybody Does It!

*"I am GOD, your God. Don't live like the people of
Egypt where you used to live, and don't live like
the people of Canaan where I'm bringing you."*
LEVITICUS 18:2–3 MSG

As teenagers, we wanted to copy the popular kids. We wanted to
dress, act, even think like them. When our parents gave us the old
argument, "If everybody jumped off a building, would you jump off,
too?", we rolled our eyes.

God's people displayed the same immaturity. Wherever the
Israelites lived, they tended to adopt the morality—or lack thereof—of
the people around them. God may have used their disobedience and
subsequent forty-year punishment of wandering in the wilderness to
protect them from bad influences. He wanted His children to learn to
love Him and His ways. So God emphasized they were to forget the
gods of Egypt. When they would finally reach the Promised Land, He
wanted them to avoid the destructive ways of the Canaanites. But
Israel turned away from the Lord—and suffered the consequences.

God wants us to forget the ugliness and pain of the past. But His
plans for us do not include new evils that may tempt us. Will we roll
our eyes at Him like adolescents, crashing and burning once more? Or
will we accept the healthy boundaries He defines for us in love?

*Dear Jesus, You have healed me of my past and
filled my future with promise. Please give me the
maturity to welcome Your plans with open arms.*

Wish List

But they cried the more, saying, Have mercy on us,
O Lord, thou Son of David. And Jesus stood still, and called them,
and said, What will ye that I shall do unto you?
MATTHEW 20:31–32 KJV

The two blind men heard that Jesus was passing by. They called out a generic plea. "Have mercy on us!"

The man they addressed as Lord and Son of David stopped in His tracks. He responded with a simple question: "What do you want?"

Wasn't it obvious? Jesus knew their thoughts and what their hearts desired. But that wasn't enough. They had to verbalize their request: "We want our *sight.*" The one thing they could not receive without divine intervention. Jesus answered their prayer by opening their eyes—and they responded by following Him.

God wants us to bring specific needs to Him. Do you need a job? Tell Him how much salary you need, what kind of work you like to do, and where you want to commute. Do you need a new home? Tell Him exactly what you'd like.

God doesn't *need* us to tell Him our desires. He already knows them. But He delights in going above and beyond what we can ask for. He loves to demonstrate His lavish love. Even if He doesn't give us what we want, it's because He has something better in store.

God wants us to bring the wishes of our hearts to Him in prayer.

Heavenly Father, I thank You that You care about the smallest details of my life. Teach me the joy of specific prayer.

A Satisfied Tummy

"The wolf and the lamb will feed together, and the lion will eat straw like the ox, but dust will be the serpent's food. They will neither harm nor destroy on all my holy mountain," says the LORD.
ISAIAH 65:25 NIV

During the summer in Alaska, it's not uncommon to see grizzly bears at the mouths of rivers, feeding on salmon. The bears need all that protein to fatten up for a long winter's hibernation.

Grizzlies are solitary animals. Normally, they'd fight over food. But at the rivers' mouth, there are plenty of salmon for all. With the bears' tummies satisfied, they can live in peace with their neighbors.

What a glimpse into heaven! Our basic needs will be filled. We'll live in perfect peace. In the complete absence of sin, our doors won't need padlocks. Our windows can be left open. We won't hear an endless recital of problems and disasters on the evening news. We won't worry over our future, because it is secure!

Our lives can be stressful. But it's good to remember what we can look forward to as children of God: One day, we'll live in perfect safety and peace, satisfied to be in the presence of God. Our tummies will be full.

Thank You for the promise of heaven, my God.

What Is Your Request?

*And pray in the Spirit on all occasions with all
kinds of prayers and requests. With this in mind,
be alert and always keep on praying*
EPHESIANS 6:18 NIV

What burdens your heart today? Is there a trial that engulfs you or someone you love? Present your request to your heavenly Father with the assurance that He will act on your behalf—either by changing your circumstances or by changing you. He is always concerned for you.

But be patient. What we may view as a non-answer may simply be God saying, "Wait" or "I have something better for you." He *will* answer. Keep in mind that His ways are not our ways, nor are His thoughts our thoughts

God knows what He's doing, even when He allows trials in our lives. We might think that saving a loved one from difficulty is a great idea—but God, in His wisdom, may decide that would be keeping them (or us) from an opportunity for spiritual growth. Since we don't know all of God's plans, we must simply lay our requests before Him and trust Him to do what is right. He will never fail us!

*Father God, here are my needs. I lay them at Your feet,
walking away unburdened and assured that You
have it all under control. Thank You!*

Powerful Prayer

*The prayer of a righteous
man is powerful and effective.*
JAMES 5:16 NIV

"Never underestimate the power of prayer." We hear those words time and time again—especially when we find ourselves in obvious and desperate need. Often, well-meaning Christian friends or acquaintances, who don't really know what to say, come up with the handy, pat answers given to them in their last crisis. It's easy to quickly dismiss these common sayings as silly and unhelpful.

But whether we dismiss it or not, this particular saying is true. Prayer *is* unmistakably powerful and effective.

When it comes to the best interests of our own children, we mothers have a remarkable ability to seek God with all our hearts. This scripture promises us that God considers the prayers of a righteous man (or *mother*) powerful and effective.

While we may not see immediate results, there is no doubt that God pays attention to our prayers. They may not bring the results we thought we needed, but we can be confident that our prayers are bringing what God has planned for us.

*Lord, Your Word says You consider my prayer to be powerful and
effective. You know the burden I am carrying on my tired shoulders
and I give it to You to work out. Thank You, Father.*

An Hour Apart

And he cometh unto the disciples, and findeth them asleep, and saith unto Peter, What, could ye not watch with me one hour?
MATTHEW 26:40 KJV

An old hymn describes a "sweet hour of prayer," but let's be honest: Few of us have an hour to spend with the Lord every day. When those rare opportunities come, we don't even know how to handle them. But simply trying to fill an hour with spiritual things can be a real blessing.

Picture yourself sitting at a table, Bible in hand. You have an hour in front of you. What do you do?

First, choose a passage to study. Read through it at least five times, in different translations, if possible. Use a dictionary—both an English and a Bible dictionary—to check the meaning of any unusual words. Use a concordance to find other places where key words appear in the Bible. Check out the cross-references found in many Bibles.

Ask the five W's (*who, what, when, where,* and *why*) about the passage, and summarize what you've learned. List any lessons you can apply to your life.

Ask God to make you a doer of His word, not only a hearer. Then, as a final step, share what God has taught you with someone else.

Lord and Savior, show me when and how to carve out an hour with You. Make me hungry for that intimate time.

Defective Lions

*Daniel answered, "O king, live forever! My God sent
his angel and he shut the mouths of the lions. They
have not hurt me, because I was found innocent in his
sight. Nor have I done any wrong before you, O king."*
DANIEL 6:21–22 NIV

Daniel had lived most of his life as an exile in Babylon. Dragged from
Jerusalem, probably around age fifteen, he kept his faith intact and
uncompromised. Now, at about age eighty, Daniel had refused to
comply with a decree to pray only to King Darius. The punishment for
this rule-breaking? Daniel would be thrown into a den of hungry lions.
King Darius ordered a stone to be placed over the mouth of the den and
sealed it with his own signet ring so that "Daniel's situation might not
be changed" (Daniel 6:17 NIV). The old prophet's fate was sealed. Or
was it?

Maybe those lions weren't so hungry after all. Or maybe they
were defective. Vegetarians, perhaps?

Or maybe those who sought to harm Daniel underestimated
the power of the almighty God, sovereign over even the most basic
instincts of hungry, ferocious cats.

Somehow, even in a hostile foreign environment, Daniel never
compromised his beliefs or trust in God. And God never disappointed
Daniel.

Few of us will become lions' lunch for compromising our faith,
but we all face situations that are hostile to our trust in God. Daniel
reminds us how to respond: firmly, boldly, trusting that God will
never disappoint us.

*King and Lord of my home, I want Your holy
presence to shine in my family's life. Reign here today!*

Not My Will

*Jesus walked on a little way. Then he knelt down
on the ground and prayed, "Father, if it is possible,
don't let this happen to me! Father, you can do anything.
Don't make me suffer by having me drink from this cup.
But do what you want, and not what I want."*
MARK 14:35–36 CEV

It's easy to believe that our righteousness would determine whether
or not our prayers will be answered. Often, people think that
unanswered prayers signify unconfessed sin. But there once was great
and godly man who prayed with deep conviction without receiving
the answer He most desired. In case you hadn't already guessed it,
that Man was Jesus.

The Lord faced a cup of suffering from which He was to drink.
In His humanity, Jesus didn't want to endure the trial ahead, and He
asked His Father, if it were possible, to take the cup away. But we
all know how the prayer was answered. From His own Father, Jesus
received an answer of "not yet." God proceeded with His plan of
Jesus' arrest, trial, and crucifixion, before the suffering was ultimately
overcome by Jesus' resurrection.

In faith, we can boldly take our needs before God's throne of
grace. But, like our Lord Jesus Christ, we must delight ourselves in
the will of our almighty God, subjecting our own desires completely
to His.

We pray in obedience; we surrender in obedience. Blessed be the
name of the Lord!

*Blessed be Your name, Lord. I will come to you with
my needs and I will trust in You. Please work
in my life according to Your perfect will.*

Beauty for Ashes

Get wisdom, get understanding;
do not forget my words or swerve from them.
PROVERBS 4:5 NIV

The decadent, triple chocolate fudge cookie recipe called for real butter, but the young mother could only find a container of lard. Hoping it would make little difference, she went on gathering ingredients. Then, another item missing. . .no baking powder. *Could baking soda be that different?* Mouth watering, proud of her ability to improvise, she mixed, scooped, and baked the ingredients with great anticipation.

As she watched the cookies bake through the oven window, they didn't look quite as she had expected. Actually, they appeared rather flat. *Well,* she thought, *at least they'll taste good.* As the cookies were removed from the oven and cool enough to bite into, she gingerly nibbled one of her creations. Though she had expected a delicious chocolate cookie, she ended up with a worthless glob of goo—and an embarrassing lesson. The right ingredients make all the difference.

We've all made embarrassing messes by trying to "substitute" our human insight for God's infinite wisdom. When His Word said "no," we've countered with "well, maybe." And the results were, predictably, poor.

But God is completely faithful to us. As we acknowledge our errors of judgment in "substitution," He will graciously offer us perfect chocolate chip cookies—rather than the tasteless mess we should have received.

Father, please help me to trust in Your wisdom
rather than rely on my own brand of human reasoning.
I appreciate Your faithfulness to me.

Light My Path

Your word is a lamp to my feet and a light for my path.
PSALM 119:105 NIV

Amy was walking a usually well-lit path around the lake. But tonight, the street lamps had not come on—and the moon, though large and full, was covered by thick clouds. She had often walked around the lake, but this night, Amy stumbled over unnoticed tree limbs and half-buried rocks. Then the street lamps flickered to life and a golden light illuminated the path. Amy could speed her pace, easily avoiding the dangerous obstructions.

God's Word is like a street lamp. Often, we *think* we know where we're going and where the stumbling blocks are. We believe we can avoid pitfalls and maneuver the path successfully on our own. But the truth is that without God's Word, we are walking in darkness, stumbling and tripping.

When we sincerely begin to search God's Word, we find the path becomes clear. We see everything in a new light, a light that makes it obvious which way to turn and what choices to make. God's light allows us to live our lives in the most fulfilling way possible, a way planned out from the very beginning by God Himself.

Jesus, shine Your light upon my path. I have spent too long wandering through the darkness, looking for my way. As I search Your Word, I ask You to make it a lamp to my feet so that I can avoid the pitfalls of the world, and walk safely along the path You have created specifically for me.

Creating Margin

*"My Presence will go with you,
and I will give you rest."*
EXODUS 33:14 NIV

From the very first chapter of Genesis, God teaches us to take rest. He rested on the seventh day of creation and declared it good. Later, as the Israelites entered the Promised Land, God ordered the people to give the *soil* a rest every seven years.

When we short ourselves on rest, illness can result. That's our body's way of saying "Slow down! I can't keep up! If you won't listen to me, then I'm going to force you to."

God believes in rest! But most of us live lives that are packed to the brim with activities and obligations. We're overwhelmed. With such a fragile balance, unexpected occurrences, like a dead car battery, can wreck us emotionally, spiritually, and physically.

That's not the lifestyle God wants us to have. "He grants sleep to those he loves," wrote the psalmist (Psalm 127:2 NIV). God wants us to create a margin for the unexpected: a neighbor in need, a grandparent who requires extra attention, a friend who needs encouragement, our own kids as they grow and mature.

Life is busy. But in God's presence we find rest.

*Help me, Father, to listen to Your
instruction and heed Your words.*

Marvelous Thunder

"God's voice thunders in marvelous ways;
he does great things beyond our understanding."
JOB 37:5 NIV

Have you ever reflected deeply on the power that God is? Not that He *has*, but that He *is*.

The ailing woman who simply touched Jesus' garment was healed. That's power. Lazarus walked out of the tomb alive. That's power. Jesus could walk on water and calm a storm with His words. That's power.

Only a God who *is* power could do such things.

Job's friend Elihu made some false assumptions about his suffering companion, but he certainly understood God's power. Elihu described God as telling lightning where to strike (Job 36:32), and generating thunder with His own voice (Job 37:2–4). That's power—full-blown, mind-boggling, earthshaking power.

Now, consider this: the One who controls nature also holds every one of our tears in His hand. He is our Father, and He works on our behalf. He is more than enough to meet our needs; He does things far beyond what our human minds can understand.

This One who is power loves you. He looks at you, and says, "I delight in you, my daughter." Wow! His ways are marvelous and beyond understanding.

Lord God, You are power. You hold all things in Your hand and
You chose to love me. You see my actions, hear my thoughts,
watch my heartbreak. . .and You still love me. Please help
me trust in Your power, never my own.

Rachel's Saddlebags

Now Rachel had taken the household gods and put them inside her camel's saddle and was sitting on them. Laban searched through everything in the tent but found nothing.
GENESIS 31:34 NIV

Why did Rachel feel a compulsion to steal her father's household idols and hide them in her saddlebags? The idols were probably little statues of gods common to the time and culture. She risked the wrath of the true God, and jeopardized the safety of her family. Didn't she know better, as the wife of Jacob—the great patriarch of God's nation of Israel?

From our twenty-first century vantage point, it's easy to wag a finger at Rachel. Living in a western culture, we find such idols, of sexualized bulls and multi-breasted women, to be grotesque. But in Rachel's day, those little idols were pervasive, part of the culture. She didn't dismiss Jacob's God—she just added to Him. Naive, ignorant, or sinful, she allowed idols to replace God's primary position in her life.

Household idols probably don't tempt us. But we can all identify with Rachel. Think of the importance we place on material things, financial security, the achievements our careers—those ambitions can easily consume us! They can occupy our thought life, fill our spare time, and become our life's focus.

Let's take care to keep God exactly where He belongs, in first place.

Lord, clean my house! Open my eyes to the worthless idols in my life. Teach me to desire only You.

Rock of Ages

You will keep in perfect peace those whose minds are
steadfast, because they trust in you. Trust in the Lord forever,
for the Lord, the Lord himself, is the Rock eternal.
Isaiah 26:3–4 amp

You and I can have peace. Authentic peace. God-breathed peace. Not because we live in some make-believe world, repeating positive-thinking statements in an attempt to alter reality. Not because we've been able to avoid adversity or opposition. No, we can have peace simply and only because we trust our heavenly Father.

It's not our incredible faith or extraordinary, over-the-top godly lives that brings us peace. God simply wants our complete trust. He calls us to lean confidently on Him and His faithfulness, rather than fretting over, and focusing on, our circumstances.

This doesn't imply that we'll live without difficulties. All single moms have those! But when we make the commitment to trust our heavenly Father, come what may, He guards us and keeps us in His peace.

No matter what we see with our eyes, no matter what the hardship, God is our solid rock. . .our Rock of Ages.

Father God, grant me the ability to trust You, come what may.
Cause my eyes to focus on You, not the challenges I face.

More Faith

We live by faith, not by sight.
2 CORINTHIANS 5:7 NIV

Faith is a word often carelessly used. People rich and poor, single and married, content and miserable randomly toss the mysterious term around. But what is faith, really? It's believing in something without first having to prove it.

Imagine the scene: At a family barbeque, you watch in mock horror, trying desperately to contain a giggle, as Aunt Sally plops herself onto an unsteady lawn chair—only to have it fold in on itself, spewing the red-faced woman onto the lawn. Amazingly, after she peels herself off the ground and finds some composure, she snaps open *another* chair and sits right down, trusting this one will support her. We live by faith, not by sight.

Faith is what we have in Christ. Our daily circumstances may point to failure and frustration, but faith says God has all things under control—and He never fails. God is the object of our faith. He will never fail, even when it seems like we are drowning. He will lift us up, keep us strong, and put a song in our heart. We live by faith, not by sight.

*Lord, I need more faith. I know You will never leave
me or forget about my troubles. Life seems overwhelming
at times, so I ask You to increase my faith in You.*

Prayer Changes Things

*"The LORD says you won't ever get well. You are going to die,
so you had better start doing what needs to be done."
Hezekiah turned toward the wall and prayed. . . .
The Lord sent [Isaiah] back to Hezekiah with this message. . . .
I heard you pray, and I saw you cry. I will heal you.*
2 KINGS 20:1–2, 4–5 CEV

Had Hezekiah not prayed to God for healing, he would have certainly
died. It was God's plan was for the king to die, and the Lord even
gave Hezekiah advance warning of his coming demise.

But Hezekiah cried out to God and prayed for healing. He begged
for more time, reminding God of the life he had lived and the kind
of man he was. And, graciously, God agreed to give Hezekiah fifteen
more years.

Sometimes, somehow, the Lord will allow our prayers to effect
changes in our circumstances—even in His own plans. As His
children, we are in such a close relationship with our Father that He
knows our every need and responds to our heartfelt prayers.

When we pray out of obedience, with faith, we can be sure that our
prayers are heard by God. And we can know that He will always answer
in the best way, whatever the answer may be.

*Thank You, Father, for hearing and answering my
prayers according to Your will. Remind me to present
my petitions before You as an act of obedience—
and then to accept Your will and walk in it.*

Support Staff

Pile your troubles on GOD's shoulders—
he'll carry your load, he'll help you out.
PSALM 55:22 MSG

Moms are the unsung heroes, the support staff, the ones everyone depends on. Our purses hold everything from bandages for skinned knees to granola bars for hungry tummies to tissues for runny noses. If you need it, we'll find it. But there are days when we tire of carrying the weight of the world. Sometimes, we run ragged, taking care of everyone—everyone, that is, except for ourselves.

There came a time when Elijah grew tired of caring for Israel. Worn out, he ran for the hills, contemplating early retirement. In fact, he hoped God would give him a break and end it all. "Just kill me," Elijah begged God. He was *that* exhausted. *That* depressed.

Was God angry with Elijah for seeking an escape? Did God stand over Elijah, wagging a finger, telling him to pull it together?

Just the opposite! Tenderly, oh so tenderly, God sent angels to care for Elijah. They provided food and rest and encouragement.

Sometimes, we're so busy and tired we have nothing left to give. During those times, remember Elijah. Rest, eat, nourish yourself. Just let God be in charge for a while.

Dear Lord, teach me to ask for help. Prod me to take
better care of myself. Thank You for Your gentle response
to my low periods. Remind me that things will
get better again! They always do.

Lacking Nothing

*Consider it pure joy, my brothers, whenever you face trials of
many kinds, because you know that the testing of your faith
develops perseverance. Perseverance must finish its work so
that you may be mature and complete, not lacking anything.*
JAMES 1:2–4 NIV

Trials are never fun. Nor are they pain-free. But they're still
necessary.

When people speak of trials, they might mean anything from
sleep deprivation to the loss of a loved one—or anything in between.
How can we "consider it pure joy" when we face such trials? It's
not the trial itself that we celebrate, but the personal growth and
expansion of our faith that can lead to joy. Unfortunately, our attitude
in the midst of the trial often leaves us empty and hurting.

Trials don't get easier from one to the next. But when we get
through one—battered but not broken—we can look back to see
growth and strength, which we can take into the next. We have
become better equipped to face the next trial with perseverance,
comfort, and hope. And we can walk straight ahead, knowing that in
the end we will be mature and complete, lacking absolutely nothing in
Christ Jesus.

*Abba Father, I know You go with me through these trials.
I know that any perseverance or strength I have is only
because of You and Your faithfulness to me. Increase my
joy through these trials and help me remember the purpose
of them—that I may not lack any good thing.*

You Are an Answer to Prayer

Praise God, the Father of our Lord Jesus Christ!
The Father is a merciful God, who always gives us comfort.
He comforts us when we are in trouble, so that we
can share that same comfort with others in trouble.
2 CORINTHIANS 1:3–4 CEV

It's part of our maturing process. At some point, as Christians, we should arrive at a place where we are comfortable using our own past experiences and current circumstances as tools to reach out to others in need. A maturing believer is one who is beginning to look back on the things she has gone through with gratitude, as her purpose in the body of Christ begins to unfold.

For various reasons, it can be difficult to move past that point of being ministered to, in order to minister to others in need. But, according to the apostle Paul, one of the reasons God comforts us is so we can share that comfort with others when they need it.

We might say, "I'm just a new Christian," or "I wouldn't know what to say," or "I'm only a single mom." But as members of the body of Christ, we are an extension of the Holy Spirit.

So when someone is praying for comfort, be ready—it might just be you God will send to minister to that hurting soul.

Jesus, please help me open my heart and eyes to see the needs around me. Give me the grace and wisdom to comfort others with the comfort You have shown me time and time again.

Inside Out

*"Don't you see that nothing that enters a person from
the outside can defile them?" . . . He went on:
"What comes out of a person is what defiles them."*
MARK 7:18, 20 NIV

People have generally focused on keeping the outside clean. The Jews of Jesus' day made sure they washed the same hand first each time. In keeping with the law, they refused to eat certain foods, declaring them "unclean."

We act in much the same way today. Some foods turn our stomach, and become "unclean" to us. Americans consider daily baths the norm.

If only we exercised the same care in keeping our *minds* clean. Jesus listed some of the unclean things that flow from our minds: lust, pride, envy, and slander, among others. Unfortunately, once we have allowed images or thoughts into our minds, we can't "scrub" them away the way soap washes away dirt.

Safeguarding our thought-life starts with what we allow into our minds. As much as possible, we should "see no evil" and "hear no evil." Music, television, movies, books, even our friendships must be filtered.

We can't erase bad thoughts from our minds, but we can crowd them out—by filling our minds with noble, lovely, and true thoughts. How can I stay pure? "By living according to your Word" (Psalm 119:9 NIV).

The blood of Christ cleanses us and the Bible helps to keep us clean.

*Lord, search my thoughts, and show me my impurities.
Fill me with Your Word.*

But Even If

*"If we are thrown into the blazing furnace, the God whom we
serve is able to save us. He will rescue us from your power,
Your Majesty. But even if he doesn't, we want to make it
clear to you, Your Majesty, that we will never serve your
gods or worship the gold statue you have set up."*
DANIEL 3:17–18 NLT

Shadrach, Meshach, and Abednego were men of faith who stood on
their belief in God's power. They trusted God to take care of them, no
matter what King Nebuchadnezzar did.

These three faithful men said, "But even if he doesn't [rescue
us], it wouldn't make a bit of difference" (Daniel 3:18 MSG). Even in
the face of earthly consequences—like a blazing furnace—they were
committed to obeying God.

Every day, our faith is tested by fiery furnaces of one sort or
another. The baby needs a coat; do we tithe? The boss gave us cash;
do we report it as income and pay the tax?

We need to be so grounded in the Word of God that we know His
truth and trust Him above all else. Regardless of the circumstances
or the temptations to disobey, we can stand firm in our faith in God's
ability to rescue us from all situations. That's a faith that says, "But
even if God doesn't rescue me, I'll obey Him no matter what."

Is our faith like that of Shadrach, Meshach, and Abednego?

*Heavenly Father, I trust You no matter what and will obey
Your word. Help me stand in faith and face any fiery furnace
that comes my way. Please give me total confidence in You.*

From Pasture to Palace

*Then King David went in and sat before the LORD;
and he said: "Who am I, O LORD God? And what is
my house, that You have brought me this far?"*
1 CHRONICLES 17:16 NKJV

When Samuel the prophet asked Jesse, the father of eight sons, to introduce his family, Jesse almost forgot David! He was the youngest, who looked after the sheep. But God made special plans for this low man on the totem pole. David killed the Philistine giant Goliath and became a great warrior, winning King Saul's daughter for his wife. Unfortunately, he then spent years trying to escape his insanely jealous father-in-law. After more than a decade of danger, intrigue, and battle, David finally was crowned king and achieved the stable regime God desired for His people.

Like most kings, David built himself a beautiful royal palace. Unlike them, he began to think of ways he could say thanks to God for His goodness. David decided to build Him a large, ornate temple.

To the king's surprise, God objected because David was a man of war. David's son Solomon, a man of peace, would build the temple. But God told David his family would possess the kingdom forever if they followed God's ways. David, the ex-shepherd, could only sit and marvel. David had wanted to give to God; instead, God had given the unthinkable to him!

*Lord Jesus, how good You have been to my family and me!
We can never out-give Your generosity.*

A New Day

God, treat us kindly. You're our only hope. First thing in the morning, be there for us! When things go bad, help us out!.
ISAIAH 33:2 MSG

There are days that start off wrong and finish worse. Days in which we feel out of sorts, like a tire out of balance, clumsy and inefficient. We say things we shouldn't say those around us, using a voice that is too harsh, too loud. We experience days full of failure, tinged by sin. Wouldn't it be great to re-do our bad days?

We have that opportunity. It's called *tomorrow*. Lamentations 3:22–23 tells us that by God's mercies, He gives us a fresh canvas every twenty-four hours. Anger, grudges, irritations, and pain don't have to be part of it. No matter how stormy the day before, each new day starts fresh. And He is there for us first thing in the morning and every step of the way in our day, even if things begin to go wrong—again.

Every day in parenting is a new day, a new beginning, a new chance to enjoy our children. Tomorrow, we can do it better.

Each day is a new day with God, too. We can focus on the things that matter most: worshipping Him, listening to Him, and being in His presence. No matter what happened the day before, we have a fresh start to enjoy a deeper relationship with Him. A fresh canvas, every twenty-four hours.

Before I get out of bed in the morning, let me say these words and mean them: "This is the day the LORD has made; et us rejoice and be glad in it"(Psalm 118:24 NIV).

Finding Balance

But the Lord said to her, "My dear Martha, you are worried and upset over all these details! There is only one thing worth being concerned about. Mary has discovered it, and it will not be taken away from her."
LUKE 10:41–42 NLT

With people in the house, needing to be fed, Martha jumped in to accomplish her tasks. Mary, on the other hand, chose to spend time in the presence of Jesus.

Because of Mary's choice, Martha had to do all the work by herself. She was even chastised for criticizing Mary. But if Martha hadn't done that work, who would have?

The two sisters from Bethany are a perfect example of the inner struggle that most women face daily. On one hand, we want to please people, entertain, multitask, and control the many facets of our lives at one time—because we believe those are marks of a strong woman. On the other hand, we crave rest, spiritual growth, and peace. The challenge is to blend the two into a healthy whole.

Each of us should consider our own role. Am I the person who is always working in the kitchen during the worship service, or always filling in for the nursery worker who didn't show up? Or do I never take a turn, leaving others to bear the bulk of the work?

God has called us to good deeds, but not to stress and worry. Ask Him to show you the line.

Dear Lord, I want to do my part, like Martha—but, like Mary, I also need to be strong enough to say no, in order to have time with you. Please show me how to find that balance in my life.

Pick Your Battles

To these four young men God gave knowledge and understanding
of all kinds of literature and learning. And Daniel could
understand visions and dreams of all kinds.
DANIEL 1:17 NIV

Daniel was one of the first Hebrew exiles taken from Jerusalem into friendly captivity (if there is such a thing) in Babylon. Separated from his family, forced into servitude, given a new identity and new gods, Daniel was probably only a teenager! He was now living in Babylon, the pagan center of the earth.

Did Daniel completely reject his new lifestyle? Did he argue with his master and refuse to learn? No! Amazingly, there were only a few areas where Daniel refused to compromise: He would not bow down and worship any other god, or eat food that had been offered to idols.

We live in a type of Babylon, too. We're surrounded by anti-God behavior, customs, pop culture. It's easy to be offended by just about. . .everything. Everyday language is flavored with swear words, television shows mock our faith, schools introduce curricula that make us cringe.

Surprisingly, God didn't tackle every single issue in Babylon. He picked Daniel's battles for him, and Daniel was greatly used in the midst of a pagan culture. Not indignant or antagonistic, but compassionate and seeking the best for his captors.

Can we be Daniels in our communities today?

Lord, show me how to seek Your wisdom and discernment while
picking my battles. Help me to love those who oppose You.

SCHWEITZER, PATRICIA M.,

78, passed away on Sunday, February 5, 2017 at the Hosparus In Patient Unit.

Pat, born March 17, 1938 to Harry B. and Estelle (Duran) Schweitzer, was a retired infection control nurse who served for many years at various area hospitals. A 1957 graduate of Our Lady of Mercy Academy, Pat played on the basketball team and continued her love of the sport as a loyal UL fan. She was a very compassionate individual and chose the nursing profession as her career, receiving her RN degree from Jefferson Community College.

In addition to her parents, Pat was predeceased by her stepmother, Sarah Chase Schweitzer Pevlor and husband Pete; brother Joseph E; nephew, Mike; and her best friend, Polly O'Reilly.

She is survived by her loving family, brother, James D. (Dorothy); sister-in-law, Hilda; nieces, Karen and Mary; nephews, Jim Jr, Joe Jr, Nick, Joel and David and their families. She is also survived by her large extended loving Schweitzer family and many friends.

Visitation will be 3-7 p.m. Thursday at Ratterman and Sons, 3800 Bardstown Road. Funeral services in celebration of her life will be held immediately following the visitation at 7 p.m. Thursday at the funeral home.

In lieu of flowers, donations may be made to Hosparus of Louisville. The family would like to thankfully acknowledge the care given to Pat during her last two weeks in Norton Hosparus Pavilion where she received tender care in the most dignified way.

Ratterman

passed away Sunday, February 5, 2017.

Norman was a native of Brandenburg, Ky. a U.S. Army veteran during 1953 - 1955 & a member of Incarnation Catholic Church. He formerly worked for Mclean Trucking for 23 years & Ranger Transportation for 10 years.

Preceded in death by four brothers, Joe, Jim, Mike & Ike Knott.

Survivors include his wife of 56 years, Norma "Joy" (Swink) Knott; two children, Ronald Wayne Knott (Tricia) & David Bryan Knott (Cheryl); a sister, Maxine Crawley; four brothers, Frank, Garland, Carroll & Gary Knott; five grandchildren, Kristin, Sarah, Joshua, Joey & Amy; five great grandchildren, Jasmin, Makayla, Aleah, Tucker & Lilyann .

A funeral mass will be held 11:00 A.M. Thursday at Incarnation Catholic Church 2229 Lower Hunters Trace with burial in Louisville Memorial Gardens West. Visitation will be 2:00 – 8:00 P.M. Wednesday at Owen Funeral Home 5317 Dixie Hwy.

Memorial Gifts to St Vincent dePaul Society or Healing Place.

Online condolences to www.owenfuneral-home.com

Faithful Father

Be joyful in hope, patient in affliction, faithful in prayer.
ROMANS 12:12 NIV

This verse gives three straightforward instructions.

First, "be joyful in hope." It sounds simple, but that often depends on what we're hoping for. Is it a bonus at work—or just a job in general? Hoping for a raise to cover a vacation is easier than hoping for a job to simply pay the rent. Can we be joyful in either circumstance?

"Patient in affliction" is even more difficult. Our level of patience largely depends on the day. Is your child's father becoming demanding? Are creditors pushing you for payments? Or is a medical situation looming? Romans 12:12 offers no escape clause for afflictions that seem unbearable. God simply says to be patient.

Finally, we're to be "faithful in prayer." That shouldn't be a problem, right? But "faithful" implies a continuing pursuit. Sometimes we start out well, but get weary and give up. If we pray with faithfulness, though, we'll see results.

Implement these three straightforward commands, and you'll begin to see changes in yourself and your circumstances. Try it— experience God's faithfulness.

Father God, some days my life seems manageable—
but at other times it's more than I can handle. Help me to
"be joyful in hope, patient in affliction, [and] faithful in prayer"—
then show Yourself to be my faithful Father and Friend.

A Block of Marble

I praise you because I am fearfully and wonderfully made;
your works are wonderful, I know that full well.
PSALM 139:14 NIV

In 1501, Michelangelo looked at a block of marble and saw David. Michelangelo worked on the premise, an artistic discipline called *disegno*, that the image of David was already in the block of marble—in much the same way the human soul is found within the physical body. Three years later, Michelangelo had chiseled out a masterpiece. Out of a hunk of rock came the most recognizable sculpture in the world.

That's a picture of how God sees us! With His divine genius, God made us purposefully, with loving intention, as an outpouring of His joy. "For you created my inmost being; you knit me together in my mother's womb," wrote King David in Psalm 139:13 (NIV).

We look at ourselves and see the uncut sections, the rough edges, the areas that need sanding and polishing. Will we ever be considered a work of art? We seem like such a mess. But God looks at us and sees the sculpted piece, His completed masterpiece!

Do we see those around us in the same way that God sees us? Or the way Michelangelo looked at a block of marble and saw David? Our family and friends are miracles, filled with possibilities! God is accomplishing a soon-to-be revealed masterpiece.

Dear Lord, how awesome is Your artistry! Open my
eyes to Your creative ways. Give me Your vision to
see the potential of those you have brought into my life.

Temper Tantrum

He prayed to the LORD, "Isn't this what I said, LORD,
when I was still at home?" . . . But the LORD replied,
"Is it right for you to be angry?"
JONAH 4:2, 4 NIV

Poor Jonah. After he escaped that big fish, he obeyed God's call
to preach to his nation's greatest enemy. Then Jonah waited for
judgment to fall—but God spared the city of Nineveh when its people
repented.

That's when Jonah threw a tantrum. He told God, basically,
"You're compassionate. I knew You would spare them. I'd rather die
than see that."

So God asked Jonah a rhetorical question: "Is it right for you to be
angry?" Jonah had his priorities all wrong.

Like Jonah, we can be angry over the seeming injustices in our
lives. Why should our friends have happy marriages and our exes
enjoy a higher standard of living than we do? Why does God show
compassion to others—even the people who hurt us—when our own
needs are so great?

When we're tempted to grumble, God may ask, "Is it right for
you to be angry?" Others need His mercy as much as we do, like the
120,000 people of Nineveh, too lost to know the difference between
their left and right hands.

The next time we feel a temper tantrum coming on, we should
stop and, instead of venting, praise God that His grace, compassion,
and love are available equally to all—including us.

Lord God, You are slow to anger. You love us even when we fail You.
Teach us to have the same patient compassion for others.

Hide and Seek

*"And do you seek great things for yourself? Seek them not,
for behold, I am bringing disaster upon all flesh, declares the Lord."*
JEREMIAH 45:5 ESV

When we were little girls, we all dreamed big. Maybe we aspired to be a prima ballerina, to win an Oscar, or to own a mansion. Somewhere along the line our expectations fell into step with reality.

While the scope of our dreams may have narrowed, our desire for "great things" probably never changed. We'd like recognition for our talents, we want success at work, and we hope for more than just a minimum standard of living.

But God warns us: *Don't seek great things.* The more we seek them, the more elusive they become. As soon as we think we have them in our grasp, they disappear. If we commit to more activities than we can realistically handle, the best result is that we can't follow through. At worst, we neglect those we love. If we buy more things than we can really afford, we may lose them. Worse, we might make them our god. Our God—the true God—wants to rearrange our priorities.

Jesus tells us what we should seek: the kingdom of God and His righteousness (Matthew 6:33). He won't hide from us. When we seek the right things, He'll give us every good and perfect gift (James 1:17). And that will be more than we can ask or dream.

*Lord, please teach me to seek not greatness,
but You. May You be the all in all of my life.*

Joyful Songs

Sing joyfully to the LORD, you righteous;
it is fitting for the upright to praise him.
PSALM 33:1 NIV

Singing often reflects our mood. When we're lighthearted and happy, we may tend to sing more often than when we're feeling burdened and downtrodden. But the Word of God tells us to sing joyfully to the Lord, without prerequisites. The Bible doesn't say, "Sing if all is well and you're overjoyed." It just tells us to sing joyfully.

It's fitting for us as Christians to praise Him. Not only when our circumstances are conducive to a joyful spirit, but any time—simply because of who He is.

If our actions depend on our situations, we may never try a tune. But if we sing amid our situation, whether good or bad, joyous or painful, we will soon find our moods—and our spirits—rising from the ashes to reflect our joyful songs.

When we, like the psalmist, sing joyfully to the Lord, our spirits will follow—and we'll become deeply joyful moms, unshaken and steady.

Lord, I know I need to sing to You out of a joyful spirit.
For all You have done for me, and simply because of who
You are, I will choose today—whatever my circumstances—
to sing songs of praise, joy, and thanksgiving.

Bear Fruit

But the Spirit produces the fruit of love, joy, peace,
patience, kindness, goodness, faithfulness, gentleness,
self-control. There is no law that says these things are wrong.
GALATIANS 5:22–23 NCV

For a short time each fall, apple orchards are full of sweet, ripe fruit ready to be enjoyed. The rest of the year, though, the trees spend time growing, taking nourishment from the sun, soaking water up through their roots, and waiting for the fruit to grow and ripen. Picked too soon, apples are bitter; too late and they're overripe and mushy.

There's no season, though, for the fruits of the Spirit listed in Galatians 5. Those desirable behaviors are exhibited in our own lives and toward others as we mature in Christ. None of us can master the qualities on our own, as each of us has one or more areas of weakness the Holy Spirit is addressing in our lives.

Sometimes, when we don't see immediate growth in our lives, we become impatient. But just like the apples on a tree, our own spiritual growth requires cultivation and patience. We need to soak up the light of the Father, be nourished from His Word, and be patient while the Holy Spirit works within us.

If we simply remain rooted in Christ, we'll bear fruit—to the glory of His name.

Jesus, please continue to develop Your godly traits
in me. Help me to bear good fruit and be an
example of Your love toward others.

So, Talk!

*"No one can come to me unless the Father who sent
me draws them, and I will raise them up at the last day."*
JOHN 6:44 NIV

In some of the psalms, the writers seem to shake their fists at God, shouting, "Where are you, Lord? Why are you so slow? Are you sleeping? Wake up and help me!"

Interestingly, the psalmists never doubted God's existence, only His methods. They loved Him, they believed He would triumph over enemies, they knew He was the One True God. But they had some strong opinions about the way He went about His business. And they had no qualms about telling Him!

Fortunately for us human beings, God isn't easily offended. He is deeply committed to holding up His end of our relationship, and He doesn't want us to hide anything from Him. He already knows every thought we have, anyway. Why not talk to Him about those thoughts? Every concern about our lives, every worry for our future, every little thing that's good, bad, or ugly.

Our Father always wants to talk. In fact, the very impulse to pray originates in God. In his book *The Pursuit of God*, author A. W. Tozer wrote, "We pursue God because, and only because, He has first put an urge within us that spurs us to the pursuit."

So, talk!

*Lord God, it boggles my mind that You want to hear from me!
And often! Your Word says that I can call out Your name with
confidence. That You will answer me! Today, Lord, I give You
praise, honor and glory—and my heart's deepest longings.*

Rest and Restore

"Come to me, all you who are weary and burdened, and I will give you rest."
MATTHEW 11:28 NIV

Weary and burdened—such is the daily existence of the single mom. Weary from long hours of working, cleaning, and parenting—giving all we have to our children. Burdened from knowing we have to do it all again tomorrow and the next day and the day after that. It's a common place for single mothers.

Thankfully, we don't have to stay in this exhausting place. God offers rest to the mom whose shoulders are tired from carrying much more than her share of burdens. "Come to Me," says the Lord. "I want to give you rest."

When we bring Him our weary spirits, He lifts off the burden and exchanges it for His comfortable rest. He gives us strength to get through tomorrow and the next day and the day after that.

When we continually go to the Lord for rest, we'll find that, even though our situations don't change, we can get through our days with peace rather than exhaustion. We'll have enough left over to do it again tomorrow and the next day and the day after that.

Lord God, You are the giver of rest. I am weary and the burdens I carry are too heavy for me—but I come to You in faith, putting this heavy load in Your hands. I ask You to replace it with Your sweet rest, restoring my spirit, body, and mind for this journey.

A Fleece

*Then Gideon said to God, "Do not let Your anger
burn against me that I may speak once more."*
JUDGES 6:39 NASB

After seven years of judgment for doing evil in the eyes of the Lord, it was time for Israel to be freed from the Midianites. God chose Gideon, a mighty warrior, to lead the battle. He even promised Gideon that the battle would be won.

Gideon's response to this holy visit was to doubt the Lord's word! Gideon wanted proof of victory, so God gave him a sign. Audaciously, Gideon asked for another. Gideon put a wool fleece out overnight and asked God to keep it dry from the morning dew. God complied. Then Gideon asked for a reversed scenario. Again, God complied. The story of Gideon's fleece is so well known that, even today, people refer to putting a fleece before God when they try to discern His will.

Amazingly, God wasn't angry with Gideon for his disbelief. God met Gideon where he was. Gideon's faith was growing; that's what mattered to God.

When we feel inadequate about qualifications for a job God has given us—a job like single motherhood—we can take a page from Gideon's book. Gideon didn't hold back his fear of failure. He needed God's reassurance and patience in his faith walk, and God lovingly provided both.

He'll provide for us, too—if only we'll ask.

*Lord, the battles I face may not be like Gideon's, but the feelings I
have certainly are. Be patient with me, Lord! I need encouragement
today and a reminder that You are with me.*

Moving On

How long wilt thou mourn for Saul. . . ?
Fill thine horn with oil, and go.
1 SAMUEL 16:1 KJV

Samuel invested a lot of himself in Saul. He anointed Saul as Israel's first king and prophesied about him. He warned the brash leader against sinful pride. After the prophet delivered the news that God had rejected Saul as ruler of His people, the two men apparently never saw each other again. Samuel went into deep mourning.

God nudged Samuel. "How long wilt thou mourn?" In other words, God told the prophet to get moving. Samuel was to fill his horn with oil, a symbol of joy. God led the man to the village of Bethlehem and a shepherd boy named David—and we all know the rest of the story.

Like Samuel, we may mourn lost opportunities, relationships, and dreams. Whether we're single because of death, divorce, or other reasons, we're often tempted to brood on the past. Perhaps it's time for us to answer God's question: "How long will you mourn for [insert your issue here]?"

Grief is natural, and it often comes in waves. But God wants us to move forward. The end of a particular dream doesn't signal the end of hope. Let's fill our horns with the oil of gladness and re-engage with life.

God will provide for us—in ways we can't even imagine.

God of love, You have so much yet in store for me.
Teach me to step forward into Your abundant joy.

Know Love

*And I pray that you, being rooted and established in love,
may have power, together with all the Lord's holy people,
to grasp how wide and long and high and deep is the love of
Christ, and to know this love that surpasses knowledge—that
you may be filled to the measure of all the fullness of God.*
EPHESIANS 3:17–19 NIV

Love is not necessarily an emotion that gives us a warm fuzzy feeling.

God is love. It is who He is, not just something He does. To know His love is to know Him personally and intimately.

Paul desired the church at Ephesus to actually experience the love of God by knowing that love as a Person, rather than a feeling. Only then could the church become a body wholly filled and flooded with God Himself.

We, too, should seek to know love through an intimate relationship with God—not just by knowing stories about Him. We develop that relationship in the same way we get to know people—by spending time with them. Meditate on God's Word. Talk with Him in prayer. Listen to Him in the quiet moments. Obey Him.

As we do these things, we begin to experience love as a Person, not a feeling. And our families will benefit from that.

*Heavenly Father, I come to You, desiring to know love
in an intimate way. Reveal Yourself to me, Father.
Fill me so I may have the richest measure of Your divine presence and
become wholly filled and flooded with You.
Help me show Your love to those around me.*

The Kind Leading the Blind

I will bring the blind by a way that they knew not; I will lead them in paths that they have not known; I will make darkness light before them, and crooked things straight.
ISAIAH 42:16 KJV

Natalie felt like she needed a translator to read the insurance policy. An accident was bad enough; why make everything so complicated? Tomorrow she would file a police report, then take the car to repair shops for estimates. How long would it take to fix? Would she have to walk to work? Who would take the girls to school?

Natalie could have sworn she checked both ways before pulling out. Somehow her old minivan had smacked a shiny New Yorker.

"What are you, blind?" The gray-haired owner hadn't bought her lame explanation.

"Yes!" Natalie had wanted to scream. *"I'm blind! I have no idea where I'm going or what I'm doing."* Instead, she'd muttered a vague apology, but the other driver's question stuck in her mind like an arrow. Ever since the divorce, Natalie had felt as if she were stumbling through a maze blindfolded.

Lord, I don't want to play the game. Natalie couldn't cry aloud, or she'd awaken the children. But her tears plopped onto the insurance policy.

"I am with you."

God's words seemed carved into the air. Natalie couldn't see them. But they were more real than her troubles.

Maybe she wasn't so blind, after all.

Jesus, help me remember that You specialize in giving sight to those who have lost their vision. I love You, Lord.

Have You Looked Up?

The heavens proclaim the glory of God. The skies display his craftsmanship. Day after day they continue to speak; night after night they make him known.
PSALM 19.1–2 NLT

One afternoon, Cathy was walking around the park near her home. Her mind whirred with concerns about work and worries about her kids.

Suddenly, a man called out, "Hey lady! Have you looked up?"

She stopped and turned to see who was shouting. The voice belonged to an elderly man, seated on a bench.

"Have you looked up?" he asked her again.

She lifted her head and saw a magnificent scarlet oak tree, with leaves of crimson at the peak of their color. It was so beautiful, such a fleeting autumnal sight, that it took her breath away. She thanked the man and resumed her walk, relaxed and grateful after being reminded to "look up!"

God has placed glimpses of creation's majesty—evidence of His love—throughout our world. Sunsets, seashells, flowers, snowflakes, changing seasons, moonlit shadows. Such glories are right in front of us, every single day! But we must develop eyes to see these reminders in our daily life and not let the cares and busyness of our lives keep our heads turned down.

Have you looked up today?

Lord, open my eyes! Unstuff my ears! Teach me to see the wonders of Your creation every day and to point them out to my children.

God's Exchange Policy

*To appoint unto them that mourn in Zion, to give unto them
beauty for ashes, the oil of joy for mourning, the garment of
praise for the spirit of heaviness. . .that he might be glorified.*
ISAIAH 61:3 KJV

When the sale was on, the cute shoes with too-high heels seemed
perfect. The coat in that odd shade of green appeared an incredible
bargain. At home, however, the coat and shoes didn't look so great.
Neither did the price tags. *What was I thinking?*

So you stand in a long line, hoping to exchange them over your
lunch hour so you won't waste precious family time, running errands
after work. But the receipt's in your other purse. Will you receive the
full price back without it? Do they even accept a return on sale items?
You glance at a calendar. Does the store place a time limit on returns?
Whew! This exchange presents a major hassle for a single mom trying
to manage alone.

God's exchange policy as recorded in Isaiah seems too good to
be true. No standing in line. No hassles. For the ashes of our pasts,
He offers a beautiful future. God dispels our loss and loneliness and
anoints us with the oil of His Spirit as if we were royalty. We've
grown accustomed to dark, depressing clothes, but He points us to
dressing rooms where new outfits await: garments of praise—light,
lovely dresses that fit us perfectly.

*Lord Jesus, what an exchange! I want to wear
this garment of praise every day, just for You.*

Nebuchadnezzar's Sabbatical

"This is the verdict on you, King Nebuchadnezzar:
Your kingdom is taken from you. You will be driven out
of human company and live with the wild animals. You will
eat grass like an ox. The sentence is for seven seasons,
enough time to learn that the High God rules human
kingdoms and puts whomever he wishes in charge."
DANIEL 4:31–32 MSG

Nebuchadnezzar, king of Babylon, ruled the first known world
empire. An idol-worshipper as well as a man who idolized himself,
Nebuchadnezzar was given multiple opportunities to acknowledge
the one true God. Through interactions with Daniel, a tiny little light
would begin to glow inside Nebuchadnezzar, and he would accept
Daniel's God into his assortment of deities. But then the light would
dim. Finally, as Nebuchadnezzar's reign stretched into its final lap,
God gave him one more chance to repent—or else.

But Daniel reminded him it didn't *have* to be "or else"! God's
warnings were intended to bring repentance, not wrath. Did
Nebuchadnezzar heed God's warning? Sadly, no.

The king of Babyon didn't take God's word seriously, but God
took him seriously. Nebuchadnezzar spent seven years living like a
beast in field, until he looked to heaven.

What warnings has God given us—warnings that wo haven't
taken seriously? What habits or attitudes or influences need to be
pruned out of our life? Gossip? One drink too many at a party? An
attraction to the wrong man? We need to take God at His word and
heed those warnings. They're intended to draw us closer to Him.

Show me, Lord, the areas that steal my affections
and turn my heart away from You.

For His Own Good

And we know that in all things God works for the good of those who
love him, who have been called according to his purpose.
ROMANS 8:28 NIV

One day, as Jesus walked down the dusty roads of Jerusalem, He
came upon a blind man. Jesus spat in the dust, made a clay paste, and
rubbed it on the man's eyes. When the man washed the mud from his
eyes, he could see!

Many people thought the sightless man was blind because of sin
in his parents' lives. In response, Jesus said, "Neither this man nor his
parents sinned. . .but this happened so that the work of God might be
displayed in his life" (John 9:3 NIV).

It wasn't the dirt that held the healing power—we never find
healing in the dirt of our lives. The miracle was in how Jesus used the
dirt. And so it is in our own lives. The dirt and pain of life are simply
tools that God uses.

Sometimes life's circumstances cause us to cry out, "Why, Lord?
Why?" And God's response is always the same: so that His good work
might be displayed in our lives. And like the blind man's story, our
stories—our testimonies of God's involvement in our lives—could be
the light that points someone else to true faith.

Father, help me to trust You more. Help me to see Your
hand at work and to let go of my desire for control.
May Your glory be displayed in my life for all to see.

A Time to Give

"Is it a time for you yourselves to be living in your paneled houses, while this house remains a ruin?"
HAGGAI 1:4 NIV

Requests for donations bombard us. Feed the hungry, save those endangered animals, support a political candidate—so many appeals are made that we run the danger of developing calluses on our hearts. And, of course, our local churches need our giving to continue their important work.

We may think, *I can barely afford to provide for my family. How can I give? I'll worry about that when I get our finances straightened out.*

God once sent a message to the ancient Israelites through the prophet Haggai. Describing that experience of never having enough to go around, Haggai said, "You earn wages, only to put them in a purse with holes in it." (Haggai 1:6 NIV). Through His prophet, God didn't say that work, food, and clothing were unimportant. But He did stress that God's house—in our day, His work—needs to be a priority for us. The Israelites responded, and God poured out His blessing.

Do we need to examine our own spending habits? Are there times when we seek luxury at the expense of God's work? Do we set aside money to support "the Temple," or do we just say, "Someday"?

God has chosen to use us to carry out His work in the world. When we're faithful to that calling, we can be sure He'll provide for our needs.

God of all, may we make You the Lord of our financial and physical resources. Show us how much, when, and where to give.

David's Diary

God! God, save me! I'm in over my head, quicksand
under me, swamp water over me; I'm going down for
the third time. I'm hoarse from calling for help,
bleary-eyed from searching the sky for God.
PSALM 69:1–3 MSG

We think of the book of Psalms as poetry, or even a peek into King David's private diary—over half of the psalms are credited to him. But they were originally verses set to music, compiled as a hymnbook for corporate worship in the temple. Unfortunately, we have no known record of their tunes.

There is a psalm to match every emotion and mood experienced by human beings: joy, anger, frustration, discouragement, loneliness, doubt. Thousands of years after they were written, they still speak to our needs and desires.

But the psalms are much more than beautiful words that parallel our emotions: God is their central focus. Psalms often begin as a heart cry of pain from the psalmist—but they invariably end with a focus on God.

The psalm writers had a very real, genuine relationship with God. They sang praises to God, they got angry with God, they felt abandoned by God, they didn't understand God's slow response. . . and yet they continued to live by faith, deeply convicted that God would overcome.

These ancient prayers remind us that nothing can shock God's ears. We can tell Him anything and everything. He won't forsake us— His love endures forever.

Oh Lord, You know the secrets of my heart. Teach me
to talk to You through every emotion and every circumstance.

He Keeps His Promises

"For I know the plans I have for you," declares the LORD,
"plans to prosper you and not to harm you,
plans to give you hope and a future."
JEREMIAH 29:11 NIV

Unimaginable. That must describe the hopelessness the disciples felt as they saw their Master die on the cross. All the promises they held dear—all their feelings of hopeful expectation—were shot down with those final words: "It is finished."

Some of Jesus' followers may have remembered His earlier words assuring them of His return. But in the face of certain death, those words of victorious life must have been hard to accept.

We all experience moments of hopelessness in our earthly journeys. The death of our dreams, the crashing down of our hopes, the promises of God seemingly unfulfilled. . .we are no more immune to disappointment than Jesus' disciples were.

In the end, though, Jesus' promises held true—He did prevail no matter how dark that first Good Friday looked. We can always trust the words of our Lord. He knows the plans He has for us, and He has the power to see them through.

Hope and a future, prosperity and peace—we can trust that, even when things seem hopeless, God is still at work, carrying out His promises.

Thank You, Jesus, for being at work in my life.
Thank You for having a perfect plan and for keeping
Your promises. Give me faith to believe in You even
when it seems like everything is going wrong.

Not Now, God!

The end of a matter is better than its beginning,
and patience is better than pride.
ECCLESIASTES 7:8 NIV

Sarah's pastor told a story that really hit home.

"The other day I was driving," he told the congregation. "And I began to talk to God. I prayed that He would give me patience, and at that very moment, a slow-moving tractor pulled out in front of my car, blocking the road. At that moment, I thought, 'I didn't mean *now,* God!'"

Patience may be a virtue. But it's a virtue that many of us struggle with on a daily basis—particularly when others are involved. Though we may *pray* for patience, it's hard to actually *be* patient in every situation.

So beyond praying for patience, we ought to *practice* the patience we seek. Really. Maybe you could choose the longest line at the checkout counter or allow other shoppers to go ahead of you. Perhaps you could slow down a bit, and drive the posted speed limit. (And don't be angry when others drive even a bit slower.) Maybe you could even allow your kids five extra minutes to chat with their friends before rushing home after an event.

It will probably be difficult. But gaining patience will be worth all the trials.

Dear Lord, please give me patience. Remind me to be
patient not just when I want to be, but in all situations.
Help me to practice that virtue and model it every day.

The Babylonian Brain Trust

When the magicians, enchanters, astrologers and diviners came,
I told them the dream, but they could not interpret it for me. Finally,
Daniel came into my presence and I told him the dream.
DANIEL 4:7–8 NIV

Dreams were important in the ancient Babylonian culture. It was believed that they revealed the future or relayed a message that a god was angry. Dreams were not to be ignored.

So when King Nebuchadnezzar had a troubling dream, he nearly executed his entire brain trust in trying to have it interpreted. That was when Daniel intervened, praying to God for divine wisdom to figure out the king's vision.

Why, then, when faced with another troubling dream, did Nebuchadnezzar immediately turn back to his incompetent magicians for answers? Again, the brain trust failed him. Again, Daniel intervened. How could a brilliant man like Nebuchadnezzar make the same mistake twice?

When a troubling circumstance intrudes into our life, do we "get it"? Do we hit our knees and take the problem to God for wisdom and guidance? Or do we return to ineffective habits—like anxiety, despair, or anger?

Habits are hard to break, even the ones that have failed us before. Let's learn from old King Nebuchadnezzar. The next time trouble hits, forego old habits and turn instead to the God who never fails.

Reveal my tendencies, Lord, to respond to problems in
the wrong ways. Show me a better way—Your way.

Be Still and Know

A woman must quietly receive
instruction with entire submissiveness.
1 Timothy 2:11 NASB

Five minutes of rest. That's all she needed before studying God's Word. But the moment her head hit the pillow, sleep became the priority. Spiritual instruction would have to wait until another time.

Even in the craziness of life, we will benefit by taking a few minutes (or longer) each day to receive guidance from God's holy Word—the Bible. The apostle Paul, in 1 Timothy 2:11, reminds us that we as single mothers should receive instruction from the perfect male influence in our lives—God Himself.

It's often difficult to find five minutes to spend in God's Word or prayer. And right before bedtime—when many of us try to squeeze in our devotions—may not be the period most conducive for study.

For a few days, watch for breaks in your schedule—times when you're alert and ready to receive instruction. Maybe that's first thing in the morning, or perhaps it's in your car five extra minutes before you head off to work. You could read the Word instead of the newspaper while you're drinking your coffee. Or maybe it's some other time and place.

What's important is that we make time for regular Bible reading and prayer.

Dear Lord, help me to carve out time for You today.
Remind me that Your instruction comes from Your Word—
and that I should immerse myself in that Book every day.

The Best

*"But the father wasn't listening. He was calling to the
servants, 'Quick. Bring a clean set of clothes and dress him.
Put the family ring on his finger and sandals on his feet.
Then get a grain-fed heifer and roast it. We're going to feast!
We're going to have a wonderful time!'"*
LUKE 15:22–23 MSG

The prodigal son had wasted his wealth. He had made mistakes—
big ones. He had forgotten his position as a son and made foolish
decisions based on his own selfish desires.

One phrase in this story reads, "When [the son] came to his
senses" (Luke 15:17 NIV). When the wasteful young man remembered
who his father was and what he could provide, he acted differently.

In his own eyes, the prodigal son saw himself as deserving
nothing. He was ready to offer himself as a servant to his father. But
his father could see his son only through the eyes of compassion. He
saw a son in need of the best things a father could give him—and he
lavished his love on the young man.

In the same way, our heavenly Father sees *us* through eyes of
compassion and love. When we believe in Jesus, God sees only the
blood of Christ—not our mistakes, faults, and failures. He views us as
worthy of the best He has to offer. If we see ourselves as less worthy,
we discount His amazing love for us.

Forget the past, and don't worry about the struggles of the
present. Our Father rejoices when we trust in Him, and promises us
His very best.

*Father God, I thank You for loving me the way You do. I know You
want the very best for me in all things. Help me always
to remember that I am Your child—and to act accordingly.*

Why Pray?

"Why were you searching for me?" he asked.
"Didn't you know I had to be in my Father's house?"
LUKE 2:49 NIV

Most of us have heard the story. Mary and Joseph unknowingly leave the twelve-year-old Jesus behind in Jerusalem. When they discover He's missing, they spend a frantic three days looking for him. Finally found in the temple, Jesus responds with an interesting question: "Why were you searching for Me?"

What makes us seek God out? Perhaps, like Mary and Joseph, we've missed our connection with the Lord for a few days. Often, we don't realize our mistake until an emergency arises—then we search for Him. God may seem far away, though, of course, *He* hasn't moved. Heaven is still His throne and the earth His footstool. But we seem to have lost our way.

Maybe we're rushing to God because we're worried. Then, in the presence of the Lord, who is our light and salvation, we no longer feel afraid. We trust Him to provide for us.

Or perhaps we're doubting God's goodness. We might repeat the anxious question of Mary and Joseph in our prayers: "Why have You treated us like this?" (Luke 2:48 HCSB). When we hurl anger at God, He simply absorbs it, reprimands or encourages us as needed, and renews our strength for another day.

So why do we pray? There are as many reasons as there are minutes in the day.

Heavenly Father, I know that when I seek You,
I will find You. I praise You, and pray that I will
learn to come to You with every detail of my life.

From Badlands to Glad Lands

I will restore to you the years
that the locust hath eaten.
JOEL 2:25 KJV

Have you ever tilled a garden in the spring, breathing the earthy fragrance as sharp blades turned the moist, rich dirt? Perhaps you planted seeds and envisioned fresh vegetables: rosy radishes, plump pods of peas, and sweet carrots that taste nothing like their grocery-store counterparts. Or maybe you and your children have patted soil around tomato plants that promise a tasty harvest. Everyone loves flowers; we may get carried away with circus-colored visions of zinnias, marigolds, and petunias.

Then Japanese beetles and green worms discover our gardens and destroy our dreams. Without a twinge of conscience, they bore holes and riddle leaves until our seed-catalog-perfect scene succumbs to their greedy appetites.

When God sent fierce enemies to punish their willful wrongdoing, the Israelites felt as if giant locusts had wiped out years of their lives. His people had invested all their energy in defying God, yet had nothing to show but spiritual, emotional, and physical devastation.

But God still loved them. He even promised to restore the years they lost because of their sin.

When we make bad choices, it's hard to believe anything good can grow in our lives again. But when God plants His seeds and rains His love down on us, we can expect the best!

Lord Jesus, I have not cultivated my life according to
Your directions. But You, the Resurrection and the Life,
can bring springtime to me today and every day.
Thank You, Lord, for raining Your blessings upon me.

Type-A Prophet

Elijah was afraid and ran for his life. When he came to Beersheba in Judah, he left his servant there, while he himself went a day's journey into the desert. He came to a broom tree, sat down under it and prayed that he might die. "I have had enough, Lord."
1 Kings 19:3–4 niv

Did Elijah take on too much and suffer for it? He seems a classic Type-A guy. He had a calling. He felt consecrated. He had a plan. He was doing God's work. He had even been part of many miracles!

So how did he end up alone in a remote place, exhausted and depressed, begging God to let him die?

Isn't it comforting to read about a flawed prophet? One with the highest of highs and the lowest of lows. At one point, Elijah led Israel in righteous living! In the next chapter, we read of his bone-deep weariness. James tells us that Elijah was a human, just like us (James 5:17). Elijah was *real*.

God used Elijah, flaws and all. Just like Elijah, we can honor God and be used by Him—flaws and all—if we give Him our whole heart.

Lord God, sometimes I feel so wholly inadequate to do Your work. I don't feel as if I have much to offer, but I give You my heart, knowing that You can do more with my life than I could ever ask or imagine. Use me as You will!

Hunks of Rust

*Then Deborah said to Barak, "Go! This is the day
the Lord has given Sisera into your hands.
Has not the Lord gone ahead of you?"*
JUDGES 4:14 NIV

Sisera, a powerful warrior, led a coalition of Canaanite rulers. For twenty years, he had cruelly oppressed the Israelites. He had a fleet of nine hundred iron-plated chariots, chariots that caused dread among the Israelites. What ill-armed, ragged tribe of former slaves could withstand that kind of power? Small wonder no one challenged him.

The Lord told the prophet Deborah it was time for Israel to confront Sisera. General Barak was tapped to lead the charge—but he refused! He insisted that Deborah come with him. So she did—and in a brilliant stroke, God sent rain! Lots and lots of rain. Sisera's greatest strength—iron chariots—became a liability. Oozing mud gripped the chariots like sticky glue.

Barak and the Israelites saw those iron chariots as intimidating, insurmountable obstacles. Deborah saw them as trivial details. She knew that God was sovereign over all things, including the weather! Those iron chariots turned into big hunks of rust.

How do we look at dire circumstances? Do we see only the obstacles? Hopefully, we have the faith to believe that God can turn any situation into a victory. After all, as Deborah reminded Barak, has not the Lord gone ahead of us?

*Lord, the very things we fear the most are nothing to You!
You are sovereign over everything—material objects,
spiritual battles, emotional crises, even the weather.
Thank You for going ahead of me and leading me to victory.*

Talking to God

One of his disciples said to him, "Lord, teach us to pray,
just as John taught his disciples." He said to them,
"When you pray, say: 'Father, hallowed be your name,
your kingdom come. Give us each day our daily bread.'"
LUKE 11:1–3 NIV

Ruth was a Christian, but she struggled in her prayer life. How could she be worthy of speaking to the supreme Creator of the universe? He already knew everything in her mind.

Lord, she thought, *I don't know what to say. How can I possibly pray to You? Do You even hear my insignificant requests?*

Yes, God hears—and, although He knows what we need before we even ask Him, He *wants* us to pray. He even gave us instruction on how to pray. Our prayers don't have to be long or eloquent or even particularly organized. When Jesus taught His disciples to pray, the sample wasn't wordy. He simply taught the disciples to give God glory and to come to Him and ask for their daily needs.

But Luke 11 teaches us something beyond just an outline for prayer. The story shows clearly that if we ask God to teach us how to pray, He will. It's all part of the prayer—ask God to lead you, then speak to Him from the heart.

Let's make it a habit to pray every day. Like we tell our kids, practice makes perfect.

Dear God, teach me how to pray. Remind me that
my words don't have to be profound. You're just
looking for earnest thoughts from the heart.

Starry Skies

Lift your eyes and look to the heavens: Who created all these?
He who brings out the starry host one by one, and calls
them each by name. Because of his great power and
mighty strength, not one of them is missing.
ISAIAH 40:26 NIV

The first night of summer vacation found Hanna and Becky enjoying
the multitude of stars in the wide sky. The girls giggled while
reminiscing over their middle school years, now completed. Thoughts
of their upcoming high school years were enhanced by the awesome
display above them.

Everyone should spend some time stargazing. When we slow the
frantic pace of our minds and look to the heavens, we begin to sense
the unmatchable power, the sustaining strength, and the intimate
love of God. As we gaze with admiration at the stars, we can drink in
the very essence of our heavenly Creator.

It was God who hung every star in place. It's God who knows
each star by name. Nothing in the farthest reaches of the universe
goes unnoticed by God, because He's a God of order and intimacy.

If God cares that deeply about His starry creation, how much
greater is His love for us, His cherished daughters?

Father, You are the Creator of all. I thank You that I can take in the
awesome vastness of the universe and rest in peace—knowing that
You are not only the master Creator, but that You hold me in the
palm of Your hand, caring about every detail of my life.

No Vandalism

You realize, don't you, that you are the temple of God,
and God himself is present in you? No one will get by with
vandalizing God's temple, you can be sure of that. God's
temple is sacred—and you, remember, are the temple.
1 CORINTHIANS 3:16–17 MSG

Church buildings—from giant stone cathedrals to quaint country chapels—pepper the landscape of North America. Wouldn't you be appalled to see any of these beautiful buildings vandalized?

The Bible says we as believers are a type of church building—but even more than that, we're the actual temple of God on this earth. It's amazing when you really think about it: God actually resides in *us*. Our bodies aren't just a temporary dwelling for our spirits—they are the actual home of the God of the universe. So wouldn't "vandalism" of God's temple—our bodies—be even sadder than that done to church buildings?

But how do we "vandalize" God's temple? Maybe by eating that second piece of pie. . .or drinking soda instead of water all day. . . or ignoring physical exercise. (Who really uses a gym membership anyway?)

Sure, it's hard to exercise. Sometimes it's easier to grab fast food than to cook. It's tempting to fill our lonely times with sweets. But our bodies are holy and sacred. Don't vandalize God's temple!

Father, I thank You for dwelling in me, and I
commit to take care of my body as Your temple.
I will treat it with respect, in honor of You.

Home-Based Business

If any of you lacks wisdom, let him ask of God, who gives to all liberally and without reproach, and it will be given to him.
JAMES 1:5 NKJV

As home-based businesses become increasingly popular, researchers have listed steps necessary to be successful in such endeavors. The top five recommendations: Plan ahead, put money aside, organize your time, organize your space, and stay focused.

We as Christian parents are running our own home-based businesses—the business of Jesus. To be good managers in our homes, we need to plan ahead. Only with careful planning can we set aside time for study, prayer, and teaching. We must be good stewards of our finances so we can serve God with our resources as needs arise.

With proper time management, we will be available to serve our family inside the home and the body of Christ outside. May we always stay focused on our reason (Jesus) and our goal (leading others to Him).

Though serving God is much more than a business, looking at our choices practically can help to bring order to our chaos— and bring success to our spiritual lives.

Father, help me order my priorities and focus my energy with the singular purpose of letting Your light shine through me. Help me to be a good steward of all that You have put in my charge.

Restoration

*He maketh me to lie down in green pastures: he leadeth
me beside the still waters. He restoreth my soul.*
PSALM 23:2–3 KJV

Dumb, helpless, straying sheep. The fluffy creatures don't know
any better than to wander away from the herd and get tangled in
underbrush. The animals need a shepherd who acts in their best
interest and protects them from harm.

That's us—sheep. We wander away from the fold and get caught
in the underbrush of the world. We leave the flock and become tired,
hungry, and thirsty. Our wandering ways leave us sick in mind, spirit,
and body.

We need the Good Shepherd—Jesus. He searches for us when we
go astray. He pulls out of the pits we've fallen into. He removes the
thorns from our hides. During the heat of tribulation, He places us in
His shadow where we can rest. He slakes our thirst with His living
water, the Holy Spirit. He restores our souls. We know His voice and
follow Him.

God watches over us day and night, no matter where we are. He
tends our wounds, guards us, and builds us back up for the challenges
of life. When we are lost, we need only listen for the voice of our
Shepherd.

*Lord, my Shepherd, I shall not want. Teach me to
lie still in Your green pastures and drink of Your
quiet waters. Please restore my soul.*

This, Too, Shall Pass

Weeping may stay for the night,
but rejoicing comes in the morning.
PSALM 30:5 NIV

There may be night feedings that destroy your sleep. Terrible twos that seem never ending. No money for dinner and a movie. Trouble paying the electric bill. Rebellious teens. Disagreements with the other parent. Loneliness, discouragement, physical aches and pains. Being a single mom can be downright tough.

But you know what? Every season has one thing in common—each has a beginning and an end. As with the calendar seasons of spring, summer, autumn, and winter, these "seasons" of your life will pass, too. By God's great design, no season lasts forever. No trial goes on endlessly.

The psalmist eloquently reminds us, "Weeping may endure for a night, but joy comes in the morning." He's not saying that if we can just hang on until sunrise, life will come up roses. The psalm writer is revealing that, though we may go through tear-filled night seasons, we can look forward with joy to the certainty of a new day. A new season of life. This, too, shall pass.

Heavenly Father, I often feel as if my night season will
never end. Thank You for the hope of a new beginning—
a new season of life. I thank You that no trial lasts forever.

A Teary Prophet

*My eyes fail from weeping, I am in torment within; my heart is
poured out on the ground because my people are destroyed,
because children and infants faint in the streets of the city.
They say to their mothers, "Where is bread and wine?" as
they faint like the wounded in the streets of the city,
as their lives ebb away in their mothers' arms.*
LAMENTATIONS 2:11–12 NIV

Jeremiah was known as the prophet with the broken heart. He had a
mother's heart—tender and compassionate—for Judah. He was a man
in tears most of the time. He saw the destruction of Jerusalem and
the Babylonian captivity.

When Jeremiah focused on the terrors around him, he felt
overwhelmed, even personally assaulted by God: "He pierced my
heart with arrows from his quiver" (Lamentations 3:13 NIV). Only
when he focused on God's past mercies did he find strength and
encouragement: "Yet this I call to mind and therefore I have hope:
Because of the LORD's great love we are not consumed, for his
compassions never fail" (Lamentations 3:21–22 NIV).

Every day we face crises small and large. Sadly, we often focus
on the problem from *our* point of view, which is, of course, rather
limited. Incomplete. Earthbound. Missing the big picture.

Jeremiah's perspective changed from despair to hope by
remembering God's faithfulness. What a good reminder! We do not
face any crisis, big or small, without God's loving presence.

*Faithful God, when I feel under siege, turn my eyes
toward heaven. Help me remember Your past mercies.*

Million-Dollar Smile

A happy heart makes the face cheerful,
but heartache crushes the spirit.
PROVERBS 15:13 NIV

Ever seen a million-dollar smile? You know the one. It shines like the sun—and it's contagious. The million-dollar smile makes everyone else light up, too.

Maybe the face encircling that smile is yours. Or maybe it's not. A million-dollar smile can't spread itself across a face weighed down by a broken heart or a wounded spirit. It can't be faked. You have to have happiness bubbling up from your heart in order to exhibit such a cheerful, honest smile. Where do you find that kind of happiness?

Only God can offer us joy—the true, long-lasting, nobody-can-take-it-away kind of joy that comes from knowing and trusting Him. We may carry a heavy load—but Jesus Christ wants to fill our hearts with joy so our faces shine like the morning sun.

Happy hearts are vital for us as single moms. May our faces reflect the love of Christ in million-dollar smiles that spread like wildfire to the faces of our children.

Jesus, I want my cheerful face to speak of Your goodness.
Though I've been hurt and I carry heavy burdens,
I ask You to release my heartache. Please cause my
face to be an expression of Your joy.

Almighty Whisper

*A hurricane wind ripped through the mountains and shattered the
rocks before GOD, but GOD wasn't to be found in the wind;
after the wind an earthquake, but GOD wasn't in the earthquake;
and after the earthquake fire, but GOD wasn't in the fire;
and after the fire a gentle and quiet whisper.*
1 KINGS 19:11–12 MSG

Have we ever become slaves to inaction because we were waiting for
the wrong thing?

As parents, we might want God to force us to move with shouted
directions. Wouldn't it be so much easier and clearer if He wrote our
next move across the sky, then mightily and unmistakably imposed
His will on us?

But God doesn't work that way. He speaks to us gently, through
our spirit, while He waits patiently for us to listen and obey His gentle
prodding. He never forces us to act because He desires that our
actions grow out of our own desire to please Him.

Elijah searched for God in the hurricane winds, the earthquake,
and the fire. He expected a mighty God to use all the forces of the
universe to announce His presence. In reality though, God was found
in none of those things. When the chaos abated, His presence could
be realized—and His voice heard as a quiet, gentle whisper.

*Almighty Father, help me to hear Your whisper amid
the chaos of life. Guide me with Your still, small voice.
Thank You for patiently leading me through life.*

Powerful One

He who forms the mountains, creates the wind, and reveals his thoughts to man, he who turns dawn to darkness, and treads the high places of the earth—the LORD God Almighty is his name.
AMOS 4:13 NIV

Ever pondered the power of our Lord God Almighty? Meditating on God's power can soothe our biggest worries and calm our deepest fears.

The Word of God speaks often of His power—we know He created our universe in less than a week. But if that's too much to comprehend, consider the enormity of a single mountain or ocean. Those vast, mighty things came into being simply by God's voice—and they're only a tiny fraction of everything He made. What power!

The Lord opens the morning curtains to reveal the dawn, and pulls the sky shades back at night to bring darkness. He plots the course of the wind, arranges for rainfall, and causes grass, crops, and trees to grow. He feeds the gigantic whales of the ocean, and every tiny little bird. If our Lord has enough knowledge and power to handle these jobs, surely He can (and will!) look after us.

Problems that seem insurmountable to us are simply a breath to Him. Let's not be anxious today—God holds each one of us in the palm of His hand.

Lord God, You are my provider. Thank You for holding such power—and for choosing me to be Your child. Please give me a greater understanding of who You are, helping me to remember that You, the Lord God Almighty, love me.

Unloved

She conceived again, and bare a son: and she said,
Now will I praise the LORD: therefore she called his name Judah.
GENESIS 29:35 KJV

Leah, through no fault of her own, found herself in a loveless marriage. Jacob had contracted for her pretty sister, Rachel. But their father, Laban, conned Jacob into marrying Leah as well, plus working seven additional years on his farm. Laban's friends toasted him as a shrewd businessman.

But Leah paid for her father's schemes. Never attentive, Jacob grew more indifferent every year. Still, God blessed Leah with beautiful babies, and she gave them names that reflected her faith in Him despite her pain. She delivered Reuben, which means, "He has seen my misery," and Simeon, which means, "one who hears." Leah named her third son Levi, "attached," hoping for a true bond between her and her husband. But Jacob forever identified Leah with her father's scam. He didn't like losing—and he didn't like Leah. After their fourth son's birth, Leah said, "This time I will praise the Lord," and named him Judah, which means "praise." Although she continued to struggle, Leah did not lose sight of God's love.

She had no idea God planned a special blessing for her: the Messiah, the glorious hope of all mankind, would descend from Leah, the unloved.

Jesus, I want so much to be loved here and now. But until You lead that person to me, help me to cling to You and know Your loving plans are bigger and better than I can ever imagine.

An Eye for a. . .Tooth?

But if there is serious injury, you are to take life for life,
eye for eye, tooth for tooth, hand for hand, foot for foot,
burn for burn, wound for wound, bruise for bruise.
EXODUS 21:23–25 NIV

God gave the law of retaliation to Israel to ensure that punishments fit their crimes. Using clear, spelled-out deterrents, it was intended to preserve the sanctity of human life.

This law was also designed to stop the human tendency to extract revenge. Bitterness has an insatiable appetite—nothing really satisfies it. It's been said that bitterness is a pill we swallow, hoping someone else will die. The truth is, we don't just want someone to pay for his offense to us. We want him to pay and pay and pay. We want an eye for a tooth. We want justice! Not mercy.

Jesus amended the law of retaliation by invoking over it the law of love. "You have heard that it was said, 'Eye for eye, and tooth for tooth.' But I tell you, do not resist an evil person. If someone strikes you on the right cheek, turn to him the other also'" (Matthew 5:38–39 NIV).

Forgiveness can be so hard. Only God can give us the desire to forgive. Only God can do the impossible in us.

Father, I need Your on going help in this process of
forgiveness. Prompt me to pray a blessing on those
who've hurt me. Make a miracle out of my heart.

He Never Leaves

I will always be with you and help you . . .
So be strong and brave!
JOSHUA 1:5–6 CEV

Joshua faced a difficult task. He was to take over for Moses, the man who had led the children of Israel out of their bondage in Egypt.

For years, Moses had been preparing Joshua, teaching him to seek the face of God. Joshua had walked by Moses' side and been through each battle with him. He had been led by the cloud by day and the fire by night. He had walked on dry land through the Red Sea.

Yet with all the training and preparation, God knew Joshua still needed reassurance. So God told him—more than once—"I will be there to help you wherever you go" (Joshua 1:9 CEV).

God tells us the same thing. No matter what we face or where we go, He is with us. He will help us through it all.

Not only has he assured us of His help, He has commanded us to "be strong and brave." So release your fears to Him, and rest in the peace of knowing He is present. There is no need to be afraid or discouraged.

Lord, You are my God and I trust You. Thank You
for never leaving me. I draw strength and courage
knowing that You are always with me.

Welcome Back!

After arriving back home, his disciples cornered Jesus
and asked, "Why couldn't we throw the demon out?"
He answered, "There is no way to get rid of this
kind of demon except by prayer."
MARK 9:28–29 MSG

One afternoon in Galilee, the disciples were arguing with the teachers
of the law while a grieving, desperate father listened. When the
man saw Jesus approaching, he poured out his problem to the Lord:
"Teacher, I brought my mute son, made speechless by a demon, to
you. . . . I told your disciples, hoping they could deliver him, but they
couldn't" (Mark 9:17–18 MSG).

So Jesus gave the evil spirit its marching orders: "Out of him, and
stay out!" (Mark 9:25 MSG). Afterward, He explained to His disciples
that prayer was the only way to rebuke that demon.

Was it a particularly difficult demon? The worst of the worst?
More likely, the disciples had taken for granted the power given them.
Jesus indicated that they had a lack of prayer. His emphasis was *on*
prayer.

Somehow, having seen the miracles Jesus performed through
prayer, having observed the importance Jesus placed on prayer in His
daily life, the disciples still took prayer for granted. If they could do
that, the danger exists for us, too.

Lord, strengthen my prayer life! Your Word tells
me to pray about everything. I want to pray with a
more muscular faith. Forgive me for my silences.
Thank You that You still welcome my prayers.

Warm Fuzzies

Yet you are near, LORD, and all your commands are true. . . .
All your words are true; all your righteous laws are eternal.
PSALM 119:151, 160 NIV

Have you ever read a scripture and thought, *That's nice. . .but is it real?*

At times, we're all tempted to think God might try to placate His children with tales of comfort or miracles that don't ring true with our day-to-day experience. But that's not the case at all. Whether we need money for groceries or comfort for a broken heart, child care or a car that runs, patience or a paycheck, vindication or a vacation. . .God provides real substance—not just warm fuzzies.

Our God is forever faithful. He'll never tell us, "It'll be okay," when it won't. He is God. Though He may not remove the various difficulties, He has promised to be with us in the midst of them and walk us through to the other side.

As the psalms tell us, God's Word is the sum of Truth. Trusting that Word is much more than a positive thinking exercise. . .it is our faith in action.

Father God, what a comfort it is to know that You aren't
simply trying to give me a warm, fuzzy feeling. You care for
me and are faithful to walk me through whatever I face.

Strong Enemies Require Stronger Power

*He sent from on High. He took me; He drew me out of
many waters. He delivered me from my strong enemy,
and from those. . .too mighty for me.*
PSALM 18:16–17 NASB

The toilet overflows, the car breaks down, work hours get cut, the
gas bill is twice what you budgeted for. Taken one at a time, these
challenges are minor nuisances. Coming in a bunch, they can send
even the strongest among us over the edge.

Though the "strong enemy" in Psalm 18 is a human opponent,
our "enemies" as single mothers are just as real. We may face illness
in our homes, financial trials, or the strain of raising children on our
own. Feeling as if we're drowning in responsibility, these "enemies"
can quickly become too mighty for us.

Thankfully, we have an even mightier God! Though the daily
issues of life may seem overpowering—even insurmountable—God
has promised to deliver us from our "strong enemy, and from those
"too mighty" for us. He uses His Word to bring hope to our weary,
worn-down souls. He may use a sister or a coworker or a friend from
church to send an unexpected check or drop us an encouraging note.
Or He may find some other way of helping us, something we never
would have guessed.

Of this we can be sure: God is mightier than any foe we face.

*Father, sometimes life feels like a raging flood
around me. Help me turn to You in my times
of trouble, knowing You are able to deliver.*

Beauty of the Beholder

So God created human beings in his own image.
In the image of God he created them; male and female
he created them. . . . Then God looked over all he
had made, and he saw that it was very good!
GENESIS 1:27, 31 NLT

Janet looked in the mirror and winced. *I shouldn't have eaten that extra piece of cake,* she thought as she pinched a bit of fat around her waist.

Janet's not alone. Women tend to find something wrong with themselves, no matter how they actually look. Our noses have bumps. Our hips are too large. Our eyes are too small for our face. We've got wrinkles where smooth skin used to be.

Though there's nothing wrong with presenting ourselves in the best light, we should always remember one important fact: God created us in His image. We don't have to look like the models in a women's magazine to be beautiful. The One who created us loves us exactly as we are!

Those little things we see as imperfections are actually attractive to God. Just as we see our own kids as the most adorable things, God sees us as His lovely children.

When it comes to self-image, let's not view our own perceived flaws as negatives. Let's see ourselves through God's eyes, remembering that His creation is always good.

Dear Lord, when I look in the mirror, remind me that I was created in Your image and that, although I may not always see myself as beautiful, You think I look very good.

Lead Me On

This book of the law shall not depart out of thy mouth; but thou shalt meditate therein day and night, that thou mayest observe to do according to all that is written therein: for then thou shalt make thy way prosperous and then thou shalt have good success.
JOSHUA 1:8 KJV

God Himself told Joshua the news of Moses' death. Saddened, Joshua knew he would miss his spiritual mentor. But Joshua also thrilled to the fact that God was talking to him just as He did to Moses!

God had big plans. He told Joshua to guide the Israelites across the Jordan River and conquer a huge area that stretched from the Euphrates River to the Mediterranean Sea. Joshua must have been awestruck, because God lost no time in reassuring him: "As I was with Moses, so I will be with thee" (Joshua 1:5 KJV). But God also commanded Joshua to learn His Law. The Israelites' leader needed to spend substantial time meditating upon God's Word. God promised that if Joshua integrated His commands into his personal lifestyle and leadership methods, he would succeed.

We may find ourselves taking leadership positions in our families or congregations. How will we make it? God gives us the same answer He gave Joshua: Absorb My Word. Let My commands light your paths.

Joshua listened. Many of his people did not.

Will we?

Lord God, help me study the Bible, meditate on Your precepts, and listen for Your guidance each and every day. And as You grant me success, may I give You all the glory!

The Last Straw

*While Belshazzar was drinking his wine, he gave orders
to bring in the gold and silver goblets that Nebuchadnezzar
his father had taken from the temple in Jerusalem. . . .
As they drank the wine, they praised the gods of gold
and silver, of bronze, iron, wood and stone.*
DANIEL 5:2, 4 NIV

It was the last straw. Belshazzar, king of Babylon, had taken out the
gold and silver vessels that had been looted from Solomon's temple in
Jerusalem. He used those sacred vessels for the party of the century.
Though *party* might be too kind a word. More like a drunken orgy.
Belshazzar partied as his city was under siege.

God was ready to deal with Belshazzar's arrogance. A mysterious
hand appeared, writing a message of of Belshazzar's fate on the wall.
Later that night, he was killed.

Centuries later, our culture is still at odds with what God holds
sacred. And it's not just our culture that disregards what God holds
dear. Sadly, we can do that, too. Is getting to church, regularly and
on time, a firm intention for our family? Do we cut ethical corners
at work or on our tax returns? Do we slip up with a careless "Oh my
God!" on occasion, or let our kids take the Lord's name in vain?

Let's ask God to reveal any areas of neglect in our lives. Then
let's cut out anything—like a cancer—that could lead us to sin.

*Lord, I don't want to settle for what the world thinks
is right. Search my soul! Show me what needs
to change and let me be quick to repent.*

Molding His Clay

O LORD, you are our Father. We are the clay,
you are the potter; we are all the work of your hand.
ISAIAH 64:8 NIV

Many of us have had the chance to make pottery in an art class. Those of us who've tried it know making something nice is much more difficult than it appears. Only a really talented potter can create a work of true beauty.

Clay starts out hard and cold, but becomes formable after the potter beats, stretches, and works it over. Eventually, the clay becomes soft and pliable—then it goes on the center of the potter's wheel. The clay is pushed and pulled. Spinning rapidly, it rises up and is shoved back down. Sharp tools make designs and patterns within the developing work of art. Finally, in the right hands, a masterpiece emerges.

We are God's clay. Often, we're beaten down and worked over. But with Him as our potter, in His tender hands, we'll be molded and shaped into something beautiful. Sure, it can be painful and tiring. But we trust that when He is finished, we'll be glorious examples of His workmanship.

Made by tender, loving hands, no two pieces of pottery are exactly alike. And neither are we—as our characters are formed by God's perfect wisdom and knowledge. He always has our very best in mind.

Lord God, You are the potter, I am merely Your clay. Mold
and shape me today to become the masterpiece You had in mind
when You saw me in my mother's womb. I submit myself to be in
Your hands and trust You will keep me there.

Forgotten Fragrances

*He has made everything
beautiful in its time.*
ECCLESIASTES 3:11 NIV

Scuffling along a dreary path, Liza and Jane remarked on the cold, dead, sad display of the wintertime forest. The previous summer, the same path was crowded with fragrant, eye-catching flowers. Now, though, the blossoms were long gone, and their gentle fragrance only a distant memory.

But Jane and Liza knew, from years of living through the changing seasons, that the springtime sun would soon warm the air, melt the snow, and cause the flowers and trees to grow once more. The stark, cold quiet of wintertime would give way to new freshness, new beauty, new life.

It's the same for us. God indeed makes everything beautiful in its time—flowers, trees, baby animals, and us. There are seasons in our lives that are dry and cold; we wonder what good will come of our lives. In other seasons, life is radiant and wonderful—and we simply enjoy every minute of it.

If you're in one of those cold, sorrowful seasons of life, don't fear. Soon, God will blow back the gray clouds, revealing the warmth of His Son and making us beautiful once more.

*Father, I thank You for the beauty You've given me
to enjoy. You have a time for everything, and will
eventually make all things beautiful. Please keep
me faithful, awaiting Your special time for my life.*

By the River

*"Blessed are those who trust in the LORD and have made the LORD
their hope and confidence. They are like the trees planted along
a riverbank, with roots that reach deep into the water."*
JEREMIAH 17:7–8 NLT

Trees lining a river bank are often a bit strange. They're twisted
and gnarled, growing out of rocks or up through other trees. Rarely
standing up straight, they stretch over the river as if to drink or catch
a breeze off the water. Though not always beautiful, these trees
are strong and well nourished. With water always available, their
roots plunge deeper than most other trees—strengthening their firm
foundation, making their foliage brighter. Even their smell tends to be
more refreshing and sensual than the rest.

God's Word says that if we put our trust and confidence in the
Lord, allowing our hope to rest in His hands, we'll be like those
strong, healthy trees. True, our circumstances may be gnarled and
ugly—but with our roots deep in the Lord, our foundation is firm
and unshakeable, our fruit brilliant and refreshing. We'll breathe in
the fragrance of our Savior, drink in the river of life, and be strong
and confident whatever may come.

*Jesus, I thank You for Your faithfulness and ask that You'll
help me to increase my trust and hope in You. Like those
strong trees by the water's edge, may my roots go deep into
Your Word, drinking from the river of life that never runs dry.*

He's Here!

When they came to the other disciples, they saw a large crowd
around them and the teachers of the law arguing with them.
As soon as all the people saw Jesus, they were overwhelmed
with wonder and ran to greet him.
MARK 9:14–15 NIV

Jesus had just come down the mountain after being away with Peter, James, and John for a few days. When He located His disciples, He found them surrounded by a large crowd, locked in a heated argument with teachers of the law.

And then, scripture explains, everyone saw Jesus. Almost like children running to a parent who's been away, their faces were filled with joy as they surrounded Him.

Tweak this Bible passage a bit, and it plays out like a scene very familiar to moms. We've been away from home for awhile and return to the house to hear the kids arguing. But they see us and run to us, relief written on their faces! Happy that we can act as peacemaker for their argument. Happy that dinner will now get underway. Happy, really, just that we're home.

What a beautiful parallel to our relationship to Christ. He's here—even in our homes. He can solve our problems and provide for us. All will be well.

Lord Jesus, thank You for the gift of motherhood.
Your presence in my home is so comforting.

Get Plugged In

*For we are God's workmanship, created in Christ Jesus to
do good works, which God prepared in advance for us to do.*
EPHESIANS 2:10 NIV

"How can I 'produce fruit' for God, when I'm already so busy?"
Ruth wondered aloud as she read an e-mail requesting her help with
an upcoming church luncheon. She wanted to contribute, but felt
overwhelmed with other responsibilities—inside and outside her
home.

The Bible often calls us to "bear fruit" by doing good works,
showing God's love to others. That's easier said than done when
we're trying to squeeze in family, jobs, and other responsibilities. But
bearing fruit doesn't necessarily mean we have to volunteer for every
church committee. What it does imply is that we should find a way to
show God's love every day.

Seek out ways and places to use your talents, as much as you
can give now. Take stock of the time you have available to give in a
week or month, then set a goal to spend some of that time on church
and other activities. Ask where you could be of assistance, and find a
place to "plug in."

And if you can't find a plug, make one yourself. Chances are, other
people might share your interests and want a new place to join in.

*Dear Father, help me find a way to be "plugged in" without
feeling overwhelmed. Remind me to show Your love
every day, and to use my talents for Your good.*

The Ant's Lesson

*Go to the ant, you sluggard; consider its ways
and be wise! . . .yet it stores its provisions in
summer and gathers its food at harvest.*
PROVERBS 6:6, 8 NIV

Working women treasure Saturday mornings. We don't have to rush
to work or to church. We can catch a little extra sleep and spend a
quiet, contented morning (we hope) at home.

Those times to rest and recharge are necessary. But problems can
start when we allow that rest to become our highest priority. We may
set our alarm later and later each weekend, then hit our SNOOZE button
once or twice or more. It's easy to act like the man in Proverbs who
says, "a little sleep, a little slumber" (Proverbs 6:10 KJV). *No, really—
just five minutes more.*

In contrast, Solomon points us to the example of the lowly ant.
Think of what that tiny bug accomplishes: She locates food and
carries home as much as she can manage. She makes a note of where
the rest of the food is located and enlists others to help out. She stays
busy and never worries about her next meal. She's already prepared.

What might we accomplish in an extra five, ten, or fifteen
minutes a day? Has our quiet time slid by the wayside? Is there a
stack of mail needing our attention? Can we play a game with our
children or read a book together?

Let's consider the ant's ways, and be wise!

*Lord, teach me the balance between necessary
rest and laziness. Teach me to use my time wisely.*

Sit Back and Sing

*"The LORD will conquer your enemies when they
attack you. They will attack you from one direction,
but they will scatter from you in seven!"*
DEUTERONOMY 28:7 NLT

Many of us grew up watching Sylvester the cat trying to catch Tweety Bird. It never failed though—Tweety's elderly owner or the big bulldog always intervened, and the cat, usually with his hair standing straight up, would scurry away.

Ever notice that Tweety never seemed worried, even when saying, "I tawt I taw a puddy tat"? He just sat on his perch and sang. Apparently, Tweety had confidence that as long as he stayed in his cage, he'd be protected from the "bad ol' puddy tat"—even if his help wasn't immediately apparent.

When our "enemies" advance toward us, we often lose sight of the fact that God is on our side. Taking our eyes off Him, we tend to look at the enemy instead.

Unfortunately, that's totally backwards! We can sit back and sing (praising God), knowing that we're under the protection of His mighty hand. He will conquer and scatter our enemies.

*Lord God, I thank You for fighting my enemies for me.
I don't have to fear or worry because I know You are always
with me—and my enemies are helpless against You.*

Melting Point

*If anyone builds on this foundation using gold, silver, costly stones,
wood, hay or straw, their work will be shown for what
it is. . .and the fire will test the quality of each person's work.*
1 CORINTHIANS 3:12–13 NIV

Wood, hay, and straw—they all burn. We use them as kindling and fuel. Apply a flame to each and they leap to life—providing light and heat until they're totally consumed.

Gold and silver, though, are different. They don't burn, they *melt*. As they turn from solid to liquid, the impurities of their natural state burn away.

In a similar way, tribulation reveals the quality of our inner lives. Trials consume the worthless parts of our character, activities, and spending habits. What isn't consumed melts, turning our stability on its head. Then we're prepared for a reformation of what remains.

When we consider what we say, do, purchase, or pursue, we can use today's verse as our standard. Is our pursuit *ignitable*—temporary and unimportant—or is it *malleable*—something that can be reshaped and used as God directs?

What happens when the fires of tribulation blow through our lives? Do we reach an ignition point or a melting point?

*O Lord God, You test me to transform me into the
image of Your Son. Teach me to invest in what
will last and not that which passes away.*

Ups and Downs

Anxiety in the heart of man causes depression,
but a good word makes it glad.
PROVERBS 12:25 NKJV

It was Wednesday, and Marcie wondered how she would get through the end of the week. Her long list of what needed to be done wasn't getting any shorter—and she was beginning to feel anxious. Marcie really needed some help just to get through the day.

"Life is just a bowl of cherries," an old saying goes. But not every day is happy and beautiful. We have bills to pay, jobs to attend to, kids to run around, and life to live. And being a Christian doesn't make every day easy and carefree.

The good news is that we don't have to be anxious. When life becomes too much, we have a God who listens to our worries and speaks words of encouragement back to us—through His Spirit and through His holy Bible.

The next time anxiety creeps up on you, go to the one true source of joy and peace—our God. Take a minute and pray for calm. Remember that He loves you and encourages you every day. After all, if He takes care of the birds in the air, how much more will He care for His children?

Father God, I may be anxious about today, but I
know that I can rest in You. Help me to find comfort
in Your Word and happiness in Your presence.

The Eyes Have It

The God our ancestors worshiped raised him
to life and made him our Leader and Savior.
ACTS 5:30–31 CEV

The Christmas cantata was only two weeks away, and the choir director was becoming frustrated. During practice, choir members only occasionally glanced his way. Instead, their noses were buried in their music, focusing on the words and notes. Consequently, joy did not radiate from their faces nor did their voices project as they should. Unity was sorely lacking. It was obvious that all eyes needed to be on the choir director!

Who or what has our undivided attention? Trying hard to live the Christian life, we may forget to look at our leader, Jesus! It is easy to become distracted with worldly concerns—career, family, friends, homes, and so forth. Jesus may get pushed aside or left out altogether. We may even be diligently serving in our church or community. Yet when we take our eyes off of Jesus, we can get caught up in the administrative details and forget the Person we should be serving.

Jesus is our Leader. It's imperative that we keep our eyes on Him (Hebrews 12:2) for direction and instruction. How else will we be able to navigate wisely in the world? He will communicate His will for our lives, day by day. He will make our paths straight and show us the way to go. Let's keep our eyes on Jesus so we can follow our leader!

Dear Lord, help me focus on You. Teach me
the way I am to go each and every day. Amen.

Share the News

I pray that you may be active in sharing your faith,
so that you will have a full understanding of
every good thing we have in Christ.
PHILEMON 1:6 NIV

Joy was seated on a plane, awaiting takeoff. She was headed toward home—and her children—after a weeklong business trip. This was a chance for a little shut-eye before seeing her family once again.

Joy was about to doze off when a talkative older woman sat down in the next seat. It didn't take long for Joy to realize her traveling partner needed to hear the good news about Jesus Christ. *Not today, God,* Joy thought—but she knew this was an opening she had to take.

Sharing our faith with others can be scary. We could be rejected or even laughed at. But we could also help lead someone to Jesus. Either way, we must share the good news.

In his letter to Philemon, the apostle Paul penned a prayer that his reader would be active in sharing his faith so that Philemon would "have a full understanding of every good thing we have in Christ." When we get excited about other important things in our life—our children's accomplishments, a new job—we share them with others. How much more important it is—and how much more joy we'll get— sharing Christ's love with others.

Share that news! The reward is so much greater than the risk.

Father, I pray for courage and boldness in sharing my faith
with others. You have given me so many blessings—please
help me to share Your love and goodness with others.

Faith Fitness

*Ye, beloved, building up yourselves on your most holy faith,
praying in the Holy Ghost, keep yourselves in the love of God,
looking for the mercy of our Lord Jesus Christ unto eternal life.*
JUDE 20–21 KJV

Physical fitness takes center stage in our country. Stores teem with books full of advice to help us look better, feel stronger, and live longer. Everyone wears workout suits and jogging shoes. People spend thousands of dollars on exercise equipment. Not content with a basement full of fitness gear, we pay out thousands more for gym memberships.

So we can conclude all Americans are physically fit, right?

Unfortunately, our interest does not necessarily transfer to our actions. Judging from the number of sports channels, we love to watch other people exercise, but sweating it out ourselves? That's a whole 'nother ball game.

In the same way, we Christians often fall short in building ourselves up spiritually. We buy millions of Bibles and tons of literature, attend conferences and seminars, even purchase sweatshirts with scriptures on them—but we don't practice daily spiritual disciplines that make us strong. Jude, the half-brother of Jesus, urges us to devote time and energy to fervent prayer in the Spirit. He tells us to maintain intimacy with Jesus, which the Lord Himself defined as keeping His commands (John 15:10). If we also exercise our faith daily by focusing on His mercy and grace, this regimen will keep us fit for God's heavenly purpose.

*Lord, help me stay on top of my spiritual, as well as physical,
conditioning. Thanks for Your concern for me.*

God's Armor

Therefore put on the full armor of God, so that when the
day of evil comes, you may be able to stand your ground,
and after you have done everything, to stand.
EPHESIANS 6:13 NIV

Startled by his alarm, the man jumped out of bed. "I'm late!" he said
to nobody in particular. Gulping some leftover coffee, he stepped
into yesterday's pants and pulled on a sock. Throwing a coat over his
shirtless chest, he rushed out the door.

Racing down the snow-covered sidewalk, he thought, *I may*
be only half-dressed and exposing myself to frostbite and public
humiliation—but I won't be late.

None of us would ever dress so haphazardly. But, sadly, that's
often how we put on the armor of God. We rush in, quickly asking
God to bless our day and protect our minds, but going no further. As
a result, we might end up looking foolish spiritually and exposing
ourselves to the lies and attacks of our enemy.

God's Word is clear: We need to put on every piece of armor each
day, taking up the shield of faith and the sword of the Spirit. Only
then will we be prepared to ward off the enemy's schemes.

Dear Lord, I put on Your armor so that I'm fully protected
from schemes of the enemy. From the top of my head to the
soles of my feet, I pray Your peace, security, and protection.
Keep me in Your presence I pray, Father.

Beloved Black Sheep

Jacob awaked out of his sleep, and he said,
Surely the Lord is in this place; and I knew it not.
GENESIS 28:16 KJV

Many young people leave home to look for a promising future. But
Jacob left home because he had bilked Esau, his older brother, out of
his inheritance. Jacob also tricked their blind father into giving him
a special blessing that symbolized God's favor. Jacob thought he was
set for life.

Instead, he became a fugitive. His heart pounded at every rustle
behind a rock. Had Esau, the wilderness expert, followed him? The
rocks Jacob used as pillows felt less painful than the thought that he
never would see his parents again.

During the night Jacob stirred uneasily. *Someone was there.* He
felt for his dagger. Instead of Esau, Jacob faced glowing angels on a
ladder that stretched to heaven. God Himself stood above it. Instead
of judging Jacob as a con man and family disgrace, God promised to
give him the land where he stood and bless the world through him.
When Jacob awakened from his dream, he called the place Bethel,
which means "House of God."

"God was here!" he said in awe. "And I didn't even know it."

Like Jacob, we all have blown it. But God's angels surround us,
and His powerful, loving Presence stands ready to bless us far beyond
anything we could imagine.

Lord God, how can you offer me, a person who's made so
many mistakes, a glimpse of heaven? Thank You for Your angels
surrounding me, and Your immeasurable mercy.

Say It. . .Do It!

When you tell God you'll do something, do it—now. God takes
no pleasure in foolish gabble. Vow it, then do it. Far better
not to vow in the first place than to vow and not pay up.
ECCLESIASTES 5:4–5 MSG

Have you ever known people who made promises they didn't keep?
Maybe they said they would call, but didn't. Perhaps they promised
a lunch together or a movie, then simply got busy and forgot. It's
frustrating, isn't it? A person like that is hard to trust. And when you
have to work with someone who doesn't follow through, it can be
even more frustrating.

How wonderful that God never forgets His promises. If He says it,
He means it. And if He means it, He does it. Talk about keeping your
word! God is the very epitome of trustworthiness.

Remember that you are created in God's image, and He's all about
honesty. So, pray before making commitments; then do what you've
said you would do. And when the Lord speaks into your life, giving you
instruction—like ministering to someone in need or spending more
time in the Word—better get to it! Be a woman of your word—both to
people and to the Lord.

Lord, I want to be known as a woman of my word. I want to be
trustworthy. Today, remind me of the commitments I've made,
then set me back on the right track to get those things done.

God Has Compassion on Us

As a father has compassion on his children,
so the LORD has compassion on those who fear him.
PSALM 103:13 NIV

What does it mean that God has compassion on us? For some women, it means that God gives strength as they battle a chronic illness. For others, it means that He has forgotten their sins, because they came to Christ from a life of deep regrets.

Because we are all unique, God's compassion is individualized. Just as a father treats each of his children uniquely, according to their ages and temperaments, so God deals with us as individuals.

How do you need God to show you His compassion today? Do you need guidance for a decision? Ask Him, and He will show you what to do. Perhaps you long for a companion to talk to. He is always available. Maybe you believe that God couldn't love you, because you've strayed from Him. Remember that He is the image of the loving father who ran to His prodigal son when he returned.

Another wonderful aspect of God's compassion is that once we've experienced it, we long to share it with others. So when you feel that God has met your needs, ask Him how you can be a blessing to the people around you. Does a coworker need some encouragement? Or maybe your best friend could use some girl time. If you ask Him, God will give you fresh ideas on ministering compassion to those in your circle of influence.

Lord, I am so thankful for—and in awe of—
Your compassion. Help me spread it to everyone I know.

Strength for the Weary

*He gives strength to the weary and
increases the power of the weak.*
ISAIAH 40:29 NIV

Stress is part of every woman's life.

Stress is like a weight on one's shoulders. The load is heavy.

There are two "W" words in Isaiah 40:29—*weary* and *weak*. Have you felt these culprits lately?

You start out Monday morning with things under control. By Thursday, you have drawn arrows all across your calendar, indicating that although the task wasn't accomplished today, it will certainly take precedence tomorrow. Another task. Another interruption. Another arrow in your calendar. Weary and weak? Yes, you've been there.

Ask God for extra strength this week. While you are at it, ask yourself which tasks should be removed in order to reduce your stress. Give yourself permission to rest. Put it on your calendar! God desires to give you strength when you need it. Your Father also longs to see His daughter relax, enjoy a hobby, nurture relationships, and draw close to Him through prayer and the reading of His Word.

*Lord, please increase my strength and guide
me as I seek to decrease my stress level. Amen*

Don't Say It

*Do not let any unwholesome talk come out of your mouths,
but only what is helpful for building others up according
to their needs, that it may benefit those who listen.*
EPHESIANS 4:29 NIV

The sequence of events is very predictable: Random thoughts
enter our minds; negative scenarios dominate our thinking; volatile
emotions soon bubble up; and before we know it, hurtful words come
out of our mouths. We may not be able to control every thought that
enters our minds, but the good news is we *can* control what thoughts
we dwell on and what words we utter.

Learning to tame the tongue is a difficult task. First we must
acknowledge the destruction our tongues are capable of. James 3
addresses the consequences of an unbridled tongue. Although our
tongues are a tiny part of the body, they can do great harm to us, and
others, if left unchecked.

Edifying speech begins with a disciplined mind. Weigh your
thoughts against God's truth found in His Word. Dismiss lies. Yield
your thought life to God's control. When God is allowed to guard
our minds, our speech will be pleasing to Him and will truly benefit
others.

*Dear Lord, help me win the battle of the
tongue by dwelling on Your truth. Amen.*

Iron-Sharpening Friendship

As iron sharpens iron, so a man
sharpens the countenance of his friend.
PROVERBS 27:17 NKJV

Maybe you're familiar with the biblical expression "iron sharpens iron." But what does it mean? In order to keep things like knives sharp, they have to be rubbed against something equally as hard—something that can shape them into effective tools.

Godly friends will sharpen us. They won't let us grow dull in our relationship with God or with others. They will keep us on our toes and will work with the Lord to shape us into the most effective people we can be. Rubbing against them won't always be fun. In fact, we might feel the friction at times and wish we could run in the opposite direction. But don't run! Allow God to do the work He longs to do.

Take a good look at the friends God has placed in your life. Are there some who don't sharpen you? Perhaps you've been put in their lives to sharpen them. Are there a few who diligently participate in your life, growing you into a better, stronger person? Do they rub you the wrong way at times? Praise God! He's shaping and sharpening you into the person you are meant to be.

Father, thank You for my friends, especially the ones
who keep me on my toes. Thank You for the sharpening
work You are doing in my life—even when it hurts!

Thanksgiving as Sacrifice

Offer to God a sacrifice of thanksgiving,
and perform your vows to the Most High.
PSALM 50:14 ESV

It's not difficult to say thank you. So why does the psalmist call
thanksgiving a sacrifice? What are we giving up in order to be
thankful? When we list our blessings, we realize that we are
recipients of many gifts—things God has given us freely, through no
effort on our part.

Giving thanks is a means of letting go, of opening our hands
and acknowledging God's power, His control, and His goodness. In
the process, He frees us from ourselves. In the act of thanksgiving
we are letting go of the control we think we have. We acknowledge
once again that much of who we are and what we have are gifts of a
sovereign God who loves and blesses us. We sacrifice our pride and
self-sufficiency when we say thank You.

Lord, give me a grateful heart. Cause me to turn
daily to You in thanksgiving and thus free
myself from pride and self-importance.

Complaining or Trusting?

Do everything without complaining or arguing.
PHILIPPIANS 2:14 NIV

It is our nature to look out for number one. We want our opinion to count. We want our voice to be heard. We want things to go the way we plan, but life often does not measure up to our expectations. So we complain, bellyache, whine, and grumble. Resisting the urge to be the squeaky wheel is difficult, especially when we are in a situation where we feel we are treated unjustly.

Consider that maybe God tells us not to complain because He wants us to acknowledge that *He's* in control and is powerful enough to take care of everything. Psalm 10:17 tells us the Lord hears the desires of the humble. Romans 8:26 says that the Holy Spirit prays for us and helps us in our weakness. We have these assurances that our God is both hearing our prayers and helping us pray them. Why do we need to keep muttering our dissatisfaction to those around us?

Father, help me to break the habit of complaining.
Cause me to remember I can bring all my problems to You.
You will help me to pray and will hear my prayers.

Practicing Quiet

He who guards his mouth preserves his life,
but he who opens wide his lips shall have destruction.
PROVERBS 13:3 NKJV

We all have times in our lives when we wish we had just kept our mouths shut. Maybe you've let casual conversation slip into gossip or accidentally revealed a secret. Scripture tells us our tongues are powerful and dangerous and that no one can tame them. When we sin with our mouths, it is because we lack self-control; but self-control as we think of it seems impossible to attain.

The world's definition of self-control is personal discipline or willpower, but the Bible says self-control is the fruit of the Spirit, a result of God's work in our lives. His power can keep us from sinning in our speech.

Invite Him into this part of your life. Pray Psalm 141:3 (NIV): "Set a guard over my mouth, O LORD; keep watch over the door of my lips." Watch and see Him help you tame your tongue.

Lord, so many of my words have been unhelpful
and even destructive. Forgive me. By Your Spirit,
watch the door of my lips and produce control in me.

Yes, Lord, Yes, Lord, Amen

"The joy of the LORD is your strength."
NEHEMIAH 8:10 NIV

In our success-driven world, fun is an often-overlooked commodity. There's a corporate ladder to climb, a glass ceiling to break through, another committee meeting to attend. Serious, staid, and structured, our lives lack joy. We race a ticking clock with a sweep hand.

Paul exhorted the Christian community to be full of joy *now*. The Psalms encourage us to sing and dance and praise His name. How is that possible with a solemn face? A little lighthearted fun releases pent-up tension and balances life's scales. Laughter will lower our blood pressure. That cheerful heart is good medicine.

Surely it's time for a bit of spontaneity. 1 Thessalonians 5:16 (NIV) says to "be joyful always." In our cyberspace world, we can share jokes and hilarious videos. Pull one up on the screen, throw back your head, and laugh. Realize God intended for us to have joy in our lives. Say, "Yes Lord," and chuckle.

Father, I live in a world loaded with danger, serious issues,
and worry. Help me to find joy in my life this day. Amen.

Clutter

When he heard this, he became very sad,
because he was a man of great wealth.
LUKE 18:23 NIV

Donna's life was full to the brim. Known for her ability to multitask, she often worked from her laptop with music playing through the speakers. She simultaneously conversed with friends via text and online messaging. While driving to work she'd also talk on her cell phone, put on makeup, or jot down items on a grocery list. She couldn't fall asleep at night without the television on. Each morning she awoke to the sounds of talk radio.

Our lives quickly become cluttered. We think of constant noise and activity as a contemporary issue, but it's a problem that has been around for centuries.

The rich young ruler was a careful rule-follower, an expert at keeping all of them since he'd been a boy. But his life had become so cluttered that he couldn't find God. He came to Jesus looking for something else to put on his to-do list; but instead, Jesus challenged him to get rid of clutter that stood between him and God. This saddened the ruler, because he wasn't willing to part with it.

What clutters your life? It could be physical, mental, or emotional. Set aside time to take an inventory. Ask God to cleanse your heart and bring to mind things you need to get rid of to draw closer to Him.

Father, search my heart and reveal
anything that keeps me from You. Amen.

God as Our Guide

Whenever the cloud was taken up from above the tabernacle, after that the children of Israel would journey; and in the place where the cloud settled, there the children of Israel would pitch their tents.
NUMBERS 9:17 NKJV

When they escaped from the Egyptians into the desert, God gifted the children of Israel with His presence. During the day, a cloud accompanied them; at night, they had a pillar of fire. When it stopped or started, they followed suit.

Do we follow God that closely? Or do we make our own decisions and ask God to bless them? We should make Him an integral part of our daily life—instead of just someone tacked on to the beginning or end of our day.

When faced with a big decision, some of us ask our friends and family members for advice, and others of us tend to be more independent. But if we're seeking to be like Christ, we need to ask God to lead us. He desires to be the first and last person we lean on. And He promises never to lead us astray. What comfort we can take in that fact!

Today, ask God to make His will for you clear. Then read scripture, pray, and be on the lookout for His guidance. He promises to give it and to go with you wherever you go, just as He did for the Israelites.

Lord, thank You for Your promise to lead me. I'm so thankful that You want to be intimately involved in my life.

SCRIPTURE INDEX

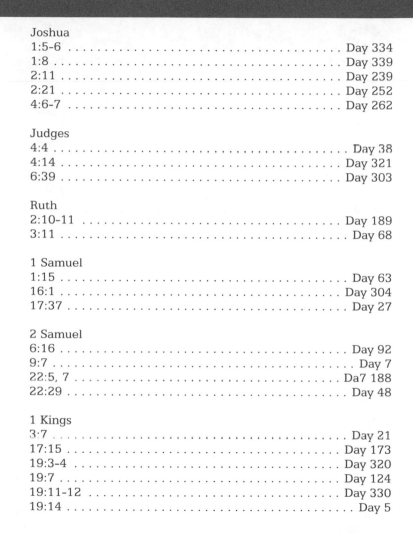

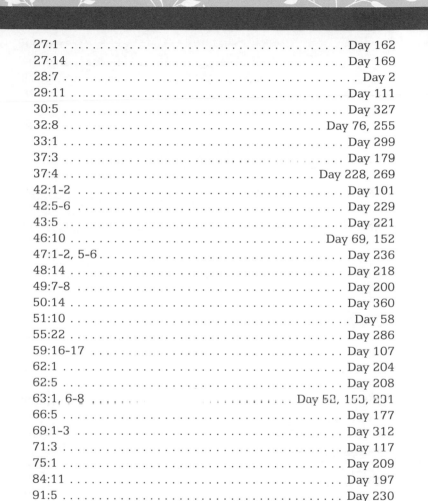

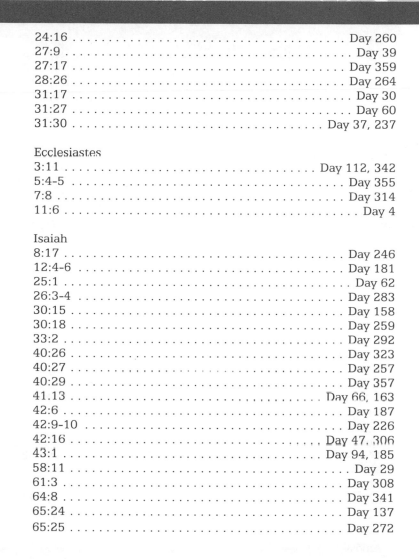